Echoes in the Rain

Ryan Miller

ISBN: 1533100551
ISBN 13: 9781533100559
Library of Congress Control Number: 2016907533
CreateSpace Independent Publishing Platform
North Charleston, South Carolina

Dedication

This story exists because of the courage of a very unique and special southern woman, my wife. Through her unwavering devotion to a dream and her perseverance in needing to give and to obtain love, she found me, although I was lost and to her knowledge killed in Vietnam. She gave me the strength, to look back, fulfilling if you will, the visions and dreams of the children we once were and to reach into our souls, bringing back to life, the designed plan of our destiny.

I would also like to thank two other extraordinary people; Leah's grandmother, for without her commitment to her granddaughter's well-being, our happy ending might never have happened. And to Mr. John Wilson, *"My Buddy"* whose love and benevolence assured that this book would be published and presented to you as a vision of hope and faith that will live on as an inspiration for those that have served proudly, and those "never" forgotten lovers, for generations to come.

Preface

Have you responded to the call of God's love?

These words resonated in my heart long before I committed the first word of our story to paper—a story of love, faith, and the casting off of sin. It began in a far off land with a single letter from a young Southern belle to a nineteen year old soldier stationed in South Vietnam. Her words brought wonder into my life and gave me the strength to endure the bitter realities of war. As letters passed between us, a rich love and a timeless bond was formed, kilned through need and youthful dreams; one we would never deny, even though we had never heard each other's voices as adults.

When I returned from Vietnam in 1971, our dreams were stolen from us; yet three and a half decades later, that which was lost was found. God embraced me in 2005 as I wept over the loss of my father, for a miracle was about to happen that would reveal the truth behind the earlier heartbreak Leah and I had suffered. This revelation brought families to their knees, challenged beliefs and exposed an evil that dominated our lives during the ensuing decades. When we reconnected, we came to understand that man may try to alter fate, but only God controls and fulfills destiny.

Leah and I responded to the call of God's love, and we welcome you to follow the paths of our lives as they unfold in the lonely and harsh days of the Vietnam War, through the loss of true love, and finally to the reawakening of destiny. We believe the hand of God opened a door for us to find each other and live out our lives together in love, and we marvel at the miracle of His great power and compassion. It is our desire that the truths you find in this book will echo in your hearts and, through faith, provide you with the hope you may need.

Part I

Far Off Land: The Beginning, 1970

1

The Love I Could Never Deny

It seems like only yesterday I was trying to understand how a love like one I had never known vanished from my life, leaving only cherished yet distant memories of her and the timeless misfortunes that took place, in a far off land. Time may heal all wounds, but it did not work for me. I never forgot nor let go of her since it was her love that guided my steps and gave me life.

Now, so many years later, I still dream of her and what our lives might have been, but she took her love and walked away to a land where I suppose children needed to play, but I will never accept that she willing bared her bosom into the arms of another man. Denial is probably the perfect word for my state of mind, but my love for her never wavered; it lay hidden in time, held reverent yet concealed from others, alive within me as vibrant as when I first pledged my life to her.

Time and toil steal precious moments from us, seemingly devoid of boundaries. Relentlessly in its quest, pillaging our strength and evilly adding new facial distinctions like valleys on our once unmarred profiles and limbs. Yet neither I assure you, can ever take away that exhilaration we felt when our first love appeared, it never fades. I know you remember it; I will never forget it. It was a life-altering and emotionally overwhelming experience that took possession of our lives and was so arousing, each of us can recall it as vividly as if it happened an hour ago.

My first love materialized in the most unromantic place on the planet, buried deep within simple words in a letter that traveled over seventeen thousand miles. Through words on a page, a special girl came into my life in a time of war when I was surrounded by hostilities such as most of you may never comprehend. The love she offered was so deeply seated in need, so desired and so cherished, I will never lose it, though we had not shared our first kiss.

Her name was Leah Heartaway and I relied on her when times were dismal. I held onto her throughout the night with dreams of passion and delight. Her playful teasing and the well-chosen Southern clichés in her letters saw me through many bleak hours and gave me purpose and the desire to press on day to day. Oh Lord, how I prayed for just one more day. One more day to talk with her, if only through letters, and one more moment to hear her words as they leapt from the pages and echoed through the storms of a war that was ravaging my sense of self-worth as it laid waste to the country of Vietnam.

Although our story began while I was stationed in Vietnam, I learned we had played together as small children. I have no recollection of those times except from stories told to me and from old and faded family pictures. We had no past, really, as we had not seen each other in nearly two decades; and it was only by chance (or fate) that she sent me the first letter. Her words soothed me, then thrilled me, but always abounded with innocence. She brought me a sense of belonging I had never felt before. Did she knowingly or accidentally choose the words she used? I may never know for sure, but she provided exactly what I craved, someone to live for and someone to love. Vietnam bombarded all of us with harsh realities, many of which I, nor any of us will ever forget, but in those special moments when I was alone with her, hidden between the pages of her letters, I escaped the fear and through her eyes experienced the beauty and splendor of her far off land.

She held my hand so many times and caressed me with her words. She helped me pray and sleep at night and fight off far too often tears. She offered me a love, no I guess she brought me a love' filled with so much joy I find it difficult to explain. I know it was because of her and childhood chum, John Wilson, whose letters and love never stopped, that I am alive today. I prayed each night to see another tomorrow with no other motive or desire than to spend time dreaming of Leah and what our lives could be together.

Fast forward three decades, and I am left wondering why and dreaming of what might have been. It's as though a lifetime has come and gone, passing me along the way and leaving a gaping void in its wake. Even though I know she is gone, I still see visions of her and find myself calling her name. Before, I had her letters, but today these are no more. She vanished into the unread pages of my life, leaving behind painful and unfulfilled memories of the past. Was she real or the product of a homesick kid whose imagination contrived the girl of his dreams? Either way, I am alone and will forever question what I must have said to push her away.

I kept my part of the bargain. I made it home alive from the war, but I came home to empty, bitter nights. She was not there waiting for me as I had hoped. No longer could I read her words or dream of a future with her by my side, but I will not fault her. She was the one who, so very long ago, kept me strong when I was at my weakest. My hope is one day our destinies will converge and allow us to love and live as I know we were meant to.

2

In Country

Vietnam was a little plot of land filled with endless hostilities, driving rains, unbearable heat and a near surreal landscape. It was as though time had stood still for hundreds of years with a single paved road which connected the North to the South below the Demilitarized Zone or DMZ. I was stationed in one of the poorer regions of the country where villagers lived in makeshift huts surrounded by endless rice paddies, lush foliage, rolling hills and the Vietcong, "Victor Charlie" in the phonetic alphabet, or VC.

I was stationed in Quang Tri Province at a firebase in Dong Ha, the farthest northern outpost of South Vietnam. Outside of our firebase, there were no sanitary facilities to speak of. The rivers served as laundries, bathing facilities, and the main source of drinking water for the villagers, who were for the most part helpless, relying on the U.S. military for protection. Sure we all detested being there, I mean really what the hell for? Then after a while I guess most of us came to realize that we did have a purpose, maybe it might be fleeting, but a purpose that might just keep us sane.

Given the part of the country we occupied, there was no doubt in any of our minds that, without our presence, the villages would be overrun and the people forced to join the Vietcong or worse. The VC used vicious and inhumane tactics to control the South Vietnamese civilian population in an attempt to turn them against their government and recruit them. Mass murders, torture, rape, beheadings and abductions were a part of daily life. Entire villages were wiped away in minutes, leaving behind the ugly stench of the mangled and decaying dead. However, our presents slowed their aggression and for the most part prevented these atrocities yet, once we stood down, they would begin anew. These memories, although ignored by the American press at the time, still awaken me with horrific nightmares.

My unit patrolled the region close to the DMZ in an attempt to monitor and stop the flow of troops crossing the border. I was the Tank Commander (TC) of a Sheridan tank which had plenty of fire power but was also a prized target. We would be out on patrol for weeks at a time with little physical contact with the rear. This meant few hot meals and a slow mail delivery system that was never enough or often enough. There was limited room on a tank and everything had its place, meaning most of our personal items were left behind at the firebase in small hooches we occupied while on stand-down. Most guys, however, took something with them on patrol—a special letter, photograph, a deck of cards, a set of dominoes—anything to help stave off the emptiness we all felt. I had two: a tape recorder and a beat-up, out-of-tune guitar. During my tour, I recorded several hundred tapes for the guys to send home to their families. Through them I understood how loneliness and fear affected us daily and how this country and this war were changing us.

Every day held the unexpected and usually unwanted surprise, but by far the most anticipated time of each day was mail call. In Viet Nam, there were no cell phones and no Internet so letters from home were our only real source of escape. Although eagerly awaited, mail call could also be filled with apprehension. Would a letter arrive? Would it be filled with joy and love, or would it have the sting of a pit viper? Generally, a letter from a family member was ripped open in a second. A letter from a love might be held for hours out of fear of what might be within. The envelope was studied; was there a kiss planted on the outside, or was it plain? Was that a clue to the contents? Sadly, these precious pieces of home were fleeting at best and crumbled far too soon from the constant rain and mud or simply deteriorated over time from too much handling.

I know serving in Vietnam was like serving in any other war. Days were never-ending at times. I developed a fear of being alone; and as it prowled through my mind, it left me with such despair that I became physically ill. I spent hours on end daydreaming about what was going on back home. Why were we here? It was a nightmare I couldn't wake up from.

I was luckier than most as I generally received a steady stream of letters and gift packages from home. One day I got a letter with the return address "Leah Heartaway, Marietta, Georgia." I had no clue who she was, how she had found me or why she was writing to me. I looked at it for a few minutes and then tore it open.

She began by explaining that her grandmother had helped raise me in an in-home daycare center in Lawndale, California, many years ago. As I read her letter, I flashed back to a kind and gentle woman named Lenna, whom I had not thought of in years but who had been like a second mother to me. I read on and began to get an uncanny feeling that fate was tempting me to open a door to a new beginning. It felt as though Leah was reaching out to me, inviting, if not enticing, me to pursue her. Her letter revealed a shy young woman whose words were so well chosen I could hear her talking to me as though she had known me all her life. I saw through her eyes as she described her life: vast fields of cotton, starry nights, the Great Smoky Mountains, and the problems and challenges of high school and life on a farm. Life on a farm? Who was this woman?

At first, I wasn't sure what to make of her letter. There was a tempered innocence in her words that was irresistible. Here I was, continents away from someone I had no memories of, yet I was smitten with a compelling desire to discover everything about her. Someone had just entered my life who would change it dramatically. I had longed for this feeling but never experienced it before. How ironic. The girl of my dreams was holding out her hand to me and where was I? Halfway around the world.

After I read her letter for the second or third time, I walked around the camp, flipping back and forth between logic, emotion, and reality, sensibly trying to comprehend how or why this was happening to me. Maybe she wrote to me as a favor to her Grandmother Lenna, or maybe she was a do-gooder wanting to keep up the morale of the troops. But hers was not a "How's it going?" letter. Maybe because I desperately needed something to believe in, I relied on faith and accepted that fate had brought us together to fulfill a void in my life and perhaps in hers—love.

I read her letter a few dozen more times and was convinced I was right. No one could speak to me like she had, not in a first letter and not to someone she didn't know, without providence helping along the way. I had memorized her words, and at night I closed my eyes and walked with her up a slight slope under a large oak tree, past the barn, then over a hill to an open pasture on her grandmother's farm in southern Tennessee.

I reached out with nothing more than a faint hope this could turn into something extraordinary, beyond our control and destined to be. I was consumed with great joy, excitement, and anticipation. Neither of us knew or understood initially just how important we would become to each other. I was barely nineteen, but I believe we recognized from the beginning there was a special bond between us, a longing to be together that would follow, if not haunt, us the rest of our lives.

I wanted to write to her right away, but I wasn't sure what to say. My biggest fear was that I was reading too much into her letter and would come on too strong. What did she really know of me? What would her folks think about us if we got close? *Wait a minute,* I thought, *I'm the perfect boyfriend! How many parents would love to have their daughter fall for a boy who is seventeen thousand miles away, will never bring her home after curfew, seriously cannot get her into trouble and might just keep her away from dating issues and peer pressures at home?* On the other hand, what if our letters bring us closer? Would I hold her back from dating other boys and enjoying the social pleasures of high school?

Wow, that's a stretch! I haven't even sent her my first letter, and already I'm keeping her away from someone else.

There was another fear making me question if this was the right thing to do. Suppose we get to a stage beyond friendship and I don't make it home or she finds someone else before my tour is up. What then? Finally, I thought, *Why not?* I had no place to go and nothing to lose.

After fretting for days, I decided my first letter back to her should be very cookie cutter and somewhat bland, but with a request and a hint. I told her I was 5 feet 9 inches tall, about 165 pounds, with blond hair and blue eyes, and living in hell. I described my duties and told her that when I first arrived in country, it was like going back in time several centuries. I described the countryside, which was like something out of a science fiction movie, with jungles reaching forever and abounding with snakes and water buffalo. In response to her questions, I listed my favorite foods, songs, actors and movies. I told her when I was due to return to the States and asked her to please keep writing and, if she could, to send a picture of herself. I ended my letter with "Take Care and God Bless. My Love to You, Ryan."

A week later we were sent on patrol to an area where hostile forces were reportedly held up. We were given orders to observe and then clear the area, which we did. Other than the VC, the biggest problem facing us was the rain, which was unlike any rain I had ever known. It never seemed to stop and carried with it a cold bitter wind. This may be hard to believe, but after you have been wet for a week or more, you freeze your butt off even in seventy degree weather. Letters became fewer and far too long in between. With the misery of our surroundings and the war in general, feelings of loss and even loss of self-worth crept in like an evil predator taking over my heart and soul. It humbled me and sapped my courage and was a feeling worse than death as it never let up.

Finally there was a break in the weather, and the birds (helicopters) could fly again. This meant a five gallon metal container of hot food or maybe even two and still more importantly, mail from home and, hopefully for me, a second letter from Leah. My prayers were answered; it could not have been more than a few days after she received my letter that she responded to me and included a few pictures of herself. They were breathtaking; she was both innocent and shy but with a mischievous look about her. She wore a pants suit in one with her hair pulled back and a look that simply said, "I'm her." She was standing in front of an old shed propped up with cement blocks, with her hair falling below her shoulders and beautiful green eyes that seemed to look right through me.

The other photos were playful ones where she sported a sexy, tomboy look. I wanted to believe she was trying to send me a message or a signal through them. In one she wore tight fitting bell bottoms with a bare midriff and a bathing suit top, barefooted, with her hair hanging straight down. The bell bottoms were covered with the Coca Cola slogan "It's the real thing." I fantasized she wore them on purpose just to let me know *she* was the real thing; and although she would never admit it, I knew that already. The sun made her squint a little, and again I fantasized she was giving me a look, saying without words, "You better get back here, boy."

She wrote how fearful she was that I was stationed so close to the DMZ and what must be going on around me. She said she had not heard the song I told her to check out, "Till Then" by James Brown, but that she would try and find it. For the most part, she offered her love and how desperately she needed me to be safe and get back home as soon as I could. Between her pictures and her words, she lifted me as no one ever had.

I wanted to write back to her right then, but I could not. The conditions where we were made this impossible, so I did the next best thing and formed the words a hundred times in my mind to be written another day. When that day came, I felt like a teenager looking for the courage to ask a girl out on a first date.

I began by telling her in this land she would be called "boo-coo #10," which in the slang used around the camp meant "very much beautiful."

I told her some of my buddies from her part of the world, the South, would say she was prettier than "a speckled puppy in an old slop bucket."

"You are beautiful," I wrote, and I asked her not to take this wrong but told her I felt there was something between us, something I could not explain that drew me to her. I promised I would come back to see her and then stay until I discovered just what this feeling was. I also told her I would try and send a few pictures of me in the field and while on stand-down, but pictures taken from this place really depressed me.

As her letters continued, I pictured her covered by the warmth of Tennessee skies, lying in the fields writing to me about her dreams and her daily activities. It was as though I saw through her eyes as she wrote of long walks, wild thunderstorms in the night, the glimmering of morning dew on old oak trees, and the lush green valleys of her home. In my mind's eye (or maybe it was my imagination running wild), I perceived her as an untamed mare roaming through the back hills of Tennessee, her hair blowing in the wind, her face as soft as silk and with a smile so tender it would tear at anyone's heart, above all mine. Of course I dreamed of being with her. I could almost touch her and felt I could turn off the lights and, without a word being said, find her in a crowded room.

Leah lit up my days and left me with a deep desire to follow her as she unfolded her life to me. Mail call became my happiest and darkest times. When her letters arrived, I was like a child with a shiny new toy; and when they did not, I was an empty shell of a man alone in this wretched land. She became my reality, and nothing else mattered. I believed we were destined to be, that I had found something I had always longed for and would never let go of. Still, I struggled with my feelings, asking myself how this beautiful young woman could ever want me. I drifted into despair, imagining she had dozens of boyfriends back home and knowing, if I ever got home, she would probably be with someone else.

Her letters kept coming. They were full of life, and I sensed she knew what I really wanted to hear—and it wasn't lovesick words. I wanted to know everything about her; how she laughed, how she played and how she saw the future, what her deepest thoughts were. I hoped she could see how amazingly alike we were. Our shared letters envisioned a future laid out before us. I often paused, recalling and then delving deeper into her words, to make sure this was real. After all, what were the odds? We had never known each other as kids, let alone as young adults. Our homes were two thousand miles apart; yet somehow she had found me, albeit far away and bogged down in the worst mud hole imaginable. I felt I had been touched by the hand of God!

She never knew how bad it was in Vietnam. I couldn't tell her what was actually happening, but her dozens and dozens of letters and the four photos she sent pushed me through some of the most violent times of my life. She brought me back to a reality that Vietnam tried to steal away. I had never longed for anyone before, nor did I ever expect to feel this way; but with every passing day, I found myself lost in her. God help me; I could not resist her.

She filled my nights with anticipation of winning her love. She teased me with her innocence, but I sensed there was also great passion within her. In several letters, she had described the harsh standards of her parents' religion. Because of that, she disguised her feelings, but I believe in her heart she knew they could not be denied. As we continued to walk together, although far apart and only through letters, we both came to know that, for today and into eternity, there was no power on earth that could keep us apart. Knowing her love was there for me made the days drag on slower than ever before, represented by marks on a calendar and always a reminder of how long it would be until I returned home.

3

Salvation

ate one night the sky lit up as bright as day. The landscape glowed and then tore itself apart. Shells were landing, and no one seemed to know what to do or where to go. We were told to scramble for cover, hunker down and wait for further orders. Everyone prayed. You can fight what is before you, but it's hard to fight what you cannot see. This was the most frightening thing that had ever happened to me. The old timers "lifers" told us we would get used to it after a while, but I couldn't see how unless I gave up on life. The night drifted on, and then there was calm. We cleaned up the perimeter and hunkered down for another round which we knew would come the next day.

The losses we suffered still haunt me. I felt anguish, hopelessness and desolation. I will never forget this day, not for the pain and anger that surrounded me in this troubled land but the fact that one special girl, my girl, delivered once again as mail call came around. Her words brought balance back into my life and gave me vitality to do what I knew I must do—and it was not giving up on life.

Leah wrote that she missed me and couldn't wait for me to come home. She said she desperately longed for me and that above all she loved what I had written about coming back and holding her in my arms. She dropped a bombshell on me when she said I was saving her life. I had no idea how or why at the time, but I knew for sure she was my only reason for living. I dreamed of her in ways I never before imagined, not out of desire but out of longing. She was a beautiful and a marvelous gift from God to whom I promised to provide everything I could. With no uncertainty, I committed myself to make it through the war, body and soul, and come home to her.

Time became an insidious curse, moving slowly, denying me the pleasures of her touch, the simple delight of hearing her voice and strolling hand in hand with her through the wooded farmlands of Tennessee. Hours drifted by as we, like robots or trained circus animals, attended to the duties and tasks at hand. These tedious repetitions, though necessary, created other dilemmas as there was nothing new or stimulating to occupy our time. Many of the guys turned to alcohol and drugs to counteract the loneliness and boredom. Although I understood their feelings, I saw little future in this and did not join them. My escape into Leah was more wondrous and never limited by chemically controlled fantasies. It was as though Leah had fashioned a Castle in the sky beyond the darkening clouds and the sounds of war, where she and I could be alone to dream and pray.

Every so often, however, this backfired on me. Dark thoughts intruded as I questioned what she might be doing back home. Were her days filled with pursuit by other boys, dating, parties, movies, and youthful experimentations? I was driving myself nuts with "what ifs." I could imagine a future with Leah as all I have ever wanted, but like yesterday, today, and many more tomorrows, my reality was here in Vietnam, trapped in the rain, desperately holding onto what might only be a fantasy. Funny, given where I was, I wouldn't have had it any other way. If war was my price for Leah coming into my life, I gladly accepted my situation. It was bad but could have been much worse if I'd had nothing to hold onto and no plans to look forward to.

The rain continued to engulf us and control our every movement. It was as if a plague had overtaken the land with such relentless fury I wondered how any living thing could survive. I watched each downpour inch toward me, a great wall of water so structured that at times I actually walked just ahead of it. On one side the air was dry and behind me it was pouring, much like being chased by a giant shower head in the hand of a vengeful deity. Roads washed away or were swallowed up by the rising waters. The areas above the water line became more and more saturated, making foot movement difficult and bogging down the tanks.

The monsoon season spawned another enemy as the once fertile land gave way to massive new lakes and pestilent-ridden swamps filled with creatures like you have never seen. These small but relentless abominations from hell, over ran us, ranging from giant centipedes to scorpions, rats the size of cats, snakes, leeches, and millions of mosquitoes, invaded everything I owned—my sleeping bag, food, clothes and even my boots. Sure, we were issued insect repellant (what a joke), but nothing stopped the onslaught; it was a miracle we were not all sick.

Day after day of constant rain broke us down, zapping our strength as our hands and feet became numb and wrinkled. Many nights I broke into tears, and as the discomfort and pain grew with each hour, all I wanted to do was go home or die.

The one cruelty of war that cripples you emotionally as it slowly destroys even your will to live is homesickness. I don't care how tough you are or how you were raised, anybody is susceptible to this pain that attacks and then lingers like a constant, throbbing ache within you. For me, this was far worse than the fear of combat. Maybe this was what the old timers were talking about during the earlier patrol. It was without question the most treacherous emotion I remember, bringing with it a feeling of worthlessness, despair and loss of all compassion. You can't stop it, you sure can't avoid it, and the only thing that slows it down is activity, good or bad. Even the fear of death was more pleasant than the disabling effects of this malicious evil. Suicide provided a quick way out, one with a lingering silence that all of us experienced as far too many of our comrades surrendered their lives to it.

When homesickness struck, most of us avoided contact. Nothing took it away, and it crippled all of us at one time or another, many times for hours on end. The only cure I experienced was hearing in the distant sky the loud clapping of helicopter blades. I felt better right away knowing they might be bringing a hot meal and just maybe, as they had so many times before and far more meaningful to me, letters from home. This is what I lived and prayed for each day—news from home, letters from anyone and more importantly, please God, another letter from Leah.

I grew tired of taking and re-taking areas that meant nothing to me. I became so lost I thought taking my own life would be a quick, though cowardly, escape. I did not want to die, but fear and anxiety made me feel I could not go on for another day. I was losing it physically, emotionally and spiritually. As I prayed for guidance and help, I heard Leah's voice calling to me through the rain, echoing above the ravaged countryside. She was all but screaming at me to be strong and never again think about giving up. Her voice was so real I found myself talking back to her and searching in the early evening for a hint of her shadow. Frightened by my actions and desperately needing her, I crafted a letter to her in my mind about hearing her speak to me. What came out of that unwritten letter was a song we would find out many years later would haunt us for the rest of our lives.

Echoes in the Rain

I heard your voice echoing through the rain,
Calling softly but shouting my name.
I felt your hands reach out for me.
Across that far far distant sea,
I heard your voice echoing through the rain.

Nothing will ever make me believe this was not real. God allowed me to hear her voice, providing me the courage I needed to treasure each new day, which as it passed, brought me closer to her. At that very moment I knew I would be fine, and again Leah was the reason.

We had become very close, but our letters continued along the lines of "wanting to get to know you," filled with insights and feelings. It was difficult for me to write to her as there wasn't a lot I could share about what was going on around me. I lied to her about where I was and made up sanitized stories about my daily activities. I focused on my feelings for her, how her letters brought me so much joy and how I could not wait to hold her. I didn't feel good about deceiving her, but I knew I had to as there was already enough strife in her life. I was afraid the issues and agony of Vietnam would be too much for her to handle and might cause me to lose her.

What would you have told her? What good would have come from allowing her to share the torment we were forced to live through? Leah awoke each morning to a warm, safe environment where flowering Bradford pear trees laced the hills like flocks of wandering sheep. She saw children playing on monkey bars and merry go rounds where the worst thing that might befall them would be skinned knees from falling off their bicycles.

I awoke to a war-defaced and desolate land where I lived in fear of mortar attacks and of losing a limb or worse from the VC-planted Claymore mines or toe poppers and the dreaded Bouncing Betty mines. Here children played in rusted out shells of disabled or discarded tanks or APCs (armored personal carriers). They knew nothing about playgrounds or ball fields or family picnics, but they did know the effects of Concertina wire and rusted barbed wire. Most lived in huts surrounded by sand bags and with metal roofs held down with heavy ropes or chains which were secured with large tent stakes to keep them from flying off during a monsoon. They were never sure when dinner (one meal a day) might be but were thankful for what they received. Through them and their playful ways, I gained a greater understanding of what I had heard throughout my life, "Jesus loves the little children." It became obvious to me He sheltered them from the violence, made them oblivious to what was happening and simply allowed them to play. From what I could see they were as happy, if not happier, than anyone's kids I had known. God bless them; they became a part of Vietnam I vowed never to forget. Their memories trouble and sadden me, but I also recall how they reinforced my faith.

Leah and I had a very special connection, and I vowed to never tarnish anything that included her name and her thoughts. Most of the guys passed around their love letters, showing them off like trophies after the big game; the more descriptive the letter, the bigger the trophy. Leah was not a trophy to me, and she was not something I was willing to share; she was my girl and my guiding light. I rarely spoke about her to the other guys as I knew that they would want to know the details of our relationship. I felt bad for the guys who never got letters and had no one waiting for them back home, but in the end I could not bring myself to share her with anyone. I kept the pictures she sent in plastic bags so that they wouldn't tear and rarely took them out for fear of losing them or having them become discolored from the rain and the mud. While she was a trophy to me in a way, she was also the most cherished thing in my life.

Leah saved my life many times, but there was one time I felt sure some greater force guided her letter to me at the perfect moment, making me realize what I was in danger of losing. Tragedy struck one afternoon while we were on patrol in an isolated area near Alpha 4. We were hit pretty hard, and a buddy of mine was killed when an RPG (rocket propelled grenade) round exploded alongside us, tearing him nearly in half. There was nothing I could have done, but this one hit me the harder than other casualties as we had become close friends. We had written to each other's parents, gone to Australia together on R&R and shared plans of getting together in California after we returned home. Within a teardrop, he was gone.

It was my honor rather than my duty to write to his parents about our shared loss. I struggled for hours trying to choose the correct words. The problem wasn't that I could not find the words as I could write volumes about him. My fear was how they would be accepted and understood by his parents. I told them how their son could take miserable times where grown men cried and change them into bouts of laughter with one of his stupid jokes or slapstick pranks. I wrote about his valor and how he never flinched under fire. I also told them I loved their heroic son like a brother and promised to call them when I returned home.

As I finished the letter, I could not get the visual of losing him out of my mind and realized through his loss I had a reason, as morbid as it was, to be there. Most of us never really knew why we were there; we followed orders and tried to get through the fighting in one piece. But I suppose I allowed Satan into my life because I honestly believed I now had a purpose. The VC had killed him, and all I could think about was getting back out there to avenge his death. Caught up in self-pity, disgust and rage, I decided I did not want to go home, at least not now and maybe never. By the time we got back to the firebase, I had convinced myself to stay and volunteer to do whatever I could to even the score. I was on my way to the Captain's office to put in for an extension of duty when a corporal crossed my path with a new bag of mail. Do you believe in fate?

As the guys gathered around, the first name called was "Miller." I had a letter from Leah, delivered via air mail and touched by the hand of God. Her words elevated me above my anger and hate; she took me to her bosom like a child and comforted me. She told me things would never be the same without me in her life and that she dreamed of wondrous nights shared only with me. I felt as though she had physically touched me, soothing and caressing me as only she could do. She had never used words such as "wondrous nights," and why she did in this letter I may never know; but as I read on, the ink on the pages ran from the tears which were rippling down my face and onto the paper. I could all but feel her breath and her warm embrace, and I was love-struck once again and in awe at the way she framed her loving words.

4

Homecoming

What were the odds of her letter coming to me at that time? Why did it arrive just as I was walking in to extend my tour? Who guided this letter to me, and why did she use those words? There was no way I could put my repugnance for the VC ahead of her love, and now there was nothing on earth that would stop me and I prayed to God in Heaven to give me the strength to help me find my way back to her. Where I thought I had found my purpose, I had only found hate, and like so many times before she brought me back from my despair and deprivation to a greater understanding and purpose of why I must get home, not to win her love but to share it.

As the months passed, our unit was hit a few more times, not really seriously, or at least not serious enough to get sent home. Leah kept writing letters, and I kept reading more into them than I probably should have. I was fighting a war and fighting my emotions. I was beginning to care more about her than anyone I had ever met, even though I had never met her. I experienced all the normal emotions of any other young man, even being jealous at times when she told me about her friends. I knew there must be a boy or two out there somewhere. Why not? I was thousands of miles away; I could not hold her, kiss her, or take her to movies. How do you hold back someone as positive, caring and as gorgeous as her? Why would she remain faithful to someone who might not even make it home? When these thoughts threatened to overwhelm me, another uplifting letter would arrive, and reading it, I knew she felt the same way I did. We both saw that our relationship had moved into uncharted waters. Two kids, thousands of miles apart, who had never met had fallen headlong and without hesitation in love.

I talked to her as though she was lying next to me at night, speaking of my dreams and desires, my passions and even how we would make it work after I came home. She was with me when we re-took Khe Sanh, and she held me through the terrible nights on Rocket Ridge. She walked with me through mountain trails on patrol, slept with me in rice paddies and kept me awake re-reading her letters on guard duty. No two people could have experienced a greater connection, shared more experiences or felt a greater need for each other than Leah and I. Vietnam, as bad as it was, will always hold cherished memories for me as it was here I found courage and passion and the girl of my dreams.

Toward the end of my tour, we took some heavy ground and rocket fire. We were really busted up and had all but exhausted our fire power. As the conflict intensified, I remember taking out Leah's pictures, and for the first time, I kissed them, thinking this might be my last chance. All I remember after that was a large explosion and searing pain; then all was quiet. I knew I was going into shock as everything started to dim around me. Before the light faded, I heard a voice speaking to me with gentle and soothing words, "Honey, please do not worry or fear. We have come too far to have any force of man hold us apart. Now sleep, my love."

Little did I know at the time I was soon in for the surprise of my life, but I believe with all my heart she spoke to me again that day, the same as when I had heard her voice so many times before. Maybe it was due to shock that I heard her this time, but as always, she never let me down. The next thing I remember was looking up at two of her pictures pinned to a mosquito net. As I stared at the pictures, she gave me strength and helped nurse me back to health.

During this time I did not write to her right away as I had no idea what to tell her about what had happened. Finally I told her we were being moved to Quang Tri and I was not sure when I would be able to write, but I would just as soon as I could. After this her letters stopped as well. At the time, I figured there was a problem with the mail forwarding service. Truthfully, this did not matter to me as I knew I would soon be home in her arms, maybe a bit busted up, but finally with her.

About three weeks later, I was transported to Fort Lewis in Washington State for my final discharge and was detained there with other injured Vietnam vets. The Army can be very strange at times as they placed us in a compound close to new (and green) draftees. We were put outside as they paraded these kids past us. Saying "kids" sounds strange since I was only twenty; but I could see the fear in their faces as they looked at us, wondering where they were going and what would happen to them. It seemed longer, but after a few days I was officially discharged and sent home; the problem was how to get there.

The Army provided no transportation, and most of us had little money. I contacted my father and asked for a loan and was booked on the next flight home. Dad wanted to meet me at the airport, but since I was flying standby and had no idea when I would arrive, I told him it would be better if I took a cab. In retrospect, I'm glad I did this as I think Pop would had gotten arrested for punching the protestors at LAX. When a few of us arrived, there was a crowd of protesters calling us names and holding up such ugly signs, I will never forget—Baby Killer and Pigs seemed to be the favorite chants of the day. Some even spit at us! How could things have changed so quickly? This was my generation not only protesting a war but slandering me for doing something they knew nothing about. I got out of there as fast as I could on crutches, grabbed a cab and made it home, kissed my parents and started to make phone calls. By now you have probably guessed who the first call went to.

I dialed the number Leah had given me. The phone rang and a woman answered. Since I had never heard her voice, I said, "Leah?"

There was a long pause, and then the woman's voice asked, "Who's calling?"

Loaded with excitement and anticipation, I almost shouted, "This is Ryan Miller. Where's my girl?"

At that very moment the phone went dead. I tried over and over again as I thought maybe she fainted since she did not know I was home, but the line remained busy for over two hours. Over the next few weeks I called repeatedly, maybe four or five times a day, trying to let Leah know I was home. Almost every time I called, I got the same woman's voice telling me, "I'm sorry Ryan, Leah's not home. She's on a date." Then click and the phone would go dead.

This was hard for me to understand. Leah had written that she never dated and was not allowed to go to dances or parties. Now, when I am home, she is out and about all the time? Fear crept into my every fiber. Could all of her letters have been lies or some twisted game leading me on? Maybe I had asked for too much from her, or maybe she had moved on and did not have the heart or strength to tell me. I sent her two dozen letters during this period, and although they weren't returned as undeliverable, she never responded. She had written to me for eleven months so openly, so honestly and so filled with love. That she had let me go without a single word made no sense to me.

I convinced myself there was no way she had been leading me on, not with letters filled with the emotions we shared and surely not with the love concealed in her words. Something must be seriously wrong. I contemplated taking the next flight to Tennessee and showing up unannounced at her home to confront her face to face. But I could only think of her, and if my fears that she had moved on were true, I could not fault her. Even as I thought this, I didn't believe it was true.

I tried one more time to reach out to her. The phone rang about five times and the same woman answered. "Hello."

"Hello, hi. This is Ryan Miller and please, please don't hang up on me again. I'm not trying to be rude, but I just got back from Vietnam, and I can't believe Leah is never home. All I want to know is where she is. I've waited so long, and all I want to do is just talk with her."

There was a long pause, but the woman did not hang up. Instead, with a trembling voice, she finally spoke. "Ryan, you don't know me, and

I doubt you remember me; but I'm Leah's mother, and I helped raise you at my mother's day care center in California. I know your mom and dad, and I'm not sure how to tell you this; but Leah has found a new love and is busy planning her wedding. She never meant to hurt you; she was just too young to understand. All she thought she was doing was helping you get by while you were in the war. I'm sure if you try, you will understand that her letters to you got way out of hand; but honestly she never meant to lead you on."

"Wait a minute, are you trying to tell me that after eleven months, this was only some kind of childish game she was playing?"

"No, I don't think that is true."

"Then let her tell me this herself. Please, I really need to talk with her, and Mrs. Heartaway, you need to know that I am in love with your daughter. Will you please, please let me talk with her?"

"I'm sorry, but that's not possible. I cannot allow you to come between her and her new love. As I said, she's planning a wedding to a boy her father and I have known for years and whom we love very much."

"Mrs. Heartaway, what harm would it be for me to just thank her for the countless letters and tell her how I adore her?"

"Ryan, I can't let you talk to her, but I know how you feel. I read several of your letters, and I know you love her. If you really do, then never call here again as all you will do is hurt my daughter."

"Hurt her, are you kidding me? Now, please put Leah on the phone! Hello, hello, hello."

The phone went dead and with it all of my hopes and dreams of ever seeing Leah. At this point all I could do was hang up as there was no longer a reason to push. Now was simply a time to cry. I had fallen in love with a dream, and I still had never heard her voice. The only odd thing was that Leah's mother's response was so matter of fact it felt like it was scripted and rehearsed, but why? She knew me; she knew my parents. Then again, why would she lie to me? The letters I had sent back, not being responded to, now made perfect sense. Leah could not face nor talk with me; her love was for another. Unwillingly I decided it was true. The obvious was before me; Leah had other plans, plans that did not include me.

All the letters, the strength, the love and the joy she shared with me were just words on barren pieces of paper, meant only to help me get through Vietnam. Maybe she felt her letters would stop me from taking any undue risks that might prevent me from coming home. Was she sadistic, or maybe I was a tool she used to keep the other boys at school on their toes and make them jealous. No matter the reason, I was hurting; and I knew, no matter how I rationalized it, the hurt would never go away.

I tried my best to hate her, but I couldn't. In my heart, I knew I would not have made it back without her. I went through bouts of depression and anger, but I could never completely let her go. Even though her love for me was not real, I had experienced something magical, a feeling I would never lose. I couldn't bring myself to throw her pictures away as they were all I had left of her. I kept them safe and showed them to no one.

Feeling as low and as rejected as any man could, I jotted this down on September 9, 1971, her birthday: "Leah compelled me to do things a man should never do, and through her letters she gave me a purpose in life, the most important one being to come home to her." I know it's corny, but I was so overcome with emotion I spent hours recreating her letters from memory, torturing myself to uncover anything I might have said or done to drive her away.

— —

As I awoke to the morning sun burning my tired and saddened eyes, a small but beautifully silhouetted shadow appeared to me through the dew drenched window of my only home, my car. I thought of a place I hoped she would fill with love, but as she had gone, the vision faded, forcing me to forfeit my dreams and surrender her to another. She lives beyond my reach in a world I cannot touch, and although I feel the urge to run to her, I will not; but if ever asked, I will crawl if it takes me home to her. Heaven brought her to me and for whatever I did to make her turn to another, I apologize with all my heart. To know she took her love and walked into the arms of another breaks my heart, for I know it could only be my words that sent her on her way. My despair is unbearable; I must resign myself to the truth that she is truly gone and remain silent. I hope her new life is beyond words, and I pray she will look fondly at our past. Her love saved my life, and I cherished her every word. Leah was the kindest and most caring person I have ever known, and her love will reside in my heart beyond time, like echoes in the rain.

Part II

Goodbye Leah: Bridges

5

Spanning Time Before and Beyond

Over the next few weeks I tried to control my emotions, but my eyes betrayed me, for in my mind I could picture her standing next to me. I hope she never knows how she left my life in ashes, and I pray to God to give me strength as I face life without her love.

The years, like slow moving Arctic ice floes, methodically and relentlessly drifted past, leaving in their wake barren memories of a distant past. I took out her pictures, generally on her birthday and then again during the holidays, just to make sure I remembered how special she was to me when life, other than with her, had no meaning. What she said to me in letters throughout my tour in Vietnam could be considered noble, and I pray she is happy wherever her life has taken her. I hope what she found all those years ago is as vibrant as the love I found in her, a love that lifted me, was passionate beyond words, and was never selfish or one-sided.

During this time of my life, I suppose I had accumulated a modicum of success; I completed College, business ventures were fruitful, and the budding albums of my life were filling with prosperous and proud times (and maybe a few of shame and regret). But no matter the gain, they were always overshadowed by my memories of Leah.

I tried over and over again to shut her out, I prayed to God to rid her from my mind and wipe away those feelings that haunted me. I tried to destroy the only things I had left of her, the photographs I had carried throughout Vietnam, but I could never follow through. Something within me, a curse or a blessing, wouldn't let me still those tender reminders of what I dreamed my life with her would be.

Losing Leah hardened me. I unknowingly, yet I suppose willingly, became callous, not only to most who knew me but to myself as well. I exploited a made-up cloak of "hard ass" to drive away people, hiding my true feelings, vowing to never be hurt again. However, in doing so I surrendered my compassion and sacrificed my ability to love anyone but Leah. I truly believed without her I was nothing more than that child soldier who should have died in the steaming jungles of Vietnam.

I moved in and out of relationship after relationship, which offered nothing more to me than wilting leaves on autumn trees, beautiful at first, then crumbling far too soon in the shadows of lonely nights. I tested the waters of long lost loves, but nothing completed me like the sensitivity and the compassion of Leah's love. Beaten down and weary, I tried to convince myself there must be someone out there, someone who could fulfill me; but in the end, as I knew from the beginning, I could never replace the love we once shared. I suppose out of self preservation, reluctantly and like a coward, I sought out a mate, knowing all the while I could never provide the love she would want and deserve. I had never backed away from anything or anyone in my entire life, and now I was willing to sacrifice the most precious gift from God, love! I asked the Lord to please forgive me, knowing I would soon enter into a life with no real foundation, but one built on lies and with a heart devoid of love.

Several Years after Vietnam, I married, not for love but as an escape from my true feelings. Foolishly I convinced myself that, if I could have a family, my life would change and force me to abandon this plight I had been in for so many years. I was wrong.

Throughout my marriage, I guess I provided expressions of love, offered an allusion of devotion and acted out the part of a husband, but my feelings of barrenness and guilt remained. No matter the beauty of my wife, no matter her passion or her desire, I could not surrender my love for Leah. I never told her the story of Leah, and for this I am truly ashamed, she deserved so much more than I could ever offer. I prayed for years for God to please find it in His heart to allow her to find someone who could provide the love she so desperately longed for, I could not.

I told myself over and over how lucky I was as there were now countless treasures in my life, riches that any sane man would have been content with; but for me there was only a hollow and nagging emptiness I was never able to escape. Subconsciously I knew it was the lingering memories of Leah which overwhelmed me. I did my best to stave off these feelings; but deep down, hidden and disguised from everyone I knew, I was living in denial, too cowardly and afraid to share my secret torment with anyone. Had they known, I believe they would have thought me a bit insane. How could any grown man hold onto a dream of being with someone who dumped him over thirty-five years ago? Maybe it was insanity.

Don't misunderstand; there were happy and meaningful times throughout my life. I was blessed in many ways—children, sports, business and good friends. I had reached the pinnacle of what any rational man dreamed of, but to me, all the accomplishments, the money and the promotions were vacant and empty rewards in my shallow and lonely life. I suppose this may have been God's punishment for defiling, in his sight, the words I spoke upon his alter. I tried to love my wife, but it was hopeless. Leah, or the dream of Leah's love, held me captive and rendered me unable to open my heart to another.

As I grew older, what made sense in my life and gave me any feelings of love were my children. Without them I'm not sure what might have happened to me, as I was so filled with self-pity and guilt. They were my rays of sunshine, allowing me to feel the sense of wholeness I craved. They also provided me with a respite from the realization that my married life was nothing more than an immoral lie that I had hidden from everyone for many years.

The decades marched forward, the seventies, the eighties, the nineties, and then suddenly the new century was upon us. I did not know it, but within this decade a miracle would happen that would alter my life. No one saw it coming nor would they have believed it to be possible, but the lives of everyone I knew, loved and cared for and the families of many others would be turned upside down; and in the wake of these changes, lives would be reborn and begin to love again.

By this point my kids had left to pursue their own lives. Without them close to me, I was worried how I would survive. My marriage was in shambles, and to add to my woes, I lost my father in the fall of 2005. I was fifty-four years old, semi-retired, depressed, bored and alone. Frankly I felt like throwing in the towel and walking away. There was too much pressure, too much anxiety and far too much loneliness in my life. I knew I had to do something to end this madness or go crazy or even worse. To pass the time, I started poking around for part-time job opportunities to fill my days. God, however, had other plans for me, and through His mysterious and wondrous love, set into motion a series of events that would not only restore my sanity but also allow my life to start anew. It all began in January of 2006.

6

Truth and Lies

A job fell in my lap. I'm not sure why, but the first week in January the owner of a telecommunications company, I had done some consulting work for and selling Verizon products and services offered me a full time position heading up his agency (independent contractor) program, as well as, continuing to do some free lance selling and marketing. The position was all but perfect as I had worked in this industry for over thirty years. I gained some relief from my home life and a chance to add to the coffers of my retirement war chest.

The owner, an English chap "Mr. Wadnizak", held corporate meetings every three months or so, and he placed enormous importance on them. January 26th was one of those meeting days, and, as always, he began the meeting with opening statements on the company's financial health. As he droned on, out of the blue, my cell phone rang. If looks could kill, I would not be here today. It was obvious the owner, his staff, financial backers and my co-workers were not pleased I even had my phone on me.

I always shut it off whenever I was in any meeting and could have sworn I had this morning as well. Instead of simply clicking it off, I had an overwhelming urge I can't explain to take the call. I started to let it go to voicemail, but again I had this inexplicable desire to know who was calling me at seven-thirty in the morning. The call originated from the 931 area code, which provided no clue where the call was coming from, but I answered, "This is Ryan."

There was a long pause, and then the voice at the other end said, with a shallow yet inviting southern accent, "Hello, Ryan, this is Leah."

At first I wasn't sure who this person was and said, "Who?"

"Ryan, you knew me as Leah Heartaway many years ago when you were in Vietnam."

I could barely speak. Memories flashed through my mind like still photographs rapidly appearing and disappearing, blinking in and out as a deluge of emotions washed over me. Overwhelmed, confused, mystified and I suppose a bit delirious, I abruptly left the meeting without any explanation and went outside to talk with what might be only a memory.

As she spoke I drifted back some thirty-five years, recalling the fateful night when she left me, and then back even further, remembering her letters and the abundance of compassion and love in her words. Needless to say, my emotions were all over the map, ranging from telling her to take a hike and never call me again, to talk, oh sweetheart, just keep talking and please never stop. How many times had I wished to just hear her voice? Her voice? Oh my God, it hit me; this was the first time I had heard her voice!

The world around me stilled; no cars, no sounds, nothing existed other than the sweet southern melodies in her voice. I recalled everything she had ever written to me, and then I remembered the numbing pain of losing her. There was no way I could shut down the overwhelming feeling of needing her as I had decades ago. My only question was why would she be calling me now? Did she find an old letter, maybe my photograph; was she ill, or did she suddenly wake up today and realize how she had hurt me and, for whatever reason, feel compelled to make amends for the past? As I continued to listen, she unraveled a series of events so unexpected and unimaginable Stephen King would have had problems conceiving it, and so unbelievable that even I had trouble sorting it all out.

Leah's voice trembled as she struggled to find the right words. I felt her fighting back tears, wavering at times as though she was afraid to speak to me, unsure that I would believe what truly happened in 1971. She unfolded a story so laden in deceit and manipulation I began to cry as well as I could feel her pain and disbelief that the people who were supposed to have loved her the most stole her life.

Within a few minutes I realized love endures; it never dies and, with God's grace, *always* finds its way. You see, this was not one of Leah's letters. This was Leah herself telling me she had not abandoned me as I was led to believe. Her words pierced my heart, and as her story took shape, I felt the pain she had felt and shared her utter disbelief in what had happened to us. She pleaded with me to believe she had not abandoned me and in fact never knew of the calls I had made to her. She had never received any of the dozens of letter I sent to her after returning from Vietnam; all she knew was that I had left her alone and abandoned with lost dreams.

My calls were intercepted by her mother, who ran a business out of their house. Because of this, Leah and her sister were not allowed to answer the phone. It wasn't until after she discovered I was still alive through conversations with her aunt and her father that she found out her mother had taken all of my letters from their mailbox and destroyed them before Leah got home from school. Odd, I thought. It looks like everyone except Leah knew what was going on behind her back yet had remained silent.

Leah told me when my letters stopped, she had felt alone with no compassion from her parents, her dreams shattered and in their place a single question—why would Ryan have done this to her? As the endless nightmare of days became months, Leah became more and more depressed, wondering what tragedy must have befallen me. Otherwise, how could I have just thrown her aside? Following months of crying and disbelief, Leah's mother, either out of guilt or through some form of misguided compassion, took Leah into her bedroom and in a callous and planned fabrication said, "Leah I did not know how to tell you this before as I thought, because of your age, you would move on and forget Ryan, but honey, he was killed in Vietnam. I should have told you earlier, but I couldn't bring myself to tell you the truth until now. I can't let you on go on like this anymore, crying for a love, knowing he can never come back to you."

I guess her mother felt this would bring closure to the matter and that Leah would move on with the boy she wanted her to marry. But what it did was fashion a dream of love in Leah, keeping alive the memory of a soldier from a far off land. That dream would compel her, no matter what, to never lose the feelings of my love. It never died and left her, like me, with a void no other would be able to fulfill; Kismet, you be the judge?

It may seem odd to you, but I believe the hand of God brought Leah back to me. I was truly thankful, if for nothing else than on this one special day in time, we were together again. I prayed both of us could find closure in knowing the love we once shared was never lost or abandoned but was stolen from us.

As I look back, it is clear to me Leah never knew. She believed I had died, but the love she offered to me she kept only for me, never to be shared with or given to any other man. It is obvious her parents were so fearful I would hurt Leah, take her away from them and change the life they had wanted and planned for her that they risked tempting fate to steal from Leah the life and the love she longed for. I doubt they knew at the time how I treasured her and how much I wanted to make her mine, assure our future and build the dreams we both craved.

I will never comprehend why her parents knowingly altered and thereby damaged their child's life, sending her on a path of destruction which now so many years later may be beyond repair. As we spoke and the truth came out, many unanswered questions remained. Why? Who else knew? How had it stayed hidden for so long?

Over the Years, Leah had a few glimmers of hope that maybe I was not killed in Vietnam. One of these obscure moments happened in

2001 during a Lee Greenwood concert that she, her mother and her daughter-in-law attended. They had front row seats, and during the concert Lee Greenwood winked at Leah several times. Although she was pretty embarrassed, all she did at the time was smile, but the other two started to tease her. On the drive home, their teasing increased as they giggled and cut up, using Leah as the brunt of their jokes.

"Wink, wink. Look, Mom, Leah got Lee's attention."

"Leah, when are you going to see Lee again?"

"Come on you guy's, knock it off. I don't know why he winked at me."

Then out of nowhere Leah's mother blurted out, "That's nothing. Leah could have married a movie star."

Leah, in less than a second, shouted, "What?"

You see I was the only one in Leah's past who had a theatrical background and for Leah, who had not dated her whole life, this was a strange and disturbing statement. But her mother only said, "Never mind."

"Mom, what did you mean by that?"

As they drove on, her mother would say nothing more about it, and the once jovial car turned into a hearse with not even one word spoken the rest of the way back to their chalet. However, Leah knew her mother had done something, and she knew it had to be about me; but her mother would not utter another word about her comment. Leah cried most of the night, wondering if there could be any truth to what her mother had said. Was I dead or could it be possible I was alive? Was it possible her mother planted the whole trail of deception, forcing her into a loveless marriage?

Leah's mind raced from one conclusion to another, but nothing made any sense since every plausible assumption led her to a single conclusion she was afraid she would not be able to handle. Nothing more was said, but from this day forward Leah was forced to contend with a malicious thought lurking in the back of her mind; possibly her own mother had lied to her and set her on a path that would tear apart everything she had ever desired and remove the only man she had ever loved.

She made many inquiries and bounced from one dead end to another. No one, not even her closest relatives, would talk to her about it. No matter; this was the first time Leah had felt even a faint glimmer of hope that she someday she might find the truth and possibly find me alive.

Not long after this, Leah's mother was killed in a horrific auto accident that left her father crippled and a changed man; he was the driver on that ill-fated day. Following his release from the hospital, Leah became his caregiver, moving him into her home and nursing him back to health. It was during this time that Leah would uncover another truth.

With her mother gone, she felt now would be the time to ask her father if he knew anything about the past and the truth behind the story I was killed in Vietnam. She went into her living room, which was now a make-shift hospital room, and asked her father if he knew anything about what actually happened back in 1971 and specifically if I was alive or if it was true I was killed in the war. The conversation as she recalls, went something like this:

"Dad, a little over a year ago Mom jokingly made a comment that I could have married a movie star. I asked her over and over again what she was talking about, but she refused to say anything more about it. She apparently blocked it out, saying, 'I have no idea what you are talking about.' Was she trying to tell me Ryan was alive after Vietnam? Did he come home from the war?"

"Honey, I'm not sure exactly what or how it happened, but yes, it's true. Ryan did make it home alive. From what I was told, he was all shot up, so we thought you wouldn't want him anyhow. You were so young at the time, and it looks like everything your mother planned for your life turned out okay, so it really doesn't matter anymore, does it?"

"Oh Dad, you have no idea what you have done."

"Leah, your mother told me there would be hell to pay if I said anything, and Ryan was so messed up after Vietnam, he most likely died anyhow. But honey, how can he mean anything to you after so many years?"

"Oh Dad, what have you done to me?"

7

Unearthing the Past

This short conversation with her father all but destroyed Leah as visions of deceit by her own mother crept into her mind. But what of Ryan? Why had he not come to her? Why no letters? Why not even one call? What she thought had been a gift from God, knowing I might still be alive, turned out to be a realization that her mother knowingly manufactured a series of lies and deceptions that not only denied our love but were designed to control her future. The mere thought of this terrified Leah as it, if true, made her a pawn in a planned scheme of events set into motion to force her into a marriage she knew was wrong.

For the last thirty-four years she had desperately yearned to experience true feelings of belonging and a place where she could freely give herself to another, but her longing was vain. Now, through the rantings of a distraught and mentally reduced man she called her father, was there hope at last? What she could not figure out was her father openly admitted he had, out of fear, allowed her to throw her life away without any compassion. *"There will be hell to pay?"* Was there truth in her father's words, or were they just words he thought she wanted to hear?

Discouraged, Leah convinced herself her father's words must have been drug-induced and not true. Her religion compelled her to abandon her search and accept that the fantasy of my love was not something a married and responsible woman should harbor. So she returned to her life, which I believe she did solely to protect her children from the emotional damage they might suffer trying to understand why their mother was so desperately searching for another man.

Leah resigned herself, once again, to the fact that I was probably killed in Vietnam or died shortly thereafter. In some ways, I guess this gave her solace and allowed her to set aside the pain she had endured and the lingering idea that her own mother had betrayed her; but deep in her heart she knew she could never bury nor forget the love of her lost soldier.

Leah's words cut through my own psyche. I knew why she had called and soon so would she. Once again I could hear her voice echoing through the rain. Here we were talking to each other for the first time. I think we (without saying) had the same purpose as we walked into the past. It was apparent we still needed each other but were not sure where this path would ultimately lead. We felt a craving to bridge our pasts, the experiences we had had with and without each other, to at least the present day. What we did not realize at the time is we were actually moving forward and on our way back to each other.

Call me a romantic or a nut, but I believe love has no limit, no time lines. It is just there and will not erode even if lost for decades. A fresh breath of renewed life had come back to me, and as before, I could not resist it or stop it. Would she be strong enough to accept her feelings and live out the destiny that had been stolen from us?

At the end of this amazing call, I must admit, I wanted more, so I asked her for her e-mail address. She told me she would have to ask her Husband about that, but would let me know tomorrow. I loved hearing her voice, but there were so many voids to fill in, and I wanted a step by step remembrance should we ever come together. She called me the next day with an e-mail address, a private one that her Husband suggested she set up so as to keep our correspondences personal and confidential. I guess I was somewhat suspicious as to his motivations but still; I was elated and very thankful. Ironically, I had always felt e-mailing was a cold, heartless form of communication, but it quickly became my lifeline to a love I had lost so many years ago. Plus writing e-mails was like writing letters as we had done during the Vietnam days, except that the e-mails would become recoverable reflections of our lives that could be read and re-read as we searched for hidden tidbits of truth, love and desire.

I caught myself daydreaming about her in the oddest places: ball parks, while driving, sleeping, picking up lunch, mowing the lawn and even in business meetings. She was with me now much like she was in Vietnam, invading my every thought and giving me the hope and strength to recover that which was taken from us. "*Be strong and of good courage*" has more meaning to me now than ever before, and I will never waver on this quest to bring "*my girl*" back to me.

There were so many barriers; we were two thousand miles apart, we were both married, and thirty-five years had changed us physically and mentally. Still the dream of each other lived in both of us and grew each day as we searched for the truth and possibly the love we once shared. This was frightening, for if we found what was left behind, it would alter our futures forever—even if we never brought our lost love into the light. I knew the road ahead would be heart wrenching and demand courage. It would cause broken hearts, possibly ours, but for us there was no return. I was not willing to go back to the life I was living knowing the truth about the past, and she would no longer be able to accept the life she had known as it was built on lies and deceptions. Whatever decision we made would lead to ultimate destruction or ultimate euphoria with nothing left to chance in between. My fear was never about Leah wanting to love and be with me, my problem was how to erase the years of intimidation and fear that still controlled much of her life and her willingness to accept the true meaning of marriage and love.

I pondered for days how I could communicate to Leah that I had never lost the love I felt for her; and how she occupied my thoughts over the last three and a half decades. How could I, in good faith, tell a married woman; not only do I love you, but I have adored you, which now feels like a life time? In my mind, this was not something I could just blurt out. I needed to find a way to take her back, remembering that vibrant and gifted young woman who desperately wanted to share her life with me. Then an idea hit me; what if I could take Leah back to the days of Vietnam, when she guided my steps and shared her love? Why not write a book? Using a book as a vehicle to communicate, I could remind her of the romance and love we shared and bring back to the light, that woman she left behind.

Much to my delight, Leah loved the idea of a book about our lives and the love we experienced and exchanged throughout my tour in Vietnam; and encouraged me to write on.

Once again we found joy, hope and a purpose in our lives, but questions remained. Would the past haunt us, or would we take up anew our quest of becoming one? Without her there would always be emptiness within me, and I believed that without me she would never be complete. The irony of it all was so overwhelming it seemed fictional at times. Here we were as adults struggling with the realities of prior commitments and the vows that held us in our current lives, while at the same time searching for a way to create an Eden where our love could bloom and we could reclaim what should have been.

Her past unfolded in her e-mails in painful stories where she was rarely put first and her youthful dreams denied. As an adult, looking back and clearly seeing the deceptions that had controlled her life must have been hard for her. As a teenager, she had possessed so much life and so much talent, but her dreams were given no chance to succeed. Instead, she became second best to others and hid her inner desires and passions so deeply and so tightly that they strangled all of the creativity she had so longed for. Now, she had renewed hope that her creativity and the life she was denied would flourish. Her true desire was within reach, yet in her manipulated state of mind, the uncertainty of loyalty, spirituality, dedication and her wedding vows fought relentlessly to control her actions. However, for Leah, her time was near, her destiny all but in sight. No longer a child, she was clearly becoming a woman who could confront every step of her past life.

I cannot tell her what the future will hold, but I know that her future lies with me, a future that will not be weighed down nor denied by the lies of a distant yet ever present past. With me she will no longer be controlled by the decisions of others; she will have freedom of choice, the joy of happiness and the ability to release the passions she had knowingly cloaked all these years. I realize these feelings will frighten her at first as her loyalty and faith are challenged, but I am equally aware she will never be fulfilled until she rekindles the embers of our love that once glowed so brightly. I am convinced I am the only man on the planet who can give back to her that which was taken from her; her belief in love. They say you can never go back and that time displaces things as you grow older. Rivers run dry, buildings collapse, families move on, but I catch myself screaming in my heart, "Why not?"

Why not? I wondered if this really applied to us. The many naysayers that appeared from every hidden corridor whispering under their breath comments like "fools," "daydreamers" and "grow up, you can never go back," just didn't understand. Leah and I were not trying to put the spilt milk back into the carton. How can you go back to something that never was? We were searching for love in our lives and a person to share it with in the future.

One thing was very apparent to me. In her own special way, Leah loved only me; and I know that in my special way I loved only her as well. Our love may be deemed by many to be forbidden in the flesh, but even this may soon be inevitable, as the desires we have held for each other have not diminished over time. They will never die, pass away for the sake of others nor fade in the night. As our new story unfolds, I see in her the beginning of the joy she has so long awaited and a sense of self-worth she has never before allowed or accepted in her life.

I'm not certain what my future role will be: friend, lover, husband or a fond memory, but I know I must be there for her, if only in spirit, to guide and guard her steps along the way. If it were only possible for her to see into my mind, she would feel the desires and the love I hold for her. If she could take ownership of my essence, she would feel the gifts I have waited all my life to give to her. However, at this time I cannot allow her to know the love and passion I feel for her and the desire within me to take her into my arms. My fear is this could be our beginning and at the same time our end, as our dreams may still be too overwhelming for Leah to accept.

Much like Leah, I have always placed others above myself and spent countless hours assuring their happiness. I have fears, but how long can I avoid fulfilling the longing in my own life. When is it the right time to stand up and decide that happiness belongs to us as well? An excerpt from a poem I once read sums up for me why we must live in love and be alive in life, and not merely survive:

> *Time travels so slowly*
> *Yet it's gone very fast,*
> *You're barely aware that it's here*
> *Till it's past.*

I will not let time or the past once again steal my girl and a life that was meant to be ours from the beginning. This time I will walk slowly, trusting no one, eyes wide open, steering clear of the pitfalls and fight, if need be, those who wish to hold us apart. I have little doubt we are on a path that will reveal to all the love we once shared that was so apparent and so genuine those many years ago. I can think of nothing more loving or compassionate than to openly profess and share the joyous wonders of being in love. I know in my heart there is a greater purpose here and that a power from a higher place is guiding our actions, our words and our steps, as two people could have never held in such reverence these feelings for this long a period of time without divine intervention.

It feels as though we were brought together to save each other's lives once again. Our bond to each other is greater than before as we have lived alone, within separate nightmares, all these years. Whatever force or power that has brought us together this late in life must have a pre-designed purpose, a set course for us to follow and a faith-based message for us to share. Leah and I were blinded, in awe if you will, by the sheer and unbelievable magic we found in each other.

I have always believed God has a purpose and a plan for everyone, but what if man alters that fate or bends that design even slightly? Is it possible that a paradox could have been formed so many years ago and through it we lived lives designed for us, albeit with another person, and one who could ever complete the original design? Leah did not marry for love nor did I. The love we both searched for was already taken, her soul to me and my soul to her, and that love would not allow itself to be shared with anyone else. Our story tells me destiny can be altered but never denied and fate, no matter how long it takes, will correct all misguided alterations.

Leah and I shared many happy and sad moments together, although we were physically apart from each other. We were married on the same day, we each brought three children into this world (all the same age), and we both married, not for love, but as a matter of convenience and escape. We never lost sight of the love we held for each other. I kept her pictures as treasures of the past, and she kept every letter I had ever sent to her from Vietnam.

Leah only found happiness through her children, as did I. It's as though a greater force, one to whom we had pledged ourselves, understood our love for our children and allowed us to raise them without interruption until the right time arrived. I believe that time is now! Our children are grown and following the paths of their own lives. We have suffered and repented for our prior sins of marrying devoid of love, and we believe in our hearts the Lord of man smiles upon us and has once again fashioned a plan for us to confirm our destiny. There will be pitfalls. Without question the hardest will be the misunderstanding of our children; yet I pray they will come to believe our love must flourish, and even though some will never accept the truth, it must be unveiled.

I embark on this journey with eyes wide open and with loving arms which I hope Leah will soon fill. Without hesitation I will devote myself to her. We have placed ourselves, willingly and enthusiastically, in harm's way; but for us, there is no other way. Today we joyfully and thankfully re-join God's Team, fully aware that the devil now knows which side we are truly now on. We fully expect he will use every weapon in his arsenal to turn all others against us in an attempt to discredit and slander the path we now follow; bring it on!

Part III

Walks

8

A Journey Back in Time

Through our e-mails Leah unfolded her life, her loves, her ambitions, and her tragedies and heartbreaks to me. I am amazed, shocked, astonished and sometimes overwhelmed. As before, there is so much clarity and innocence in her words, it's as though she has waited a lifetime to share her innermost feelings and passions with me. It feels as though we are taking verbal walks together, re-learning what it means to be loved and more importantly how to share and how to give love.

As we slowly pieced our lives back together, exploring the good and the hurt, we became closer to each other and to the life we left behind. This time, however, we proceeded with a greater caution and understanding as we have already lived through the incredible pain of losing each other.

I was born in a downtown Los Angeles hospital and had what I thought was a normal childhood, but we moved around quite a bit. Dad worked in construction as a crane operator; and when he finished a job, we moved to a new one, which is why when I started high school this was my eleventh school change. In some ways this was good as it made me outgoing, maybe a bit tougher than most. It also gave me a strong passion to assure my kids would remain in the same school system until they went to college.

Leah was also born in Los Angeles, in the same hospital as I was. As a baby and little child she was taken care of by her Grandmother Lenna, who had run an in-home nursery for neighbors and friends. I attended the same nursery and was cared for by the same loving woman as well as by Leah's mother. Over the next few years, my mother and Lenna became great friends, and both have told me stories of Leah and I being inseparable. I was a few years older than Leah, and they said I carried her around with me from room to room. Lenna likes to joke about me stealing bananas and then running off to find Leah to share them with her. Lenna also told me that when it was nap time, she would settle all the other kids on their cots and then get Leah and me and lie down with us on her bed until we fell asleep. Truth or fiction? I really don't know, but I doubt if she would lie about this. Maybe it's what she wants to remember, but in a way, it seems as though fate coupled us together even from the beginning.

I actually lost Leah for the first time in 1958 when her parents moved to the South; I believe she was three years old at the time. Her grandparents had a farm and a cattle ranch they supported by working in California, but the time had come for them to move back to the South, and Leah and her parents, shortly thereafter, followed them. Life for Leah and her family these were difficult times as they lived in a home with no running water or indoor plumbing. This house was actually an old log cabin built before the turn of the century out of poplar logs with boulders used as floor supports. Leah told me story after story about her young years, her mischievous side that kept getting her into trouble, and the hard work of life on a farm in Tennessee.

[For the romantics among you, Leah and I ended up buying a portion of her grandmother's farm, as well as, that same old poplar log cabin where she had spent many hours writing to me while I was in Vietnam, and now I am telling you our story from the back bedroom of that very same cabin.]

As Leah grew, her once playful, socially active California-born parents became very controlling and stifled their daughter's social growth at almost every turn. I'm not sure exactly why; maybe it had to do with the harsh conditions or maybe it was something buried in their past, but for whatever reason, they stole the playfulness and joy from Leah's childhood. She did not experience the normal activities of youth; going to parties, dancing, and dating. I believe they were motivated, if not intimidated, via the teachings of a small but strict and uncompromising church with a doctrine of male dominance. I honestly believe Leah's parents could not comprehend how the heavy-handed structure of this church would suppress their daughter's natural creativity, stifle her development, keep her from fulfilling her dreams, and set her up to follow, without question, the church's set of standards, which appear to me, for women, to be servitude to men or face eternal damnation.

To make matters worse for Leah, her mother became ill early in her life, and many of her actions may have been a result of medications she was taking. For whatever reason, she tore Leah down to a state of hopelessness and despair, a fallow childhood in the broadest of terms. Leah became the underlying cause of her mother's stomach attacks and was told by her mother she was sick because of Leah either disagreeing with her or because Leah was bad. Leah, however, was just a kid at the time trying, as children do, to win her mother's affection, all the while dreaming of being like the other girls, having a soda with a boy or listening to music and dancing with the girls at a slumber party. All these simple enjoyments were strictly forbidden by her religion.

How tragic this must have been for a young girl trying to cope with the general problems of youth. Most of us develop social skills in our teenage years, some maybe through youthful experimentation, but we learn the boundaries between men and women, where those lines are drawn and why, but not Leah. She was sheltered to the extent that she knew nothing of relationships between men and women; she was truly innocent and naïve, not allowed to have boyfriends or even answer the phone at home. Looking back now as I walk with her through her past, I have no doubt in my mind why, even without love, a word she had never comprehended or identified with, she would ask a boy to marry her with no conception of what this might mean or how destructive it could become. It's as though she had been pushed into this appalling conclusion her entire life.

Leah's father was far from blameless, but in his mind, he had other responsibilities trying to support his family. Following a succession of jobs and several years later, he opened a family run upholstery business where Leah also worked for a while running the back office, estimating jobs, as well as helping move heavy furniture and maintaining inventory levels and stocking. As Leah's mother's illness became more and more severe, her abuse became more aggressive, verbally and physically. The tragedy was that the father figure Leah so desperately needed was simply not there. I have no way of knowing for sure, but it seemed to me the sicker his wife became, the more removed he became. He provided for his family, but those things important to nurturing his two young girls took a back seat. Her mother's actions and her father's inactions eventually set Leah up for the biggest mistake of her life.

There was one boy, I'll call him Richard, who became a big part of her life because of, once again, her parents. Richard became a household fixture, as he worked for her father and actually stayed at their house from the time Leah came home from school until she went to bed. Leah's mother also insisted that he go on family vacations with them and told Leah he was the son she never had. She even told Leah that if Richard ever went to hell, "it would be your fault young lady!"

Trapped, manipulated, brain-washed and forced, day after day, to be with Richard, she gradually lost sight of any of the dreams she had cherished. Was she completely controlled? I don't know everything, but the one thing I do know is Leah was never given the opportunity to discover who she was, never allowed to pursue her desires and never given the chance to find or experience love. All those things which should have been normal and natural were unnecessary from her parents' point of view. Everything she desperately longed for was being buried deeper and deeper, and tragically this pattern, now so imbedded, would continue to control her adult life.

It was at this time I came back into Leah's life. Her parents made a trip to the West Coast and visited old friends, including my parents, where they found out I was deployed to Vietnam. After they returned home, they told Leah about me, and she asked her mother if she could write to me. I suppose her mother thought nothing would come of this, and she agreed. So began an almost year-long correspondence. As I said earlier, I was captivated by Leah, and her letters brought me great joy and immeasurable anticipation.

As we talked some thirty-five years later, Leah told me it was my letters that kept her alive, helping her get through school and cope with the harsh times and the domineering ways of her mother. I believe a lot of the love we feel today is due to the fact we were there for each other. Leah was fighting a war and so was I, in different ways but with the same results. In all wars physically fought or those psychologically waged against you, you lose something—your innocence, your self-worth and your passion for life.

Leah told me she fell in love with me by the fourth or fifth letter, and as I look back, the same was true for me. After being told of my death, Leah was despondent. Nothing seemed to matter anymore, and as the months rolled by, her torment increased beyond reason, with her mother relentlessly pushing her toward Richard. For a meek and distraught seventeen-year-old, this constant pressure became unbearable. She held out for a year and a half waiting for something or someone who never came, and forced by others, she headed down a precipitous path of destruction and gave up any hope of happiness and sacrificed her life to stop the torment of the increasing verbal and physical assaults from her mother.

To add more fear and tragedy to Leah's young life and what would become the final and crushing blow, she discovered that she had a lump in her breast. To Leah this brought on an uncontrollable fear, as one of her girlfriends had been diagnosed just a month earlier with breast cancer and she feared the worst. Scared, alone, rejected, mentally abused and hard-pressed by her mother to be with Richard, Leah was at a point in her life where she would have turned to anyone showing her a way out.

In this regard Richard had positioned himself well; at the very least he was always there. He wanted Leah and was willing to do anything to have her, but what was odd was he made no passes at her nor ever asked her for a date. He was the proverbial "old shoe," always present but never really there for Leah. I can't help but question this. It appears he never loved Leah. He lusted after her; any man would have. But love her? I don't think so, for if he loved her, he would not have allowed her mother to treat her the way she did. He never said a word; he sat back biding his time, knowing that Leah's mother was unfolding a plan to force Leah to him.

In December of 1972 Leah had just started Christmas break when she found the lump in her breast and was advised by her doctor that lumpectomy surgery would be necessary. With little if any compassion from her mother, her mind raced to the worst possible conclusion and that night her world and will to live fell apart. The next day, consumed with destructive thoughts—Ryan was dead, no one would ever want her now with a scared and horribly discolored breast, desperately wanting to flee her mother's torment, depressed and defeated—she could take no more. It was on this fateful day she uttered these tragic words, "Richard, will you marry me?" She knew she did not love him and to marry without love was a sin, but she was willing to sacrifice love and herself and possibly her soul to evade her torment which soon, she would find out, paled in comparison to the life she was about to enter.

So on the steps that led down to the family workshop in the basement, Leah, in an almost nonchalant manner, said, "Richard, I don't love you, but do you want to get married?"

"Okay."

"But Richard, I don't love you."

"That's okay; maybe you will grow to love me."

In talking with Leah about these times in her life, I pondered what would possess a beautiful young girl to surrender herself to a man having no knowledge of what this meant, a man she had never kissed, had not discussed future plans or college plans with, who had no home and whom she did not love. How do you lose your faith in humanity; how can things be so bad you turn to compassionless servitude? Leah could not answer these questions for me, and to this day, it is still painful for her to recall what she endured throughout her childhood and then the indignities that befell her after she married.

I feel some sympathy for Richard as he had to have lived his entire life looking over his shoulder, knowing how fragile this world he helped create was. How fearful he must have been, knowing at any moment his childhood fantasy of marriage and love, like a house of cards, could come crashing down around him. He knew Leah would never stop loving me, and he knew I was alive and that someday, through faith or tragedy, I would return.

I discovered Richard carried many emotional and psychological scars as a result of his dysfunctional family unit and his deplorable living conditions. He was one of several illegitimate children sired by different men and whose biological father committed suicide early in his life. Richard's family of six lived in a ten by fifty foot trailer ridden with animals and pestilent infested living conditions, where the so-called pets ate off of the kitchen table or out of filthy dishes left in the kitchen sink for days.

Richard would go to school reeking of his environment, which I suppose he accepted as normal. This led to a hollow high school experience wherein he had no social graces, no understanding of love or even what the feelings of love were. Lost in his inability to change his environment and not possessing the skill set or the inherent motivation to change his life, he apparently built a world of fantasy and imagination. This was about the time Leah, and more importantly her parents, came into his life. For whatever reason, they provided Richard with a place to live outside of his situation; he ate breakfast and dinner most of the time with them and stayed at their house until bedtime. It was here he could escape and build memories to carry into his future; a future where he could fantasize this was truly his family.

He fashioned, like in James Hilton's *Lost Horizon,* an everlastingly happy land sheltered from the outside world. The problems he could not comprehend at the time were that his daydream was not of his making and was not supported by him, so once the reality of life set in, he would be predestined to fail. His imaginary world was built on his desire to escape his home life and on lust, not on a true devotion to love and the moral principles which most us of learn early in life. Leah's proposal made everything perfect for him. He was now locked into the family and could use Leah to perpetuate his fantasies of love. He had all to gain; a new trailer, a new family, a job with her father and a plaything he could use at will. Cruel, callous, heartless are words that come to mind. He knew love would never exist between them and that this union would cause the destruction of Leah's dreams, but he pushed forward without any concern for her, solely to satisfy his selfish desires.

What I question most during this fiasco is where were Leah's parents? What were they thinking? Richard had not asked their daughter to marry him, so what were his intensions? He had no place for them to live, no education, only a small salary from Leah's father and had not even dated their daughter. Instead of insisting on an engagement period so the two could get to know each other better, Leah's mother rushed to get them married less than three weeks later. Leah dove headfirst into a marriage that would endure, albeit through the fear of damnation, one in which she could never feel love, trapped with the lingering dream of another's love. Was this a sin? I believe it was. Leah and Richard, albeit for separate purposes, used each other and each entered a marriage they knew was devoid of love.

Leah had just turned seventeen, so her parents had to sign for her to get married. Actually, her mother insisted they get their marriage license the day after Leah's proposal. They offered their daughter to Richard, along with the down payment on a new mobile home and a pre-paid honeymoon to Disney World; as a dowry. Their wedding was curious to me in one other way. All her life, Leah's parents had lectured her and professed their religious belief that the congregation was her extended family; yet not even one member was invited to the wedding. The glorious church wedding in the sight of God and the celebration of a new union was not to be. Leah entered into her role as wife in the small mobile home her parents paid the down payment on, wearing a make-shift wedding dress made two days earlier by an elderly neighbor, witnessed by only a few immediate family members. No aunts, no uncles, no cousins and not even her precious grandparents were there as none were invited.

This one special day in their daughter's life was turned into a complete sham; they might just as well have married at the drive through window at McDonalds. I believe it to be true that Leah's parents knew this marriage was wrong and did their best to hide it and get it over with as soon as possible, maybe out of fear that Leah would discover that I was alive and bring a screeching halt to their plans. Leah and I may never know the real truth behind their motivations, and maybe we should not know as it might be too painful for Leah; but no one will ever convince me this union was blessed by God.

Reading her words from the e-mails about her wedding day, I was brought to tears. She and Richard fought the entire day as she wanted to back out. She knew, and so did he, that she did not love him and the only reason she asked him to marry her was out of desperation. She did not want to go through with the marriage, but there was also fear of the repercussions that would follow from her parents. Leah recalled one conversation on this fateful day with her mother in her attempt to back out of this insanity.

"Mom, I don't think I can go through with the wedding. I really don't like him, and I will never love him."

"Leah, your father and I have paid for your honeymoon and put the down payment on your trailer, so you are not going to back out of this. I won't allow it."

"But Mom, I don't love him."

"Too bad. He asked you to marry him and you said yes, so it's over and you will marry him!"

"That's a lie. He didn't ask me; I asked him."

"That makes no difference now, and you will go through with this wedding, and Love? What do you know of love? Now get dressed, you are going to be married!"

Intimidating? Maybe not to you, but to a mixed up and lonely naïve teenager, this was more terrifying than the thought of a marriage without love. I realize now what possessed Leah to go through with this unblessed union, but what dark secret compelled Leah's parents?

Richard, in his defense, did tell Leah that "maybe" she would learn to love him; and for a young girl who was so lost, I suppose this could be possible, but this isn't how a marriage should start. Although Leah tried through the years to love Richard, there was something missing, something she could not logically explain, that kept her from handing over her heart to him. That something was my love.

Richard knew this from the very beginning, and agreed to allow Leah keep every letter I had sent to her from Vietnam. Maybe this was his way of letting her feel love while he continued for years to use her to satisfy his physical needs, with no concern for her well-being. He mentally and emotionally entrapped her, using their religion as his instrument of bondage, from which in her mind she could not escape least she be condemned to hell. But at least through my letters she could escape, if only for a moment, and remember happy times and never forget my love. It is hard for me to understand this, but they both came from dysfunctional families where incomprehensible actions were seemingly commonplace.

9

Leah

What should have been was not and what could have been lingered and tore at her heart, but I believe her love for me gave her the endurance to sustain an unnatural and unblessed lie they called a marriage. As time passed, Leah bore three sons; and after many moves, they ended up in Tennessee, just a few minutes from her grandmother's farm in a nice home they designed and built. Her boys were her life and the only reason for her to stay with Richard. To Leah they were God's greatest gift to her, and she devoted countless hours to their nurturing and care.

Early on in the boy's lives, Leah took on many duties and responsibilities that I am not sure, even to this day, they fully comprehend or appreciate. I am convinced they were sheltered from the harm she endured having to live in a loveless marriage, but I wonder if they remember what she gave up and how hard she worked to provide for them and others? She spent endless hours, generally late at night, attending to her mother's medical needs. She tended to all of her boys basic and emotional needs and nurtured their creativity. Although Leah took on many additional tasks and jobs throughout the years, including running a successful Rainbow Vacuum Cleaner business, her sole motivation was to do whatever was necessary to support her family, and more importantly, to be there for "her boys" as a devoted mother.

To all who knew Leah and Richard, they appeared to be a loving and complete couple; they gave off an outward appearance that a special love existed between them. Church folks, family and friends saw them as a gentle, compassionate and loving family; well, all but one. Leah's grandmother knew the hidden truths that lurked behind closed doors. Everyone but her was about to learn of a change that was taking shape that would shake them all forever and change their lives in ways they could not imagine.

It began in late 2005 when my father passed away. It was my place to inform family, friends and old pals of my Pop of his death, so I drafted hand written letters, made copies of the newspaper article about him and searched every old address book of his I could find. I must have sent out over three hundred letters to people I had either forgotten or never knew. As I dropped these in the mail slot, I had no idea a single handwritten letter would set into motion a chain reaction that would alter my life forever.

Lenna, Leah's grandmother was an old friend of my parents, and her address was in one of Pop's old books, even though my parents had not seen her in fifty plus years. She received one of these letters simply because; she was in one of the books. When I addressed the envelope, I remembered bits and pieces about her, maybe from Leah's letters while I was in Vietnam, and yes, I hoped she would show the letter to Leah. I'm sure she had reservations after receiving my letter, but she knew how her granddaughter loved me and how she had not been able to let go of the memories we once shared. In her heart she could not remain silent any longer as Leah needed to know the truth, so she called her granddaughter that same day. All Leah could recall of the conversation was her saying, "Ryan's not dead, and I know where to find him."

Leah told me she almost fainted; it was quite a shock after more than three decades to find out her suspicions and dreams that I might be alive were real. She was consumed with an overwhelming desire to find me and tell me the truth about what had happened. Empowered by this desire and new hope, Leah began asking questions. She recalled her mother's comment at the Lee Greenwood concert and the conversation with her father, which now made perfect sense. She later found out other family members had known about the deception all along. Even Richard knew that her mother had done something to keep her from me, but he and all the others had kept silent. Given this, she found herself in a place where she could trust no one.

She came to the painful realization she had been cheated out of a love and a life she had so deeply desired by those who were supposed to have loved her the most. In the blink of an eye, Leah's world derailed. All the frustrations of her sheltered youth, all the pain wrongfully bestowed upon her, all the deceit and now the new and greater emotion, having to face the reality she feared following her conversation with her father two years before, came crashing down on her. The truth had been exposed, and she was forced to accept that she had been lied to and pressured into forfeiting her life and the only man she had ever loved. It was her aunt who finally broke down and told her she knew of my calls and letters and of the fact her mother had burned them to keep us apart. Others beside her aunt had known the truth for years. When the truth became known, most turned a deaf ear to her, not wanting to hear anything she had to say and not caring how she had been manipulated. She was told, "You are married, and no matter what happened before or how you were treated or how you feel, you are married and that is all that counts."

Leah was trapped between two worlds. One world contained a young girl's dreams, filled with desire and a passion for life; the other housed a mature woman trapped in a marriage devoid of love and passion. What she had uncovered frightened her, for no matter what she decided to do, in her heart and by her faith, she felt condemned and was afraid God would forsake her. If she stayed in her present life, she was condemned as it was built on lies and deceit. If she moved on to reclaim a life stolen from her, she was condemned as well, as she would be considered an adulteress. She prayed, "Oh Lord, guide my way."

Her days were filled with endless questions of what ifs and why not's. How could she cope, and for that matter, remain faithful to her husband, knowing she would always long to be with another? Confused, bewildered and alone, she knew she must find me and talk with me, if for no other reason than to silence the cries of the past.

Common sense and logic, I assume, reared their ugly heads and crept quickly and relentlessly into her thoughts, drawing her back into the place where she had lived for so long; denial. Like a cold slap in the face, she convinced herself there was really no logic or future in her harboring desires for a lost love of thirty-five years ago. However, there was no question in her mind she desired the life she had always dreamed of and the love she wanted to share. She tried to convince herself too much time had gone by, that my love for her must be dead and buried in the past. Maybe I had completely forgotten about her; maybe I was happily married with loving children and a happy, successful life. Maybe there was no chance for her to retake that lost part of her life? She knew I thought she had dumped me without even a call. Why would I want to talk to her now? There were many questions, but the one thing about Leah you need to appreciate is her incurable stubborn side, and thank God it kicked in. Her compelling urge to tell me the truth, reinforced by the love she once held for me, hardened her resolve. She would find me, but in her own way.

Fate is a queer bird at times, but I believe it always seeks to restore those things which were meant to be. Things happen in our lives we may never understand; the doors to our future open and close, sometimes without our knowledge and beyond our control. Fortunes are made and lost, careers come and go, but true love and true faith can never be displaced, no matter the evil actions others may impose. Fate breathes life back into our dreams, even those from long ago. All we need to do is keep our faith, and even those things that appear implausible will be made whole, for through God, all things are possible, even the impossible.

My father passed away on the same date Leah's mother died. My father's death left my mother, at eighty-eight and blind, needing assistance.

Somehow Lenna got my parents' old phone number and attempted to contact Mom, not knowing that she had moved in with me. I suppose she wanted to call to say she was sorry about Dad's passing and maybe relive some of their happier times, but I want to believe she really wanted my number.

Here's the eerie part. When Mom moved in with me, we terminated the phone service at her house. I know this is true because I handled all her bills and had paid no phone bill in three months. However, when Lenna dialed the number, it rang. My son had stopped by his grandmother's house to pick up a few things for her; when the phone rang, it startled him since he knew the number had been disconnected, but he answered the call. He had never heard of anyone named Lenna and was hesitant to give her any information, but she was persistent, and after some prodding he gave her my home phone number.

Could the phone company have made a mistake? I guess so. Think what you want, but I will always believe fate had a hand in this!

Lenna immediately called Leah to give her my number, and the pressure was on. Can you imagine her apprehension? She was a fifty-year-old mother of three who had been married for thirty-two years, and although she had never been happy, she was still highly religious. But in her heart, she knew she must contact me. She held in her hands a pathway in the form of a phone number to a young girl's vision of love that she believed was killed three decades earlier. What would she say to me? How could she choose the right words? What if she mistakenly used words that could be construed as insincere or even misleading? How could she hide her enthusiasm at finally hearing my voice? Yet most freighting of all, what if those desires hidden for all these years resurfaced?

These thoughts tormented her day in and day out and invaded her reasoning and desire to contact me. Weeks rolled by, and her zeal to contact me waned as her insecurity and lack of self-confidence created uncertainty. Logically she thought, *Should I seriously try to contact Ryan? I want to let him know I did not throw him aside, yet my story may be so unbelievable, he won't listen. And what if he still has feelings for me? What do I do then?*

Another day: *Should I leave Ryan buried as a lost love? I can't do that! I need to know if Ryan wanted me and was truly in love with me. I have to know this; I must know this! Who am I kidding? My love for him was never a mistake, so how can I withhold the truth?*

Later: *Should I call just to clean up the past? Yes! This is what I need to do, just a simple call, no emotions, but how will I hide the feelings I have always held for him? I must be strong and make this call even though I will not and cannot let him know how much I have loved him and that I still do. Oh stupid me, I have dreamed of him coming home to me my whole life. To let him go again, knowing he's alive, is beyond cruelty; not again! Oh God, I am so confused!*

Common sense won, but with a taste of reality. *Come on Leah, get a grip; you are a married woman and there is no way Ryan will still have feelings for you. But what if he does? I never gave up on my love for him, so what's to say he won't feel the same? I will be devastated if he is rude, or I will be rendered helpless if he still desires me. Honestly, I'm not sure which would be worse. I do know I have an undeniable desire to contact him, if only to hear his voice. Please God forgive me for I know which I would prefer. The love I have sought, yet never found, will it overshadow my sworn duty? Duty! I am so sick of hearing this word. Can't anyone have an ounce of compassion for me? I hate my life, being forced to stay where I am or face damnation. I'm not sure what to do, but I cannot ignore, with each breath I take, the euphoria I feel of finally welcoming my lost love home even though maybe not to me? God, please help me.*

Leah was torn between her beliefs and her desire for the truth, yet it was her honesty to herself that would ultimately give her the courage to call me. She talked again and again with her husband about what she should do, looking for his compassion and understanding as to why she felt such a need to contact me. I understand her motivations. She had been held so captive to and guided by her vows and her religion that she was all but lost. Unknown to her, Richard knew the details of her mother's deception, and he also knew he should let her confront her past, in part to bring closure to his fears.

Ultimately, it was Richard who persuaded Leah to contact me. He even asked her each day if she had made the call. After three months of debating and soul searching, Leah convinced herself that, through talking with Richard and his insistence that she call, she could now make the call with a clear conscience. Only she knew her true motivations in wanting to speak to me. It had nothing to do with latent passions or hidden desires, it was something Leah simply needed to know the answer to; did Ryan ever really love me?

To Leah this call was her one day, one time and one single call to reach back an entire life time. However, I believe deep down Richard viewed this as his opportunity to bury me once and for all. He knew I was alive all along, and he knew Leah harbored a love for me. Because of those unresolved feelings, he could never completely have her love. I am convinced he believed there was no way I would be attracted to her and that her religious beliefs would hold her to him. The problem he never contemplated, which exposes his arrogance and his contempt for Leah, is that by having her contact me, her true feelings of love would be uncovered, no matter what happened between us. He falsely assumed I was the problem holding Leah's love from him, but what he did not realize is his perpetual belittling of her and treating her like a possession prompted Leah to consider leaving him for years. She just had not acted on this because of her boys.

With her heart all but in her throat, the final decision to contact me was made. With number in hand and a self-assured mindset that this call would be nothing more than an explanation of the past and an expression of condolence for the loss of my father, she would dial the number her grandmother had given her. She had no idea she was about to put her life on a collision course with destiny.

10

Turning Point

Leah refused to make the call from her home. She wanted this verbal meeting to be private, though not necessarily in secret, as she believed this would be her only chance to talk with me. She needed a place where she could, without interruption, candidly explain to me she wasn't the monster I must believe her to be and a place where she could openly tell me the truth about what had transpired back in 1971 and how the lies and deceit altered both our lives.

She was scheduled to go on a business trip the following day and knew of a place along the way where she could call me. The next day she drove over one hundred miles to this place that had good cellular connections and where she could talk openly—a Cracker Barrel parking lot of all places. She parked her car, took out her phone and dialed a number she had by now read a thousand times. Her fingers trembled with excitement and she could all but see her blouse move with the heavy beating of her heart. The phone rang once, then again and again, until a voice like a gift from God and one she had waited for her whole life answered, "This is Ryan."

At that moment the feelings held dormant for so many years engulfed her in a tsunami of emotions and passions which left her searching for words. All she could manage was, "Hello, Ryan, this is Leah."

From this first call, that in her mind would be completely platonic, quickly turned and became, well at least in my mind, anything but platonic.

Within days and through our e-mails, she allowed words that had been held, sealed away for thirty five years to flow from her like poetic and graceful rivers, meandering through her past as the reality of her life became very clear, to her and to me as well. It became almost painfully obvious, this was the first time in her life she had openly expressed and accepted the truth behind what she had done, revealing a secret she had veiled, even from herself, for over three decades.

As we continued to walk together through these pathways of time, I could sense that the love we were now sharing and the affection Leah had dreamed of frightened her. To some, reliving the past can be a wondrous journey, but to Leah this was a painful remembrance which brought into view every emotion connected with loyalty, fear and faith. Bewildered and not knowing where to turn, fighting so many emotions and hearing the echoes of the past, Leah knew she must make a stand, she could not simply walk away from her feelings and return to the life she detested as she had so many times before.

These reawakened feelings consumed her, rekindling what she believed was the purpose of love she felt over three decades ago. No longer consumed by guilt and the feeling of duty, like a beautiful butterfly she was emerging from her cocoon, delighting in and wanting to indulge in long lost passions. She told me I had brought back hope and the strength to fight off the fears; she had lived with her entire life.

Leah was on a mission to find the truth, but the situation frightened her. The truth she had uncovered had already changed her. Passive and subservient behavior had given way to a new reality of self-acceptance and the knowledge that she was a person brimming with boundless love and desire. Instead of accepting the norm, as she had for so many years, she almost brazenly asked the questions, what if and why not.

Our future is no clearer to me. Maybe my role is to be the vehicle she needs to restore the Leah that was lost so long ago. Then again, maybe I am destined to share the rest of my life with her. As we continued talking, sifting through our pasts, a sense of oneness was developing, a feeling that we would never be able to leave each other, not again. No greater love had ever befallen me, and I felt great joy. Although there is fear on both sides, there is an uncontrollable desire to walk on.

I cannot completely describe my fear, though I know it is selfish and one-sided. What if I give myself to her and my love is not welcomed or returned by her? What if the young man she fell in love with so many years ago is not me? What if the past has corrupted and tarnished her in such a way that she is unable to express her love and accept my love?

Leah and I are obviously tormented by our feelings, but I believe we have the will to overcome the selfishness all around us. My torment is less painful than Leah's as everyone close to me knew of or was aware of my marital issues. However, Leah's pain is quite different, as no one had even an inkling of her marital issues and the hidden secrets of her life. The one thing I am sure of is that I will be there for her to assure no one alters the course of her destiny, no matter which direction her new sense of self may lead her. Family, friends and children may lack the compassion to see we deserve to be happy and live a contented and fulfilled life. Leah was actually told, "Nowhere in the Bible is it written that you are supposed to be happy." Maybe this is true, but I can't find any place in the Bible where it says you have to be unhappy either.

I have no doubt some members of Leah's family will turn away from her and refuse to show her the empathy she has earned through her sacrifices for them. I am also afraid they will not accept her transformation or be thankful for the love she can now express and enjoy. Rather, I believe they will hang onto their selfish need of her and focus only on how she has upset their world. Leah's search for the truth and for love was never meant to harm them and certainly never meant to be used as a vehicle to leave them, but I realize they will never allow themselves to understand this. Hypocritically, they will label her with disgusting and vile condemnations using their sanctimonious and trigger happy Bible passages, but I wonder if they ever contemplated that Leah was not doing this solely for herself but for Richard as well.

Richard has never known the true beauty of a mate completely giving herself to him, never known the unbridled passion of genuine love. Maybe through Leah's searches, she will come to love Richard as she has been unable to, or maybe he will find someone who will provide him with the love every man desires. They both need to understand a simple statement: *Life without love is nothing, and life where love lives is all.*

I believe life passed them by, as well as most who have known them, for to live where no love exists defies God's design and dishonors the beauty of love and marriage. Richard and Leah have lived day to day without challenge yet devoid of the gentle touch of warmth and contentment, never completely giving or knowing each other, and never finding the compassion that molds our lives and leads us, not on the path of performing acts we believe makes us one but on a path that glorifies God's beauty and design of being one.

I am reminded of I Corinthians 13:

> *[1]If I speak in the tongues of men and of angels, but have not love, I am only a resounding gong or a clanging cymbal. [2]If I have the gift of prophecy and can fathom all mysteries and all knowledge, and if I have a faith that can move mountains, but have not love, I am nothing. [3]If I give all I possess to the poor and surrender my body to the flames, but have not love, I gain nothing. [4]Love is patient, love is kind. It does not envy, it does not boast, it is not proud. [5]It is not rude, it is not self-seeking, it is not easily angered, it keeps no record of wrongs. [6]Love does not delight in evil but rejoices with the truth. [7]It always protects, always trusts, always hopes, always perseveres. [8]Love never fails. But where there are prophecies, they will cease; where there are tongues, they will be stilled; where there is knowledge, it will pass away. [9]For we know in part and we prophesy in part, [10]but when*

perfection comes, the imperfect disappears. ¹¹When I was a child, I talked like a child, I thought like a child, I reasoned like a child. When I became a man, I put childish ways behind me. ¹²Now we see but a poor reflection as in a mirror; then we shall see face to face. Now I know in part; then I shall know fully, even as I am fully known. ¹³And now these three remain: faith, hope and love. But the greatest of these is love.

Leah must complete this journey, not for me, but for her and for Richard. It will be painful, but until she brings to life the woman she was meant to be, there can never be any fulfillment for her as she will always be trapped by the past.

Richard, I hope you can understand this, but I feel you are self-ishly content with what you have; I will always wonder if you could even envision what it might be like to live with a woman who is truly free and unconditionally willing to love you. Maybe you are too blinded or just in denial, but before your very eyes a woman is blossoming within Leah. I only pray you and everyone about her remain strong and supports her on this path she has chosen, for the once unfulfilled young girl is now a lonely misunderstood woman of great talent craving to find her way. I must admit I am selfish as well, and I pray I am strong enough to be there when she arrives, to either win her love or be man enough to support her love for another.

Dear lord, give me wisdom and the strength to let her go if I must; yet I pray you humble me and allow me to know her in the ways of your ministry and within the miracle of your love.

Part IV

Kentucky Rain

11

Heartaches to Happiness

L eah and I have discovered a new purpose and a new enthusiasm to pursue life, as we have never done before. There is a new certainty that has emerged and one where neither of us will ever again remain in lives where love does not exist. Though hidden from almost everyone, the buds of love are beginning to bloom petal by petal, nourished by the feelings we shared so long ago. I told her of a song that described how I felt back then and how I had searched for reasons why she would run, but they were always in vain. She knew this song, being the Elvis addict that she is, but she never knew the meaning it held for me. How could she? I told her for many years I avoided this song as the lyrics did not speak *to* me, but *about* me; and every time I heard them, all I could think about was her. In some ways I lived within them.

Seven lonely days
And a dozen towns ago
I reached out one night
And you were gone

Don't know why you'd run,
What you're running to or from
All I know is I want to bring you home

So I'm walking in the rain,
Thumbing for a ride
On this lonely Kentucky back road
I've loved you much too long
And my love's too strong
To let you go, never knowing
What went wrong.

If I could upend the hour glass of time, I might find the precious moment that was lost and turn that which was cruel and heartless into something beautiful and everlasting. But for today there is an ever present evil corrupting the air, much like a plague clouding our visions of each other, disguised and hidden behind references to scripture. Although conceived solely out of selfishness and lust, I fear it preys heavily on Leah. I am in California and cannot reach for her hand. I cannot wipe the tears from her face and give her strength. We live only through e-mails, which is difficult in the same way the vanished letters of yesterday were; yet still we write on, searching for that gentle touch, that late night kiss and the endless love we pray soon will see the light.

In the beginning our e-mails were very light, exploring where we had been, what we had done, learning about our families and about our dreams and visions. But as time moved us forward, visible changes in both our writing styles took shape as emotions, needs and desires slowly became more prevalent. We began sharing our most intimate secrets and becoming more aware of each other's frailties, not as a weakness but as a longing to lift each other out of the shadows of the past and into a new world of compassion. *Amazing,* I thought. *We have already become closer than I ever dreamed possible.*

A new place where dormant dreams come to life and suppressed passions and desires flow freely was slowly developing. We both recognized what was happening and it scared us, but we knew there was a hunger developing. We both longed for this and could not run away from it. We probed deeper into each other's very beings, and our e-mails became filled with the language of love and touched on our desires and the fear of what might happen should we finally meet. I opened my soul to Leah and told her things about me that I never uttered to any living person, and she revealed to me the emptiness she has lived with and all that has been missing in her life.

My every day is filled with happiness or sadness based on her e-mails, much like mail call in Vietnam. I am so captivated by her. Her love now draws me like the proverbial moth to the flame, irresistibly yet dangerously attracting me even though I know she may never be mine. In my heart I feel as though we are already one, yet I know she is still confused and bewildered, not for lack of love for me but for reasons of her convictions, her family and her faith. I often wonder just how strong this woman might be, and then again, I wonder how I will ever be able to live up to her expectations of me. Will she allow herself to give her love to me as she has never done with any man before, or will she again fade into the memories of a distant past? I feel such oneness with her, yet I dare not tell her. A miss spoken work or a misunderstood phrase could send her reeling back to a life where "her duty" might once again control her. Still, and yet unknown to her, I am experiencing all of the pressures and all the anxieties she is feeling.

Her words, more than break my heart, they cripple me emotionally. She is being pressured to remain in a loveless life via feeble and one sided attacks, using eternal damnation as the sole motivation to hold her captive. I'm not sure how we can make this happen, but I am convinced our being together is meant to be and that God will provide a place and a time for us within his loving grace.

As you will recall, Richard was adamant that Leah contact me in the beginning, but it is obvious now his original intent is backfiring on him. Not only do I find Leah exciting, I find her playful, and although somewhat guarded, she has begun to open up emotionally to me. Richard, now realizing this, has become more aggressive and his constant smothering of her is agonizing. Leah's cell phone was now either a life line to me or an insatiable sinister device used by Richard to track her every step. I can comprehend his actions, but I cannot justify them as he has known that Leah never loved him and has always held a love for me. I wish I could make him understand that unless she completes this journey with me, she will never be his and her doubts about staying with him, even if she does, will haunt them forever.

I can't tell Leah what to do; she is still married, and what gives me the right to counsel her on this? The lost years and the love I believe we still have for each other weighs heavily on her heart but soon I pray will also guide her way. Patience is painful but necessary, for she must come to this on her own and she must be absolutely secure in her resolve. I don't believe leaving Richard would take a major leap of faith as it is obvious that, even though Richard may desire her love, he would be content to live without it as long as she simply stays with him. The fact that she never loved him and is in love with another man is something he has become accustomed to and is comfortable with. His objectives are so transparent it's frightening; to me he emerges as a self-serving and manipulative man, cruelly seeking to fulfill his distorted fantasies. His intentions are disturbing as he continues to hold on to her as long as possible without love or any concern for her soul.

What is curious to me is how he continues to be this hero to his family. What has he really ever done, other than to say "I do" to show his love and support for Leah? His lack of compassion not only began to surface through our e-mails but also through my conversations with Lenna. Through her I discovered Leah has been the driving force behind their relationship; she is the provider and the glue that holds her family together. She willingly set aside all her desires and passions for the sake of her boys, allowing herself to be held captive in a relationship solely based on her harsh religious convictions. I keep asking the question: At what point in Leah's life will she wake up and realize the life she desires is within her reach? This time, if not acted upon, she may forfeit herself forever.

As the weeks go by, I can see and feel more changes in her as our e-mails escalate to a new and uncharted intensity; the words of physical desire and even divorce have appeared. With each one, she probes deeper into my feelings for her as if she is searching for the one elusive path that will unite us. Oh Lord, let it be so, for I am still lost within her search. Where there was anxiety and fear, there is now glee as we have entered into a stage where Leah is blossoming into the woman she always knew was there. She freely welcomes the emotions of love in the way she had dreamed of all her life; no longer will she back down or give up a single day. Within the feelings she is having of possible infidelity, insecurity, despair and the realization of the dishonesty of her parents, there is a spark of a new Leah, one of incredible passion and zest for life. At first it was so faint it could hardly be felt, so frightful it was even denied by her, yet so precious she would not allow it to be put out, not again.

She stands at the threshold of a fresh future and welcomes it with loving arms; no longer will she deprive herself of her feelings or reject the beauty of her self-worth. Shortly all who have known her will be in awe of her new purpose in life. She will have new creativities, new styles and new desires, and a passion for life like they have never seen. I only hope she shares all of them with me.

"Thank you, God," for no matter what happens to us, I will always remain thankful that you chose me to walk a little while with this wonderful and gifted woman. I pray my strength is enough to guide her through this transformation and continue to be there for her in any way that allows me to be a vital part of her future. I am so attuned to what once was and what she is becoming, it frightens me just a bit and could soon make me sad. The flourishing of this changed woman within her may lead her to take wing and leave me behind. My solace is that if I am not to be the lover she has waited for all her life, I will know I played a part in her freedom. I will l never stop loving her, no matter what path she takes. My dream shall never change, and tonight before I sleep, I leave behind a lasting hope:

> *So trace not my love those silhouettes of time,*
> *when I was yours and you were mine,*
> *look only now with reverent grace*
> *to a land anew where our love will again embrace.*

12

Love Lost Again

As Leah moves closer to freedom, Richard, instead of being supportive and nourishing, has released a military-like barrage on her emotions, trying to bring fear and doubt back into her mind. It's as though he seeks to corrode her ambitions, hopes and dreams, as he uses biblical references coupled with verbal assaults to demand she remember her place in life and accept the status quo, no matter the cost to her.

I find this hard to comprehend. He must know Leah longs for a new life, but he is not willing to accept or support any change. Maybe he figures he can convince her she should not have these feelings, that her place in life is only with him; but I believe his real reason for holding her back is that this scares him. God forbid she becomes independent or starts to enjoy new challenges and, oh Lord, what if she makes new friends? If he can hold her back, then his life will continue the way it has always been. What he is unknowingly doing is throwing away his only shot at having the passionate and compassionate mate he has always wanted.

In addition to his controlling tactics, Richard grills Leah in a rhetorical fashion, apparently trying to catch her in a lie. He tests her over and over in an attempt to intimidate her. He will say to her fifty times a day, "I love you," and when she does respond back, he will only say sarcastically, "Do you really?" Could he be applying this pressure to drive her away? I doubt it, but what if he figures she is already lost to him; what then would his actions and motivations be targeting?

Leah will not lie to him, but I fear she is regressing as the pressures and fears of the unknown (me) mount. Richard, her family and her close friends push her daily to give up this silly pursuit of a past love. Comments like "It's your duty to stay with him, "You said 'I do' so now you must," "You have no authority over your own body, only your husband does," and "Do you want to be condemned?" are now common place. Richard sets her up daily, initiating heated arguments with her about me and how I am only interested in one thing, sex! He tells her he knows this to be true, for if he had the chance to meet her after so long, he would never fly all the way from California to Tennessee, and not expect to have sex with her. He follows all these arguments with, "Are you seriously willing to throw away your life for this guy?" It's obvious these people really don't know me very well, for if they did, they would understand how Leah is a cherished part of my past whom I would never harm nor cheapen solely for a night of seduction and lust; something Richard obviously cannot comprehend.

This moves me to another disturbing conclusion. In the minds of these God-fearing folks who declare to Leah; you're married and "It's your duty," to obey your husband! I'm completely bewildered as to how this mentality can this still exist? From the beginning of Leah's relationship with Richard, their surreptitious wedding looks to me to be nothing more than a chattel wedding, much like during the days of slavery, a property possession. But even worse for Leah, her so-called duty not only obligated her to service her mate, it condemned her to service his distorted pornographic disorder or face damnation.

Another disturbing twist surfaced as Richard began to use my words and actually started showing signs of affection. This was something completely uncharacteristic of him as over the last thirty two years, he had never once show a romantic side. These expressions ironically paralleled, often the very next day, what I had written to Leah in our e-mails. Valentines Day became the perfect example.

Just prior to Valentines Day I told Leah that Valentines Day is a special romantic day, between lovers; a day when a man could show his compassionate and loving side by doing something extra special for his love. I guess subconsciously I was trying to tease Leah, just a bit. I told her that if she were mine she would be treated to a soothing oil scented bath, filled with rose petals, surrounded with candles and soft music, just to set the tone for the night that laid before.

The very next day, Valentines Day, guess what? For the first time in thirty-two years, Richard drew Leah a bath filled with foamy bubbles and prepared their bath room, complete with flowers and candles to celebrate Valentines Day with his wife.

Richard however, cunning to a fault, knew he could use this to his advantage. He initiated a heated argument, obviously about me, using the same tired lines of fidelity and commitment he new would enrage her. Leah lashed out, "don't you get it, I though he was killed years ago and all I want to do is bring closure, but he has brought back to me feelings I thought were dead". "You still love him". "I DON'T KNOW, I DON'T KNOW!" And she ran away from him and into their bathroom that Richard had decorated. Intimidation or love, I guess it really doesn't matter, but I could sense Leah's resolve fading. Oddly to me though, is how did he know to do this for the first time ever? Like I said, he was never the romantic type, he had never done anything like this before, and why now just a day after I sent Leah that e-mail?

Through all of this, and it was becoming more unbelievable to understand by the minute, I needed to and began talking more frequently with Lenna. She's the only person other than my mother I can be open and honest with. She is ninety-two years old but has a great zest for life, and she urged me to pursue the truth and give her granddaughter the life she should have had. She is a strong woman who has a love for me and an abundant love for Leah, as well as, the only one who is concerned with Leah's happiness. She has become my go-between to understand the pressures surrounding Leah because this is something I cannot ask Leah directly. Although I fear telling Lenna too much, she fills in details about Leah's past; how she was raised, her dependence on her religion and, to the extent she knows them, her innermost thoughts and feelings on her marriage to Richard. I realize Lenna holds things back, but between our talks and Leah's e-mails, the adult Leah is becoming clearer to me. As this happens, fear creeps in as well. Often after talking with Lenna, I want to rush to Tennessee and catch Leah off guard, in a store or maybe at her church, just to ask her a simple question, "Do you love me?" Like I did with the girl behind the letters sent to me in Vietnam, I have fallen in love, not with the young girl of so many yesterdays, but with the person she is now. I pour my heart out to her, but I fear the time is not right for her to trust my words and follow me through the night.

I do my best to make her understand that our love must be open and honest and without doubt, for if we do come together, we must be totally committed as our actions will no doubt rip apart two family structures. Our relationships as husband and wife may have been devoid of love, but this was hidden from our children. I realize they are all adults now and I really believe my children will accept and love Leah, but I also believe Leah's children will have difficulties. We both know Leah, no matter the pain, needs to confront them if we decide to come together.

Leah and I talk about our children all the time, how they were raised, what they like and don't like, their interests and their fears. As parents we shape the lives of our children using the patterns we were taught, or self-taught through trial and error, from our life experiences. Using this template, we hopefully train them how to react to life's ever changing surroundings. Leah, as I have said, came from a very demanding religious background, not only going to church three times a week but growing up in an extremely muffled environment where she developed little, if any, social skills. She was trained to believe this was the correct way to live and raised her boys to hold the same beliefs. Adding to the prohibitions of their religion, living so far from the city, there was little for them to do socially. Parties, dances and other youthful activities were, for the most part unavailable, so her boys grew up in the same somewhat sheltered environment, but not nearly as harsh as she had known.

My kids were raised quite differently as we lived in a big city with numerous options for dating, parties, dances and many more opportunities to fail or make grievous misjudgments. I talked to them about dating, respect and how a relationship can quickly get out of hand and did my best to candidly discuss sexual relations, protections and the consequences; that should any of them make a mistake, would change their lives forever. My intent was not to be their best friend but their guide and protector. The child I worried about the most was my daughter. April had an incredible athletic body, long flowing hair and eyes that could mesmerize you. I told Leah it was very difficult for me to talk with her about such things, but I tried to impress on her the value of marriage and fidelity and how she should take her time and seriously size up any boy prior to becoming serious. Leah seemed to take a step back as I discussed this with her as this was completely foreign to everything she had ever been taught or how she lived her life.

I got the distinct impression her religion made it hard for her to accept the way I raised my kids. To date, to dance, and to have more than one boyfriend was completely foreign to her. To her way of thinking, girls go to school, find a boy, get married and raise children in their image. When we hung up the phone, I had the strangest feeling that although we had talked for over an hour, she had exited the conversation about halfway through. Like being hit, in the back of the head with a two by four, the lights came on. I had fallen into Richard's trap. Leah had never been that distant during any of our conversations. I may be paranoid, but I believe Richard took a calculated risk as he kept instilling in Leah the unknown fear of losing her life, her sons and even her soul, knowing I might slip up and say something to cause her to back away from her dreams and from me.

The next morning was Wednesday, March 8, 2006. I went to my computer, but there were no "Good Morning" e-mails from Leah. The fears that kept me up most of last night washed over me and left me weak. Something had changed; I just wasn't sure exactly what. At 10:30, her e-mail arrived with the subject line "Second Thoughts." Panic raced through my veins as I opened it and saw my concerns from our talk last night were justified. She told me she had second thoughts and had made the decision to stay where she was at, as this was her lot in life. I couldn't wrap my brain around how someone could express so much love and then discard it so easily in an e-mail?

As her e-mail continued, I could tell what Richard and her family had said to her over the last few weeks had taken hold. She said she felt like I was only sizing her up to "see if she fit," and she could not take the chance if she didn't. I had made a fatal blunder, but I still believed nothing could be hidden between us. I should have been more cautious, moved a little slower, but I was too blinded at having her back in my life to see how insecure and frightened she was. I had told myself this might happen, but this day, as the one so long ago, was a truly lost and lonely day for me.

I imagined how difficult this decision must have been for her. The pressures of leaving her family, defying her religion and giving up everything she had ever worked for had become too great. I knew her love was not mine to lose, but I couldn't help this huge sense of loss. Following our call last night, it felt like she was looking for a way to back out. I have little doubt she took some of my words out of context to justify her decision. Many years ago when we were writing to each other, I had a fear of going too fast, and it looks like I made that grave mistake this time. We had only been talking for just over a month; expecting her to completely change her life must have scared her to death. I had lost her again, and it was my fault.

Side Note: *Well, Richard I hope you're happy as you have stolen my girl again, not through love and compassion but through intimidation and lies. Like the thief in the night, as you did so many years before, you have condemned Leah to a life of servitude and lack of self-worth. But know this, pal. . . .I will always be there, and this time I am alive and she knows it! So look over your shoulder each and every day just to see if I am there. Remember this one thing, Leah will always love me, so don't slip up. If I find out you have abused her again, I will be there in a heartbeat, and I assure you, you will not enjoy my visit!*

13

Wherever Life May Lead

There is no way to express how brokenhearted I feel; all I want to do is be alone and dream of what could have been. I cannot imagine all the things she wrote could be thrown aside in a moment, but maybe I read too much into her prior e-mails. Maybe she cannot accept the changes in herself, or maybe, as I thought so many years ago, she simply used me like a fantasy to fulfill her hidden desires.

I want to go after her but I will not. I know she feels great passion for me, but I have caused her and Richard too much pain already. I still can't believe she abandoned our path, but I will stop communicating with her and will not come between her and Richard ever again. I have been through many tough times in my life, but I have never felt so abandoned, except for when I lost her thirty-five years ago.

Her decision has ripped me apart as I cannot stop loving her. It's harder this time because it is her decision and not the lies of others that hold us apart. I am very confused as I know in my heart she loves me and will never be able to let go of those precious sensations and the anticipation of sharing our love will never leave her. On a lighter side and I guess in a morbid sort of way, *I waited over three decades the last time just to hear her voice, so what's another thirty or forty years out of my life to hopefully get to meet her?* I pray she has not allowed someone else to change her fate for the wrong reasons again. If she is truly in love with Richard and I am destined to be no more than an old memory, I can live with it. I would never want someone who was not completely in love with me, and I will always wish only the best for her. "Still"

I search each day for an e-mail, but they are no more. Why am I doing this to myself? She made her decision and is where she wants to be. I should be happy for her, but I have become so close to her that her rejection left a huge void in my life. I have not been able to go to work since her e-mail arrived, and I do nothing but wonder what she is doing and how Richard is treating her. My mind wanders from one undesirable scenario to another and how Richard will use this to his sick advantage, like rubbing a dog's nose in it. I know how much I love her, and I will never understand nor will I ever believe she has completely let me go. I fear Richard will not believe this either and that her life moving forward will become another living hell, but if this is where Leah truly wants to be, then I pray to God I am wrong and Richard can be man enough to see the evil of his past and love her completely.

I cannot stop myself from reading her last e-mail over and over again, looking for a breath of hope. Her words are filled with compassion, but she is gone. She told me I stirred feelings in her she thought were dead and that even though these feelings are not for Richard, her place in life is there. She also said she wants to be friends; friends? During our e-mails and phone conversations, I laid open my heart to her, telling her secrets and how she never left my heart, and now you ask me to be friends? Are you kidding me? I suppose I'm may be weak, but the visions of your future leaves me wanting to be blind to her future fait. Additionally, she wants me to continue to write the book I started about us; I wonder if she really knows how cruel a torture it would be for me to try and create a story line about a love story that started thirty-five years ago but ended with the two characters never meeting each other. Does she expect me to create a fairy tale ending to a story that has for me turned tragic? I will not write such a book as it would only serve as a reminder of what she could have had and what I believe is still destined to happen.

Perhaps I could handle it better if we had met and discovered that the feelings we once held were only childish fantasies and not genuine. I wish to God she could make me believe and understand that she is truly in love with Richard and all the things she confided in me were exaggerated. I can't shake the feeling she has made a terrible mistake and that she will once again be trapped in a relationship where she will never be able to give her love, only sacrifice it in sin and servitude.

I need to send her an e-mail wishing her well and saying I understand her decision. Maybe this will trigger a response; so what's holding me back? Every time I go to write the e-mail, the words will not come and I get this overwhelming feeling she is still dreaming of being with me. I tried again just a minute ago to write to her but I kept hearing this voice telling me to wait. But wait for what? Everywhere I look I see her standing just out of reach. Does she feel this way as well? Who am I kidding? She made her wishes perfectly clear.

Today is like yesterday which was like the day before. I check for an e-mail, but there is none. It's now four a.m. on Friday, March 10, and like the last few days I have not slept much. My batteries are running on low and so is my emotional state. I have to get over this somehow, and I seriously need to tend to my business, which I hope will take my mind off of her. Right! Who am I kidding? I have to write to her. This has to stop; somehow I have to know about her and Richard. I have to know the truth.

Bloody Mary in hand and a fresh pot of coffee brewing, keyboard in front of me and a heart filled with far too much emotion, in my mind a letter to Leah is taking shape. First Pass:

Dear Leah,

Please read this and then share it with Richard. It is my earnest attempt to say thank you and to express my heartfelt wish that all of your dreams have come true. As this will probably be my last communication with you, please allow me to express what you have meant to me and assure Richard that I will, in no way, pose any threat to him now or at any time in the future. You opened your heart and showed me a side of you I will never forget nor regret. Always remember that you have a loving heart and an inner glow that I pray never fades.

You see, Leah, you brought back into my life a reason to dream and a breath of love so long ago lost; I will never let it go again. I cannot deny my feelings for you for they will never die, but I am happy you have found your true love. I never wanted to put you into this position, but I never wanted to stop the path we were on either. I turned my heart over to you and allowed you into places I always wanted to share with someone and I guess I expected or hoped for too much. For this I am truly sorry.

I hope you have found what you have wanted, and I wish you all the love your heart can hold. I know now that Richard is the one you wanted, and I will not continue to write after this as I may be a distraction he will not understand. Also, I need you to understand that the love I thought we were sharing was a love I could never give to anyone else. You see, little one, you were my dream that came to life, and I will hold onto your memory for the rest of my life. Please do me a favor and do not respond to this e-mail. I have lost you for a second time, and now that you have brought closure to the past, please leave it alone and only remember me as a man you once cared for.

I would like to see Lenna, but I will not. If you can please think of me every so often, that would be nice as I will be thinking of you always. Just for old time's sake: "All my bags are packed, I'm ready to go. I'm standing there outside your door." Well, I guess you know the rest. Be safe and loving and never forget that in my heart I will always be with you.

Love Eternally,
Ryan

Will she figure out I lied when I said I did not want her to respond. Do I have the guts to send it? *Come on, Ryan, all you have to do is hit "Send." What if she doesn't respond? If I don't get a reply, I will be left with the thought that Richard stepped in, forcing her to follow my instructions.* This would be worse as then I would never be able to accept her decision to remain with him. But this has to be done, and if she does not reply, I guess I will find some way to accept it. I'll give her a few weeks, and if I hear nothing, I will move on. My son Matthew has been bugging me about moving to Colorado. *What am I talking about? Running away? Oh My God! Have I finally gone insane; I can't seem to click the 'Send' button! Okay, enough, you stupid ass school boy. Send the e-mail!* And with one click of the mouse it was gone. What do I do now?

Exhausted emotionally and physically, I slept for a few hours, fully dressed, sprawled out like an old rummy in my uncomfortable office chair. I woke up groggy and with a stiff neck. *What time is it anyhow?* I wondered. *It's still dark outside, so it must be too early to try and get any work done. I'll tackle some of the stacked up e-mails; I'm probably in trouble with everyone for not keeping up, but I have to admit one thing; I actually feel better now that I sent her the e-mail, even though I have most likely killed off any hope of being with her.*

I logged in and clicked on the Inbox. *It's only 6:25 a.m., and I'm already getting e-mails? Must be from Florida. Don't those bastards ever sleep? Wait a minute; it's not Florida, it's from Leah! She must have sent it a few hours ago. She is two hours ahead of me time wise, but why now? Is fate back in my corner?* Based on the timeline, there is no way she could have received my e-mail before she wrote this one. I am all but trembling with excitement. Even if it's bad news, it's still her. Funny, first I could barely send my e-mail, and now I can't seem to open hers. *Okay, Ryan, just open the e-mail. It's going to be alright; she is just responding back to say thank you and wish you well. But there is no way she could have gotten my e-mail first.*

I can't seem to move my hand over the mouse; I know what I want to hear from her, but I am terrified of what I might find? *Silly ass, have you reflected back to Vietnam and this might be the "dear john letter??* I talked to myself for maybe another fifteen minutes and finally convinced myself I wouldn't be able to do anything until I opened it.

The e-mail began with her telling me she thinks about me all the time, and in her words I, so many times before, head her inner thoughts. Her feelings for me have not changed, and her desire to move on to wherever life may lead us has not changed. The love is still there and stronger now than ever before. She says I have taken possession of her mind. I hope she never knows how I felt the last few days, but I will not judge her or tell her how her last e-mail hurt me. Reading her words, I know we are destined to meet soon.

I cannot wait to respond as she has once again opened the door to us and to my heart. I will tell her of my dreams of the future and promise I will never lose her again, no matter what! I will tell her how I think of her constantly and about the emptiness I suffered without her. *Whoa*, I think, *better take it easy this time.*

Later that day I called Leah. Her voice was soft, serene and so amazingly pure. I felt like I was talking to someone whose words have not been polluted with the slang of our times. I could hear the truth, the honesty and the compassion in her words. She described how she told Richard of her decision to stay with him and how she thought I was only sizing her up to use her as a sex object and then cast her aside. He agreed with her and told her it was a good thing she found out now before she did something that would condemn her eternally. She told me how elated Richard was with her decision, but she said she felt empty and alone again almost immediately.

"Ryan, when he said the part about being condemned, I flashed back to the past and thought 'I've done it again; I'm right back in the place I hated being'. I felt the urge to call you at that very moment, but I needed to think."

"Leah, honey," I said, "take your time. This decision will alter both our lives."

"Richard is so anxious; I know he can see how blue I am without you in my life. You have taken possession of me, and I cannot let you go; I feel free with you, but here with Richard, I feel trapped. Please help me."

"Leah, I promise I will always be there for you, and it's sure nice to have you back. Want to take a walk?"

14

The Vision

After she sent the "goodbye" e-mail, Leah told me she searched hourly for a response from me, but it never came. I told her I did not write her back because I did not want to cause her or Richard any more pain, but that now I was sorry I had not. My only excuse: "Honey, I am just a man."

Maybe this brief separation was exactly what we needed. Leah, being who she is, could not just drift away into the night with me, no matter how much she desired to. Emotionally she had to return to Richard, and I suspect subconsciously she needed to feel the emptiness once again. She is an amazing woman with boundless compassion for the feelings of others but far too often neglects her own needs to keep everyone else happy.

I remembered she wrote in her e-mail, "At this point, all I know is for now I need to be here." She did not write, "All I know is for now I need to be with Richard." What she failed to admit even to herself was her need to stay in her old life had nothing to do with Richard. Her decision was only because of her boys, and I fear this will challenge us for quite a while; but for now I will continue to do my best to build a bond so strong nothing will side-track it again.

— ~

After a deep breath, I heard Leah reply, "Yes, Ryan, I want to walk with you."

"I am so sorry," I began. "I did not nor will I ever need to size you up or. . . ."

"Ryan, wait. No matter where I am, you will always mean so much to me. If it were not for the memories of you all these years, I don't know how I would have made it. Even if you were only a dream, you were my dream."

"Leah, I was so frightful you forgot who we once were and couldn't understand how today I feel the same."

"There is no way I will ever forget you as I think about you all the time. My only problem is how to go on, especially now that Richard knows how I feel. Understand this, I need you in my life, and I believe this is the right thing for us to do. I check all the time for a message from you, and I feel so empty when there isn't one. Walking and talking with you is all I long for, but if you grow tired of me, please let me know."

"I will walk with you throughout time if you wish, but I dream of us as I did once before, and you are the meaning in my life. I will not give you up again. By the way, I suspect Richard has known how you feel for over thirty years."

"Ryan, I am also a dreamer; sometimes I think I have trapped myself once again in this world with Richard, with dreams of you my only escape. Richard says since my decision to stay, I am different, and I guess he's right, but I don't know what he expects. I am really trying, but I'm not sure why. It is just so hard. I hope you understand what I mean."

"Just be who you are and try and do what you want for a change, and please let me be a part of it."

"Silly, you are it. I have to pick Richard up in a few minutes, but please write to me; tell me everything about how you really feel about me!"

"Goodbye, Love!"

I love talking to Leah because there is an instant response. I can hear the small inflections of tone and volume when she makes a point or shows emotion. I want to have endless time to just talk with her, but I would settle for a few days right now alone with her.

Over the next week or so, our e-mails became super-charged, intense to a level that is beyond understanding as we have never met. The most pressing topic is always when and how can we meet. Leah tries to avoid this subject, but I know she feels the same all-consuming desire I feel for her; and I realize we cannot continue on this path without knowing how we will react physically to each other. From my side it is plain; I would like to take her into my arms and make love to her. I will try to avoid this should we meet, but I make no promises. What I want most is a chance to see her and take real walks and have true and genuine talks about anything and everything. I want to know every thought she has ever had—her fears, desires, needs, cravings, politics (no way), beliefs, love, her past, her plans, her innermost feelings and what she feels we must become.

It's late March and the industry I have worked in for the last thirty years has an annual telecommunications show in Las Vegas. I am obligated to attend, and I wish she could go with me. Leah would love Vegas, not the gambling but the sights and sounds of the dinner shows and parlor acts working their way up the entertainment ladder. Vegas today has an international flair, and I could show her a partial view of the world as the new attractions and theme hotels come to life each night. Nice dream, but as usual I will be alone on this trip. I guess I have been alone for a long time, but now I feel selfish for taking this trip without her.

Generally on these trips I spend hours prepping for the next day's activities and the meetings I am scheduled to attend, but all I seem to be focused on is writing to her. I picture her with me, walking the streets, laughing, dancing, talking and just sharing each other. She has completely captivated me, and all I can think about is her touch, her embrace and how so willingly I accept my fate.

As I look out into the night, the lights of the Strip are all but blinding. I can feel the excitement in the air and hear the laughter of couples from every direction. Here I am in one of the most exciting places on earth; yet I feel such emptiness within me I don't even want to leave my room. If Leah were here, I could show her so much and give her memories she could carry for the rest of her life.

Later that night I had the oddest dream. I was back in the funeral parlor after my father's death and was speaking about his life and his passions. There was a very tall man with a long robe passing through the aisles, and as he tapped on the shoulders of the guests, they vanished. This happened time and time again, and I asked what he was doing. All he would say is "Ryan, there is only room for one; carry on."

As I did, I noticed there were fewer and fewer people, and then in a breath there were none. The room became darker and darker, and a pinpoint of light began to illuminate one of the pictures I had blown up of my father, which made it seem to come to life. In the original picture, Dad was standing next to a horse, which now had vanished. He was holding my guitar, not in the picture but holding it out of the picture as though he wanted me to take it. He said over and over, "Ryan, play the song for her; it is hers isn't it?" As I took the guitar, he started to fade, and then he said, "Time to go son; there's only room for one." Then he vanished.

In the middle of the room a bright light appeared, and a lady dressed in white stood there so serenely I thought she must be an angel. In a gentle tone, like an echo from the past, she whispered, "Play my song, Ryan." All I could think was "What song?" Then it hit me. The song was "Leaving On a Jet Plane." Many years ago I sang this song to our church group the night before I left for Vietnam, never knowing who it was truly meant for.

As I sang she came closer and closer until she was standing right next to me. I could not make out her face because the light was so bright, but I sensed she was pale, not very tall, with shimmering blond hair. She leaned over to me and whispered to me again, this time saying, "I'll wear your wedding ring; it's been missing from my hand far too long a time." With that she seemed to meld into me as though her life could only live within me as one.

I woke up in a panic as the dream ended, but for me the meaning was clear; Leah and I were destined to become one. That's what Dad was trying to tell me as he kept saying that there is only room for one. That one would be the life we were meant to share, bonding ourselves to each other, becoming one.

Arriving home the next day, I called Leah right away to tell her about Vegas, but to my surprise all she wanted to talk about was my dream. We had never talked about it before, but "Leaving On a Jet Plane" had a special meaning to her; she told me she had dreamed of me singing this song to her, as though it was written it solely for us, and even though I only sang it to her in a dream, her dream had finally come true.

Music has always held a special meaning for both of us, and we used the lyrics of songs from the past to help us express feelings and the desires which were sometimes too difficult to shape into words. Leah asked me to remember how I lived within the lyrics of "Kentucky Rain", and how she struggled and found herself re-living her life through another song "Yesterday".

"Ryan, this was my uncle's favorite song of all time, and he played it at least a hundred times. Every time I heard it I thought only of you. Every time I heard the lyrics "Yesterday love was such an easy game to play now I need a place to hide away. Oh I believe in yesterday." I believed I needed a place to hide, as yesterday was all that I had left to hold onto.

My whole life I have prayed for the guidance and the strength to make the commitment I have longed for ever sense I lost you, a commitment to love. Maybe it is with Richard, but I will never know until I face my past and accept it with or without you."

"Leah, we must meet to dispel or to accept that our love is either born in and lives within God's grace or is merely a dream that should be left in the past."

"Ryan, not now...and PLEASE do not come back here!"

I feel she is avoiding this, not out of fear of falling in love with me but out of fear of finding that her secret love was just a fantasy she had created in her mind and not the key and pathway to a completely new world?

It is still abundantly obvious, through her words, that her life is becoming more unbearable with each passing day. She tells me Richard has become more controlling and more demanding and that she is afraid where his actions may lead. I wish I could understand this better, but it eludes me. Leah is being watched like a hawk circling for prey; she cannot leave the house without a constant barrage of calls demanding she tell Richard where she is or what she is doing. She visits her grandmother just a few miles away, only to be called several times while she is there to see if she is using her grandmother's phone to call me. Even at home, if she answers the phone, Richard instantly makes his presence known by standing next to her until the call is over and then insisting she tell him what the call was about. I wish I could talk with him as an adult to try and explain to him that with or without me in the picture, he is doing everything in his power to drive her away from him.

I don't think he gets it; love cannot be caged, cannot be taken for granted and most of all must be shared and not one-sided. I believe, even if Leah told him that she was in love with another man and will never love him, he would still want or maybe I should say, command, her to stay, just like he did the day they were married, knowing she did not love him.

Well knock me over with a feather! Today I received an e-mail from Richard which included two pictures of Leah and him. Don't get me wrong, I was pleased to get the pictures, but I was confused as to what his motivations were? Why would he want me to see her? Did he think I would become disillusioned because she is not the young lady I remember? Was he trying to show me they were content and a happy, loving couple? I don't think so; I believe he was trying to show me a middle-aged grandmother past her prime and one he believed I would never be interested in. What

I am sure he did not want me to see was a depressed woman posing for a still photograph, no smile, no outward sign or expression of joy, just a slightly raised brow and two sad eyes. These two pictures, from what I could see, made everything crystal clear and reinforced every e-mail she had sent to me. She truly looked like a defeated woman who had surrendered the better part of her life, standing there much like a mannequin or a piece of the living room furniture.

I was captivated by the photographs and looked at them for hours trying to see through her vacant pose and dreaming of what must be hidden behind those big sad eyes. I felt like I was looking, as so many others have, at the expressionless smile of the Mona Lisa, trying to understand what was hidden or maybe what was lost. I knew from her e-mails and our conversations there was a magic buried deep within her and a powerful desire to love unconditionally, but in these photos all I could see was a look of defeat and despair as she stood next to Richard.

He had no idea what these two simple pictures meant to me and how they ignited my desire to win back my love. I know his thoughts and motivations were completely different, but the fact that he sent them at all baffles me. Every other communication I had received from him contained very non-flattering statements seriously suggesting that I get the hell out of Dodge and remain dead.

Leah so far had no idea Richard sent the photos to me and appeared to be holding up fairly well through all of this. It was becoming more apparent that her motivations are the same as mine, but we must find out for sure. We understand much time has passed; maybe the passion we once felt and the need to be together has faded. These gnawing feelings grow more apparent with each passing day. I only wish I could be more supportive, but I have this innate fear that whatever I do will only cause her more problems.

Did I say "more problems?" Today Leah told me Richard has had her e-mail password for quite a while. What a con man! He admitted he has it but tells her she gave it to him. How? Well, here's a twist for you; he told her that she had been talking in her sleep and out of nowhere she offered up her e-mail password. Odd? He never told her he had it, and she only found out through a fluke. Yesterday she heard Richard hurry down to the basement, and then what sounded like the rustling of papers caught her attention. Curiosity took over, and when Richard left, she went downstairs to see what he was up to. Above the door in a hidden compartment she found a file folder over two inches thick. What the heck was he hiding from her?

To her dismay she discovered a personal file, a log if you will, which contained a printed collection, sorted by date and time, of almost every e-mail we had sent to each other over the last two months, as well as phone bills (dates & times of our calls) and other information he had downloaded off the Internet. Leah was confused. Richard had insisted she make contact with me, and was adamant she set up her own e-mail account, for privacy, yet all-the-while, and behind her back he was secretly building a catalog of all of our correspondences. For what purpose?

Leah immediately confronted Richard. "What's this file for and how did you get my password?"

"I don't know. I just wanted a copy of your e-mails, and I got your password from you while you were asleep."

"Asleep? You've got to be kidding. Why are you keeping a log of them?"

Richard wouldn't answer her and began to cry. When she walked away he did not follow her, but Leah was in shock, for all those things we thought were known only to us were also known to Richard and had been all along. An eerie feeling came over me as soon as she hung up the phone. If he has known all along what we talked about and how we shared our inner feelings and desire to be together, why would he allow this to continue? And even odder, why did he document our steps with her e-mails along the way?

It began to make perfect sense how Richard's behavior and mannerisms had changed over the last few months. As you will recall, he had begun using my very words and doing special things like the bath room decorations on Valentines Day. These were not words and actions he personally created; they were mine which he had stolen from my e-mails to Leah. I have personal reasons why I believe he would do this, and it is not simple curiosity. I think he built a file whose sole purpose could only be to harm or injure Leah should she complete our journey and leave him.

There is another thought I do not like having, but it seems all things now are subject to review, especially Richard's fantasy world and how far he might go to preserve it. Let's say that he is smarter than either one of us guessed. What if this new e-mail file he is building is really a vehicle to justify and support a crime of passion? What if. . . .Oh for Christ's sake, I am becoming a paranoid wreck. The problem with this "crime of passion" scenario is that he would lose her forever with this type of insanity, or then again would he? Could this be in his mind a sick triggering device to show how far he is willing to go to keep her as an expression of his love? Stranger things have happened; I just hope not to me or her.

Enough of being paranoid; I will try logic. What would you or I have done after finding the first sign of affection in Leah's e-mails? For me, if I found out my wife was communicating with a prior love and using terms that suggested anything other than a platonic relationship, I would be in her face in a heartbeat. She would have to make a decision right then and there, and if we were to stay together, counseling and sessions with our minister would begin. If she (or I) wasn't sure, then one of us would have to leave immediately. This seems likely for the vast majority of couples. What about Richard made him different?

I am not a psychic or a psychologist, but some things are just too transparent and obvious to avoid. Anyone, well anyone who truly loved his wife, would have confronted his wife at the first hint of affection for another, unless that is, they have a deep-rooted secret to protect? I believe Richard had convinced himself that if he confronted Leah, it would still not change her resolve to find the truth and answer that thirty-five year old question: Is it possible we could still be in love with each other? I believe he felt if he pushed too hard, she might just fight back and disclose to the world his sick misuse of her. Leah had grown over the last few months well beyond his controlling ways, and he knew it! So he contrived a well-plotted scheme, supported by the e-mails (if he needed them), to show it was Leah who committed adultery and would say how he tried over and over again to get her to give up this insane search for a long lost love. I wonder what their sons would have thought had they known their hero daddy knew all along their mother was in love with another man, had a file to prove it, and yet said nothing to them. My first thought would have been, "What are you hiding?"

I am convinced Leah would be far better off leaving him no matter what happens to us as she is no longer blinded by her naiveté and clearly sees this different and ugly side of him, one she should have seen ages ago. His motivations are no longer obscured; he never truly wanted to win her love or even cared about it, for if he did, he would have fought for her love and tried to stop us from the very beginning. But instead, this self-serving coward held his tongue, hid his contempt, and kept a hidden log to use against her in an attempt to keep her in her place, much as he used their religion to the same end.

Leah is one of those rare individuals who have survived more harm and more pain than most would experience in a lifetime. Through all the pain and the abuse, she has nurtured, developed and cared for her family, built a business, and all the while never let go of her dreams, just set them aside to take care of her boys. Leah's time and place has never been allowed to blossom, never seen the light of day, has been denied by all. Now she desires it with all her heart and knows it is all but within reach. There is nothing she cannot do should she cast off the burdens of others and let her sprit be free. She has also fought with me, begging me over and over again, saying, "Please do not come back." I have heard this so many times, I now hear it in my sleep. I have tried to convince her we need to meet to bring closure to this, that we are adults and should not be afraid to discover the truth, but always she says, "Please do not come back."

Then in one e-mail I sent a stupid little remark, nothing profound or logical, just one small statement, "If we do not meet, then one of us is lying."

I received a return e-mail right away with a simple, "Okay."

Unbelievable! After trying to convince her we cannot go on like this, a simple eleven words after thousands were written prompted Leah to agree. In my prior e-mails, I told her she could pick any place in the world for our meeting, and she chose a hundred-year-old rock cabin set in a secluded place high in the mountains of Alabama, a place apart from the rest of the world, not complicated with the toils of man.

There are so many things I must tell her, and there are so many things I must know about her. I have invaded her conscience like no man has ever done before, yet I am still in the infancy stage of knowing this amazing woman. Our willingness to love each other is not in question, but this love cannot have boundaries. I have no problems with the love I wish to give her, and I fully understand the consequences that will follow. To abruptly broadcast our love, as we feel compelled to do, will be misunderstood and condemned by those closest to us.

Her life to this point has only been for others, and this chance to experience self-awareness and allow her feelings to emerge may alter everything she has ever known. I read through her e-mails again. The only thing in her life she cannot lose is her children, but I have great faith in them and pray their love for their mother will overtake their misgivings as they see in her face the true meaning of love. I realize they have been brought up in a church that follows the words of Christ to the letter and that they are true believers, but I also know the deep-rooted faith Leah has. All I can hope for is that their love for their mother will guide their actions. Leah has kept them completely in the dark as to any e-mails or our planned meeting in Huntsville. I fear this may be a mistake, but we will see. Ironically, Richard has not told the boys anything either. As for my kids, well, I pray I have instilled in them the compassion for love, the ability to see through their father's eyes and understand the realization and fulfillment of a lifelong journey. All I know is that in two days I will be with the one I have loved ever since those lonely days in Vietnam.

I wonder if she even comprehends what will happen when we finally meet and how the time we spend together will change our lives forever, with or without each other. This meeting will undoubtedly become a symbol of an end to our past lives, for once we meet and those true expressions and emotions of love are realized and awakened, we will never be able to go back; soon we will either walk alone or as a couple, but either way, our lives will be forever altered.

I arranged for my current, yet soon to be ex-, wife to go to Colorado to visit our son and his family for a week over Easter vacation. Yes, I made these arrangements, God forgive me, so I could fly back to Alabama to meet someone of a distant past, I had always dreamed of and wanted to be my lover and my wife; it was difficult, even though I felt relief, I also experienced sadness, for when Elaine boarded the plane; in my heart I knew I was saying goodbye to her for the last time. I have no doubt that Leah felt the same way, when she committed to meet me in Huntsville. I suppose in her heart she was subconsciously saying goodbye to Richard as well. At this point, it was only about Leah and me and the transgressions our current spouses had committed in the past faded away; I think here you can read between the lines. Yet still, I believe Leah and I felt compassion and care for each of them, as it was these two people that helped bring our children into this world and shared our lives; good or bad.

I can't speak for Leah, but I knew I was closing a door and one I knew I would never re-open, ever again. I prayed that Leah and I were meant to become one. But if this was not to come to pass, it made no difference, as I was now completely committed to finding love and sharing the true meaning of my destiny in Gods grace.

The irony was almost too philosophical to even imagine; as I was about to leave on this day, of all days, Easter Sunday April the 16th 2006. A day we as Christians have held reverent for over two thousand years. And yet as ironic or as poetic as it may ever be, I would meet my destiny, face to face. Divine intervention or something merely by chance; you make the call, but I, without hesitation, believe fate has taken control of my life, and I welcome it with open arms!

For the last fifteen years or so each Easter, a bunch of friends of mine and my family, twenty-five or more, met for a champagne brunch and an Easter Egg Hunt for the kids. This year it was going to be at the ballroom of the Grand Vista, a five-star hotel in Simi Valley. I thought I had let only a select few friends and family members know of my plans to meet Leah, but as we sat sipping champagne, odd comments invaded the conversation. My son was the first. Out of the blue he said, "Say there, Pop, you fixin' to take a trip," followed by someone else saying, "Naw, he's just hankerin' for some banjo pickin'." Then, as the waiter came by, and some one else said; "S'cuse me, but do you have any black-eyed peas and grits?"

Okay, I think I get it. They apparently all knew what was going on and that I was leaving for Alabama the next day, so I said, "Alright, I guess the cat's out of the bag, but I hope you all know this is something I have waited for ever since I left Vietnam. I'm not sure what's going to happen, but this is something I have to do."

"We know, but there is one thing you can help us with."

"Sure. What's that?"

"Well we have a pool going on, and we were wondering just how long you think it will take?"

"How long what will take?"

"Until you get shot!"

"Wait a minute; do you fools have a pool to see when someone back there is going to shoot me?"

"That's right. We all kind of figured there would be no way, knowing you that this won't happen."

"You've got to be kidding me"

My loving friends had doled out five bucks each to see who would be the closest to pick the date and time I would get shot in Alabama.

I was so impressed I placed my own bet! What a great, maybe morbid but great, set of friends I have; I had never felt so blessed. Actually one of the bastards took my arrival time and added an hour for his chance to win the pot, but I didn't care. In a few hours, the woman I had dreamed of all my life would be right next to me, maybe holding my hand or maybe something more? I couldn't wait to see her, feel her breath, touch her hair and walk and talk with her. To get shot for something like that, well I would feel honored if someone loved me that much!

All I had left to do was to pack, drop Mom off at Skipper's and get to the airport on time. As Al Jolson sang,

> *There's a rainbow around my shoulder,*
> *and a sky of blue above,*
> *I'm shouting so the World will know that*
> *I.. I.. I'm in love.*

Part V

Alabama Mountains

15

Our Impossible Dream Meeting

I booked my flight over a week ago with a scheduled departure from Los Angeles International Airport at 10:00 p.m., which will allow me to spend as much time as possible with Leah. By leaving in the middle of the night, I will have almost a full first day with her since the flight will set me down in Alabama at 9:30 the next morning. I'm sure the flight will take its toll on me, as it is includes a three hour layover in Detroit and a total travel time of over ten hours. I was hoping to catch a few winks on the plane, but who was I trying to kid. The excitement of finally meeting Leah was racing through my veins at such a pace this will never happen.

I boarded the plane at 9:40 p.m., and as I settled in my seat, emotions filtered into my mind. Sitting on the tarmac, I am frightened and anxious. Until now, everything between Leah and me has consisted of words exchanged via letters, phone calls and e-mails, but in a mere ten to twelve hours, everything will become tangible and a new truth will be revealed. I have dreamed of this and welcome it with open arms, but I am also aware Leah and I may not be able to resist each other. The reality is our lives and many others from this day forward will be altered forever. Did I say frightened? How about scared to death!

As the plane lifted into the air, I was overcome with an amazing sense of awareness, as though a chasm in time was righting itself before my eyes, bringing closure to the void created thirty-five years ago. It was disconcerting to realize I am leaving behind a life I had spent so many years building, one I hadn't been happy with, but one, right or wrong, I at least knew would always be there. However, I have willingly accepted that once this plane lands, that life will be no more. I feel regret and sorrow for those things I leave behind, especially those I love, but I also know this meeting with Leah is not by chance and was predestined to transform my life. I only pray that those who love me, especially my children, will understand and realize I have no power, desire or ability to change the outcome of this pathway God has opened to me. I must follow it, no matter the joy or pain it may reveal.

I genuinely pray all our kids will warm to the idea that although things might be different, their father and their mother will finally be happy and with the life partner they have always dreamed of. I know I must be stronger than ever, never showing any doubt or remorse, for if these feelings I have are returned by Leah, I must be man enough to embrace our love above all others. I realize how hard this has been on her and how deeply rooted her love must be for me as we both struggle with the possibility of losing our children. Even if they turn from the truth and cannot accept our being together, Leah and I will love each other without regret or guilt.

As I flew through the night sky, I pondered how I should act when we first meet. How should you react to someone you have never seen as an adult yet loved so desperately for so long? I am anxious to hold her in my arms and make love to her, but maybe, as usual, I am being presumptuous. I read too much into her e-mails before, but her conversations have been open and honest regarding how she had always loved me and how she dreamed of sharing a life with me. Even though there is no commitment between us, I am going to do my best to make this dream come true. I only fear that she has built me up far beyond what any mortal man could live up to; yet here I sit, a fifty-five year old trying to roll back time. I pray I will not be too big a disappointment to her. I have chosen not to put on any airs, not be to anything more than I truly am when I am with her. If we are to come together, it will have to be just as we are, frailties, wrinkles, and aged beyond what we both remember. At least I still have a full head of hair and all my teeth.

The whole idea is surreal. How, after so many years, can this spark still exist between us? How could our feelings have lasted, and what drives her to risk everything just to meet me? She knows if things do not work out between us in the long term, her life will still be forever changed. I believe neither of us will be able to avoid the passion that exists between us and the unfulfilled longing to give back to each other that which was stolen from us. A miracle is unfolding as I feel the thrust of the plane moving faster and faster, guiding my way back to her. Excitement? Yes, but I also have this uneasiness that any moment I will wake up only to find I have been trapped in a long and wonderful dream.

The plane is flying at thirty-six thousand feet; and from my window seat, like a man fixed on a great movie, I search for glimmers of land below, but the cloud cover is too thick. I catch myself day dreaming about an old *Twilight Zone* episode where the plane is caught in a storm, causing it to fly faster and faster until it breaks the time barrier and goes back in time. I have the strangest sensation that I am actually going back in time and it is now 1971 and I am making my flight back after Vietnam to be with her.

I'm not as strong as I was, and I'm not as young as I once was; but in my heart and in my mind, I am that young buck once again. I will be the lover she once desired; forget what I said before, I like this better! Anticipation now drives me and I can feel the adrenalin racing through my veins, picking me up and renewing my strength. I have been up for over twenty-six hours, yet I feel fresh and reenergized. There are endless questions: Should I take her in my arms as I would have thirty-five years ago? Should I hold back? Should I shave, maybe I should brush my teeth? I wonder if they have an iron on the plane. Oh God help me, I look like someone who just walked away from a train wreck. *This is just great, she will be all fixed up and looking like a queen, and I will arrive looking like a vagabond.*

The Captain announced the final approach to Huntsville International Airport. *Funny,* I thought, *I've been talking to myself for almost three thousand miles, including layovers.* Gazing out the window again, I see the clouds have broken up. I can't get over how vastly different the terrain looks. I thought, *maybe I really have gone back in time. There are no houses or roads, just rolling hills and farm land. Wait, there's a house, and it even has a barn; but there are no freeways, and the roads are miles apart. How will I ever fit into this place, or for that matter, how could Leah ever fit into my world? Come on, Ryan, slow down. You haven't even met her, and already you are thinking about starting a life with her.* Well, why not, isn't this the reason you're even on this flight!

Thirty minutes later we were on the ground. On the way to baggage claim, I spotted a men's room. *Great, a chance to freshen up a bit. Okay, quick shave; good thing I have an electric razor or I might cut myself to pieces. Why am I shaking so? I wasn't this nervous in Vietnam.* I combed my hair, splashed on a bit of cologne, and gave a quick check of my clothes. *I look pretty good,* I said to my reflection. *Right! Puffy red eyes are a great look.*

Next stop, the car rental counter as per mine and Leah's plans. Leah. . .so far no Leah. I thought she would meet me. My anxiety vaulted several levels. Has she changed her mind? Maybe Richard changed his mind and would not allow her to leave? Have I made this trip to be alone and lost in Alabama for the next four days. *Gather yourself, Ryan. Remember the backup plan; if she could not get to the airport, I was to go ahead to the cabin and wait.* Problem is, I have no idea how to get there, but as Dick (my old boss) always said, "the journey of a thousand miles starts with a single step." Chinese philosophy, at this point, did me no good. I am so shaken up; I'm not even sure how to get out of the parking lot, let alone the airport.

I pulled out of the rental car parking spot and made a right turn towards an exit sign when, about a hundred yards ahead of me, I see a woman walking towards me. Is it her? Yes, there she is right in front of me, no longer an image from a photograph, no longer the black ink on an e-mail print out, no longer a voice on a cell phone; today she's real! She is dressed in black slacks with a red top, her blond hair pulled back.

She was smiling that simple but yielding smile I remembered so well from her pictures of many years ago.

There was an air of innocence about her, and an almost majestic if not spiritual look that lit up her face; enticing and captivating me. This was the image I carried in my heart and dreamed of ever sense I was nineteen years old. As I pulled up next to her, she did not wave or say a word; she just smiled, staring deeply into my eyes. My entire body went limp. I had dreamed of this moment for as long as I can remember. I recalled a childhood fantasy where I would fall in love with a woman with mistletoes in her eyes. And now, there she was, just inches before me, and behind those beautiful green eyes, all I could see were mistletoes!

I had practiced time and time again what I would say to her when we finally met. I wanted this first meeting to be breathtaking, and I planned to break the ice with something a bit romantic. I had planned to give her a tender hug, a simple kiss, and then say, "Leah you are more beautiful to me today than I have dreamed, and I have waited for this moment all my life. Why it took so long I don't know, but honey, I'm glad, so glad, you are finally here."

I was so caught up in how she looked and the fact it was really her, when I rolled down the window what came out was, "Hey lady, do you spend much time picking up guys in airport parking lots?"

I'm such a dope; my first words to her came off like a fifty-year-old bad joke, but at least she got in the car. I don't know if it was because of what I said, but it was obvious she was extremely nervous. She trembled as she tried to speak. I could almost hear her heart beat faster and faster. The meeting she and I had longed for was no longer a daydream lost in the past. Can you imagine what I felt? A mere three months ago I was nothing more to her than a distant memory of a soldier who died in Vietnam, but today I am alive and she is sitting right next to me. Our dreams have been resurrected; I believe in God and I believe in miracles. Lacking words to say to her and searching for a way to break the silence, I leaned close to her, and we shared our first kiss.

I offered a simple kiss, not passionate nor with expectations, just to say hello; but to my delight and surprise, it was returned by her, which caught me off guard. I was pulling away from her with a wide smile of delight when she suddenly pressed forward in an attempt to kiss me back; instead of kissing my lips, she laid one directly on my teeth and part of my mustache. I came away with a brilliant shade of red smeared on my teeth, and her lipstick actually changed the color of my mustache! From the look on her face, I knew something had gone wrong, but I was unaware what it was until she told me.

"Silly, she said, "look in the rearview mirror."

"You've got to be kidding," I said when I saw my glowing face. "Do you have any tissues?"

"Here, but it'll probably just make it worse."

"What kind of lipstick is that anyway, lacquer-based? Now I have it all over my face, and the Kleenex is caught in my teeth."

"I tried to warn you."

In an instant laughter filled the rental car. Like kids, we roared with delight, which broke the ice nicely. This may sound stupid, but the kiss that was thirty-five years in the making was perfect for us as it was probably what nervous teenagers might have done on their first date. A silence filled the air, and she hugged me as if to say, "Welcome back, honey."

I could see in her eyes the depth of the emotion she held for me, and this frightened me a bit; but there was a warmth and honesty about her, and even a playfulness I knew I would not be able to resist. All I could think to say was, "Well, we're off to a great start—a bad joke and a kiss that left me looking like a bit character with a bad makeup job. Where to now?'

"Cracker Barrel."

"What's a cracker barrel?"

"Follow me and you'll see."

She showed me where she had parked her car, and I followed her to a large but quaint looking country restaurant—the aforementioned Cracker Barrel. After waiting about fifteen minutes to be seated, our server came to the table with a carafe of hot coffee and menus.

"What's good here?" I asked.

"Try Uncle Herschel's Favorite," Leah replied.

"Alright. When the waitress comes back, order my eggs over easy. I'm headed to the men's room to repair my face."

I returned to what I thought would be a light breakfast.

"What the heck is all of this?"

"Your breakfast, of course."

"What did you order? This looks like enough food for three lumberjacks. Eggs, hash browns, biscuits, gravy, ham, pancakes and, wait a minute, what the heck is this?"

"Grits."

"Great. What are grits?"

"Ground corn. Just put some butter and sugar on them."

"Okay. As they say, 'When in Rome. . . .' Oh my Lord, that's awful!"

I'm sorry to say I spit the grits back into the bowl and washed my mouth out with several swallows of coffee. I'm finding there are some Southern delights I might not be so enchanted with.

As we chatted and ate, something amazing took place. It's not that I was falling in love with her; I had been in love with her my whole life, but this was an affirmation of the commitment we had shared all those lost years. As I talked about my past, my marriage and my kids, I found myself drifting through old memories and wishing they were ours. The love that had evaded me for so many years was back and as brilliant as a perfect ten-carat diamond. The joy and exhilaration of retracing the past and creating new memories overwhelmed me; the thought of a journey where everything we touch will be a first time for us and the enticement of finally sharing all with each other is more than I had hoped for. This is our new reality, our chance to find the oneness within and between us. As I gazed across the table at her, I wondered if she was feeling the same.

After breakfast, I followed her through the back roads of Huntsville up into the mountains. The beauty of this land took my breath away; I had never seen such rich foliage, warmed by the sun under crystal blue skies. Homes here were not the cracker boxes stacked one after another as in California, and the yards were not brown with the summer heat. Swings adorned every porch, and as we passed, people waved at us as if to say, "Your love is welcome here." Every home was beautifully landscaped with tall trees, lots of flowers and massive green lawns. As we went higher and higher into the mountains, the homes disappeared and what lay before us was the rolling hills of Alabama.

The scenic views of this timeless land atop the Monte Santo Mountain (Spanish for "Mountain of Health") abounded with deep chiseled valleys, larger than life pines and lush pastures which teemed with young deer. The musical harmony of birds filled the air. There was an ambiance of innocence in the air, and I wanted to believe this was a place from Leah's past that she had not shared with others. I hope this special place will allow her the freedom to escape and rekindle her feelings for me and be a spot where we will explore and enjoy each other without interference from our current lives.

Not far from the top of Monte Santo, we turned into a majestic old-world campground complete with a series of rental cabins that were far removed from the other parts of the park. About a mile and a half down a carved out, narrow dirt road, we came to Cabin #10, which Leah had chosen for its panoramic views of the Tennessee valley. It was nestled amid towering pine trees, overlooking rich fertile farm lands and emerald green rolling hills that appeared to stretch forever. It was more paradise than any Eden I could have imagined, and I was here to share it with Leah.

16

Cabin #10

Our cabin was very rustic and showed its age, built in 1930 out of poplar planks and native stone. It had a make-shift kitchen, a bathroom barely large enough for one, and a huge stone fire place that took up almost half of the combination bedroom, living room and dining room. It was fronted by a screened porch, which looked to be an afterthought, furnished with two chairs, a small table and a stack of firewood.

We spent hours on this small porch, sheltered in time and silent to the rest of the world, opening our hearts to each other. It was the perfect space for us to share details of our lives and our longings for each other. We knew, almost from the beginning, that our destiny was being reborn and that we would not be able to deny a future with each other. It was in this serene setting I knew we would become one with each other, maybe not of the flesh, but as a single heartbeat. Stories never before told out loud, hidden thoughts and passions, and trepidations and misgivings of the past flowed like a vast emotional river winding its way through time.

As we sat on the porch talking about what had been stolen from us and how our lives were, up to this very day, irreversibly altered and our dreams destroyed, something else shifted within me, something so amazing it still seems hard to believe today. I had never before felt secure with anyone, yet even though I hadn't seen her face since we were very small children, I had the odd sensation of finally being complete, just being with her. The way she reacted to me was as though someone greater than us was guiding our actions and shaping our words. I have never felt so self-assured; I knew I could tell her anything, and as I did, she relaxed and opened up to me, exposing memories and hidden secrets of her life she had never revealed to another soul. We spoke as one, and I knew from that very moment I would pursue her with all my heart. I could clearly see, with delight, that she was pursuing me as well.

The afternoon flew by, stealing precious time from us. As her story poured from her heart, she unveiled a childlike naïveté when it came to the real world. Looking back I could see why her e-mails were tempered and cautious; this is how she was taught and trained to act by her family, her church and her husband, leaving her all trusting to the will of man and biblically unable to resist or defy. Now, thank God, in this secluded place and alone with me, her thoughts, her desires and her dreams flowed from her without hesitation; it was as though she had waited her whole life to expose her true emotions and her desires only to me. I see why Richard fears me; I will provide Leah the opportunity to see what love should be, sadly something he could never comprehend, much less give.

There was a sense of hunger in her, a craving to have me take in every word she spoke, catch every eye inflection she made, and openly react to her playful and teasing ways. She may not have realized it at the time, but she was driving me crazy. I wanted her, not just for this evening but again and again and then once again, as I had longed for her in the horrifying long nights of Vietnam. I was as much in love with her as I was back in 1971. I might be fifty-five now, but I had the fire of a twenty-five year old ready to run a ten-mile race and then make love to her in ways she could have never imagined.

It's a good thing I promised her a few days earlier this was to be a get-to-know-each-other meeting and that I would not try and make this a love-making session. However, she had made no such promise, and a blind man could see the passion lurking behind her green eyes. I do not believe she is aware of how alluring she is or how sensuality resonates from her, but there is something captivating about her. This playful side seems to all but scream, "Make love to me!"

I know these are not signals she is consciously giving off, and it's possible I am reading too much into them. I know it may be wrong, but there is nothing whatsoever, at least in my mind, that should hold us apart. Making love to each other seems like the most natural thing we could do. *God,* I pray, *guide my way and temper my passions.*

Prior to leaving California, I had put together a collection of pictures of my life; photos of my kids, places I have been, things I had accomplished or not quite accomplished, and anything else I could think of that would let her know who I was, where I came from and where I wanted to go. She had done the same, and the collage of her life included every letter I had sent from Vietnam.

Finding them at the bottom of a box of photos, I said, "You brought all the letters I sent you from Vietnam?"

She smiled. "Of course. I want to sit back, close my eyes, and have you read them to me."

"All of them?"

"Why not? Can't you pamper me a bit? Ryan, you have the prettiest eyes."

"Leah, stop that."

"Alright—for now. Here, let me show you some pictures of my family. This one is Brent. . . ."

As she walked me through her past, showing me places she had lived and pictures of her family, it became obvious the only meaning in her life came from her precious boys. She walked me through their lives, one by one. I wanted to know more about her, but she swelled with such pride as she spoke of them, I couldn't interrupt her.

Her oldest, Brent, lives down the street from her. He has two beautiful children, Mercedes and Trent, who are very close to her as she helped raise them. He is a very skilled artist working in the field of upholstery.

This may sound odd, but his workmanship is like nothing I have ever seen. He takes simple and drab furniture and transforms it into show pieces, blending fabrics and threads in such a way I can only call it art. Brent found out early that marrying young might not have been the wisest decision. Like many youthful marriages, the rocky roads ahead were too much, and the marriage broke apart, but his ex-wife Sandra and he remain close. Hearing Leah talk, I felt there was still a great deal of love shared between them.

Scott is the middle son, currently attending college and majoring in aerospace mechanics. Although she would not admit it, she spoke of him with such tenderness and love I could see there was a special bond between the two.

Eddie, the baby of the family, is a very skilled musician and composer. Leah told me some of her happiest times were spent sitting and listening as he played his guitar and sang songs to her that he had written. Scott may have been her pet, but Eddie brought music back into her life, and she loves him with a love he may never understand. Sometime prior to Eddie being conceived, Richard had been scheduled to have a hernia operation. Their doctor recommended that, if they were content with the size of their family, this would be an excellent time for Richard to have a vasectomy. Richard and Leah agreed this was something they should do, and the decision was made to have it performed. Richard was in the operating room awaiting the procedure when the doctor came out to ask Leah if this was truly what she wanted. Leah initially said yes, but as the doors closed she had a change of heart. She knew someday she would leave Richard, and she could not live with the guilt of knowing she took away his ability to sire another child should he re-marry; so she ran after the doctor, shouting "Stop." Eddie, to this date, has no idea why she did this, but Leah knows, and to her this third child was a gift from God.

As she talked about them, I felt I could recall every cold they had ever had, every scrape of their knees, each and every one of their triumphs and their hiccups along life's way. I have known many women in my life, some good and some bad, but I have never found a woman who could so vividly tell stories and reenact every day of her children's lives like Leah could. I have no doubts she gave up her life and her soul to provide for them, and I pray someday they will become aware of this and be strong enough to see the truth. Boys, she loves you all.

After talking about her kids, she moved farther back into her past and walked me through her family's move to Tennessee and how they lived in a small cabin with no indoor plumbing and few amenities. She described going to school and their move to Georgia, where they lived in a trailer park and where she would grow into womanhood, yet still with the mentality of a sheltered and innocent child.

It was in Georgia that things changed for Leah as her parents became very religious and very controlling. She was not allowed to dance or attend parties, and she never had boyfriends. Her only escape was through music, books and old movies. She told me about her father, who was a skilled business man who owned an upholstery shop, flew his own plane and provided for his family; but listening to her, it was apparent the father figure Leah needed so desperately was never there.

Later I found out that her father was raised by a controlling woman who denied him at almost every turn. I suppose life was tough for him as his parents divorced when he was only six and possibly why he lacked the skill sets needed to rear a family, let along two little girls. His role in how he viewed marriage was to be the provider, and I believe in his heart he did what he felt was right for his family.

Her mother was forced to rule the roost. Something that should have been a shared responsibility fell squarely on her shoulders, and at first she handled it with dignity and grace. However, as Leah entered her teen years, her mother became ill, which affected her emotionally and changed her into a much more stern and dominant force in Leah's life. It was then she began the barrage of verbal and physical assaults on Leah, pushing her toward Richard, "the son she never had."

As Leah continued with story after story about her young life, more patterns of abuse began to crystallize; and it became obvious to me she had developed irrational fears and buckets full of anxieties from either unsuccessfully trying to please her mother or from fearful stimuli from her church. Her cognitive reasoning had been so damaged that by her teen years, she could only see in black or white—you go to church; you go to heaven. You attend to your duty, or you fail God. You please your mother, or you're a failure.

I'm not sure why she told me all these details. Maybe she felt she had to make sure I knew why she agreed to marry so young and without love, or maybe she needed to justify that she really wasn't a bad person, just a mixed-up kid. Finally, she made her way up to the time after she thought I was killed in the war, which led to her married life. Although she spoke about this for many hours, I will not delve into it at this time as her words were so painful and too often appalling.

It was true she asked Richard to marry her, not for love or even wanting to be with him, but as a vehicle to escape the physical and verbal torment at home. She was at a point in her life where she was convinced no one would ever want her, so she decided to make the final sacrifice of her life solely to placate her mother and end the fighting. I wanted to cry when I realized how brainwashed this seventeen-year-old child must have been to walk into a marriage knowing she did not love the man before her.

Richard, by allowing this to happen, became in my mind the ultimate coward and opportunist. What he saw was an opportunity to complete his fantasy world and join the family he had become close to, so without forethought or caution, he seized it. I will never concede the fact he knew Leah's mother was setting this up for him, but what of his humanity? Why did he not suggest that they date, if only for a few months, to make sure they loved each other? Why did he not seek out the counsel of their church? Why did he not tell Leah's parents that she did not love him? He could have cared less, as this act would bestow upon him the ultimate power over Leah, to use her as he saw fit. His new God-given right was firmly in place, and he controlled her every day of their union.

As she spoke of her marriage, Leah began to cry, so I said, "It's all right, honey; this is only our first day, so let's take a break. I think I need a hug, don't you?"

She did give me a hug, but for some reason she needed to go on, disclosing more about her past and all but begging for my understanding. I got the distinct feeling she was not just telling me her story, she was asking me for forgiveness. She unveiled the dark secrets hidden behind closed doors and bared her fears with such agonizing pain, she cried several more times; yet as she spoke, the Leah of my letters emerged. Deep within her resided the woman of my dreams, one not damaged by time, not hardened by the events of her life, but the shy and reserved beauty asking for nothing more than to be loved and appreciated.

She said she knew her greatest sin was marrying Richard under such a false pretense, and for that she must repent. But how could anyone hold her accountable? She was all but physically forced to marry as a naïve teen, never allowed to find her path, denied social enjoyments, lied to about her true love, degraded and intimidated by her mother, ignored by her father, and above all taken like a child in the night by a man who knew she did not love him.

As the day dimmed into twilight and the cool of darkness found its way through the screens, the sky filled with blustery clouds which glowed with the setting sun's golden rays. I breathed in the splendor of this timeless land and knew I had found a place where I was destined to live out my days with her. It felt as though I was meant to be here, and I truly believed I had found a land to call home and one I would soon share with her. Our prior feelings of apprehension and fear faded as we became more at ease with each other, more trusting and more attuned to each other's needs. There was nothing selfish, nothing hidden, only the longing for our dreams to be fulfilled. Her eyes followed my every movement, and I could sense the meaning behind her words almost before she said them aloud; a raised eyebrow, a whispered sigh, a slight curl to her lips or a lowering of her head spoke volumes.

The night stole the light of day, and we shared another new experience—a simple twilight but special because it was our first one together. A bit later we took a short drive to a local steak house in Huntsville. Our eyes, which had avoided contact, were fixed on one another as we sat across the table, and the shyness Leah once conveyed had vanished. We talked as though we had been together for the past three decades, and there was calm between us which I cannot explain. I'm not sure I ever want to.

She continued to entice me, and I saw a contented look in her eyes as she reached for my hand. Her hands were soft and supple, exciting me with just a simple touch. The light from the lamp above us threw a sheen onto her hair and lit up her face like an angel looking into and through me. The teasing smile she had hidden for so long, the one from her pictures of so long ago, returned and lifted my spirits, filled me with anticipation and renewed the strength of the young lover I once was.

Dinner was a wonderful experience, even though I was very tired. Not wanting to let the night end, we nevertheless returned to the cabin where hopefully I could get some sleep. Once there, we spent a few precious moments holding hands and taking in the sounds of the night. I knew I had to do something which I never realized would be cruel; I had to send home a love I had waited on over thirty-five years, but Leah needed to return to her home to make right on a promise she had made to Richard. We had waited so long to be together and now to have to say goodbye was excruciating. We had found each other only a few short hours ago and had met face to face for the first time, with both of us knowing how much we dreamed of this night and what the outcome should be. Not tonight, however; so maybe a good night kiss with the promise of another tomorrow will last us until then. Who am I kidding? But as Leah left, albeit in tears, at least we knew there would be at least one more day we would share.

After she left, the thoughts and actions of the day invaded every breath I took, carrying with them disbelief, questions, and the certainty of problems to follow. I tried to sleep, but this was out of the question as the stories she told me kept filling my mind. I knew beyond any doubt Leah was not and had never been in love with her husband; her life with him was nothing more than a contrived fabrication created by her mother through lies and deception. Although they were not prompted by Richard, they were concealed by him and then perpetuated to hold her in servitude to him.

Leah told stories of the distorted and sick physical abuses she had endured for years, never speaking out, as this is what she was taught and what her religion mandated. She actually believed that what was happening to her was normal and that this was what a woman must give into when demanded by her husband. Armed with the truth and her new sense of self, leaving Richard will not be an issue, but her sons were another matter. Still, they were grown, and how could she, even if he changed his ways, stay with this man, knowing he concealed and was part of the plan to bury her love?

It might have become obvious to her that her marriage to Richard was a mistake, a tragic, misguided move by a young mentally abused and depressed girl, but there were no mistakes when it came to her boys. *Please, God, should we ever put our lives back together, give her boys the ability to see the pain their mother suffered for their sake, and then Dear God, guide and help them to understand why she moved on.* I was left with a dilemma. I could not simply take Leah away with me; more time will be needed, not for us to secure our love, but to bring closure to and expose the past in a true and compelling way for her boys to accept.

17

Lenna

Our second day together began with another kiss, and unlike yesterday, this kiss was natural and promising. So much had been exposed the prior day, this day was meant for relaxing and a time to enjoy each other's company and affections. We left the cabin for breakfast, IHOP this time. Today promised to be special as we planned to visit Lenna, Leah's grandmother who had been such an important part of both of our lives.

Her home was exactly as I had pictured it, an old ranch house that Lenna's husband built many years ago where they raised cattle and farmed the adjacent pastures. Lenna surprised me when I first came into her home. The first thing she did was ask me to come to her and kneel down. I was a bit surprised at this odd request, but knelt before her. She cupped her hands around my face and peered into my eyes and said, "Yep, you are Ryan, and you still have those beautiful long eyelashes."

As we all took a seat in her living room, she told me how much she had always loved me and how happy she was Leah and I had made our way to each other. She asked about my mother and said how sorry she was about the passing of my father and what a great and open man he was.

Lenna is a stubborn woman who leaves nothing to chance and who feely speaks her mind. She shocked both of us when, without any hesitation, she blurted out, "Well, are you two going to get married and be together or not?"

I knew, from what Leah had told me about her grandmother, that she could be a bit to the point, but this one really caught me off guard. I was somewhat in awe, but I told Lenna that only time would tell. She gave me a little smile, tilting her head a bit and squinting her eyes, but all she said was, "We'll see."

I think she saw the wonder and love in our eyes and knew what the final outcome would be. She might have been a tad past her prime, but she could still recognize the looks of love that passed between us and the compassion in our voices. She also knew her granddaughter better than most and suspected Leah would have never allowed me to fly all this way unless she had already made up her mind about what she wanted to happen. Given this, I believe Lenna had decided long before we showed up this morning that she was going to have a little fun at Leah's expense and now would be the perfect time. She started off with, "Ryan, can I tell you something?"

"Sure, Grandma (which is what Leah asked me to call her), anything."

"Did you know Leah has always been in love with you and that all of her dreams were of being together with you?"

Leah looked like she wanted to crawl under the couch. I smiled and said, "Oh, really?"

"Oh, you bet, Ryan. She told me this a thousand times."

It's too bad I didn't have a camera with me as Leah turned a beautiful shade of crimson. I got a big kick out of this, but Lenna did not have to do any reassuring with me as I already knew, from holding Leah, that she felt that way. However, once I told Lenna I was in love with her granddaughter, she granted us her blessing and her hopes that everything we had ever dreamed of would come true. She knew all about Leah's past, her longing for me and the marital problems she had endured; but she had kept quiet, hoping Leah would find the love she so desired and above all find the love she once shared with me. She told me not to fear the feelings I held for Leah and that if I truly loved her to let nothing on earth come between us.

I knew, at that very moment, I was something special to Lenna, and someone she wanted her granddaughter to be with. Looking about her home, I was shocked that she had pictures of my mother and me on her mantel and yet another picture of me in high school. Funny, no one had noticed, but she had Leah's picture next to mine and apparently had had them positioned this way for years. Lenna was also apologetic for the actions of her daughter and son-in-law and hoped we could forgive their misdeeds. She told me her daughter was very ill and on heavy medication at the time and her actions may have been misguided, about what really happened to me after Vietnam. I tried to let her know that today, this was not a problem, and that I was just thankful Leah and I had once again found each other.

One thing she said stunned me. She told me Leah had always been shy and rarely spoke her mind. My first thought was, are we speaking about the same person? The Leah I've been with going on two days is anything but quiet, never shy around me and speaks her mind freely; as a matter of fact, these are some of my favorite traits about her.

I told Lenna I would not do anything to let her down and that when Leah and I got together, I would move to the South to make sure we were close to her. I also told her I knew her granddaughter was a good person, and I would do nothing to change that. Lenna was accepting of our feelings for each other and made it very clear that should our love prevail, she would support our decision no matter what. She simply asked that I always do the right thing for her granddaughter.

Lenna told me story after story of the family, the good times and their short comings and mistakes over the years and how today she was furious with her son-in-law, Leah's father. From what I could gather, he had started a rumor that Leah and I had already run off together, and this story had spread through the family like a wildfire. For several minutes, Lenna voiced her anger through each of her many, and I do mean many, well-chosen words. I came to realize she was quite the talker, and

I prayed Leah did not take after her in this department, but I feared they were one and the same.

I came to understand something about Lenna, I will never forget. This woman although ninety two was the most gracious lady, other than my mother, I had ever met. She has a distinct view of life, a passion for the truth, and the ability to love beyond description. She's tough, two fisted, a bit stubborn, but she has a heart filled with compassion and love. I felt so welcomed in her home, and I felt blessed that she accepted me into her family. Leah did not have to ask me to call her Grandma, I was honored she allowed to.

Although I would have liked to spend more time with Lenna, Leah and I needed to continue our walks together, alone, and Grandma knew this. There was still so much to know about each other and only a few precious days left. As we said our goodbyes, I got a kiss and a much needed hug from a very special lady. I hope Leah and I can begin our life together before she passes on, as her loss prior to our union would be tragic to both of us.

After leaving Lenna, we decided to stop for lunch, and I picked the place. The restaurant was called Shogun, much like Ken of Japan's in California, where they slice, dice and cook your meal right in front of you. Leah was so excited, and her face lit up with the show they put on for us. Since we were in a Japanese restaurant, I asked the waitress for two sets of chopsticks. Although Leah said she had a set at home, she had never tried to use them. She struggled at first, but like everything she ever really wanted to do, she mastered this new talent in no time. I could not believe how much fun it was just being with her and sharing a simple meal. God, how she completes me!

After lunch we returned to the cabin, and once again Leah talked about her life. She filled in many of the gaps from her e-mails, and I was left in awe of her accomplishments and business sense. She had held many jobs over the years but did not find her niche until Lenna introduced her to a new business selling Rainbow Home Cleaning Systems. Leah exploded! Her sales soared, and soon she was promoted to a Satellite Distributor. Over the years, she opened several offices and storefront showrooms with a bounty of dealers working for her, while compiling numerous awards and vacation trips generated from her outstanding sales activities.

I had known she was a great mother and the backbone of her family; now I discovered a different side of her that showed me how much we were alike. Her strength had kept her family afloat; her drive and her risk-taking, good and bad, had provided for her family. Richard was not in charge; he even gave up his upholstery business to work for her. *Funny,* I thought. *Here was this shy little mother of three with more guts and get up and go than most men I had met, and yet when all was said and done, she was the one who was faulted for not being there at all times for her sons. What was she supposed to do, let them go without?*

As a break when our conversation became too heavy, I told her how I ran businesses in California and how important it was to have a viable business plan to measure growth, cash flow and projections. She had been successful but had never put one together. She had daily schedules and a set routine but nothing in place to measure her progress or success financially. So sort of in jest, we penciled out a makeshift yet measurable business plan. I was trying to break the tension in our talks about her marriage and our pasts and having some fun throwing out a few ideas when it hit me; she was completely engrossed, picking my brain, looking for ways to rejuvenate her business. Through some bad advice and the turmoil in her life, her business had slipped from forty or fifty sales per month to less than five. Concepts like sales projections, employee to sales ratios and social media marketing were completely foreign to her, and she was excited to hear fresh ideas.

Leah drew from my energy, eagerly wanting to learn, and as we poured over opportunities and new marketing schemes, she glowed with enthusiasm. I could feel her anticipation grow with renewed hope of rebuilding her once vibrant business. I was delighted to no end. I have no doubt Richard will object to this, but I don't think he will have much of a say in it.

After our brief respite, we burrowed deeper into our pasts. She spoke of love and how hard it had been to wake up every morning knowing the love she longed for was never there between her and her husband and today how much more difficult it is knowing her marriage was conceived by others through lies and deceit.

Leah was maybe four or five years old when she was indoctrinated into a church that believes there are no exceptions when it comes to marriage and divorce and where Christ allowed only one plausible way "in the sight of God" to divorce your mate—adultery or death. I believe fervently in God and have served as an elder in my church, but I also believe there are many forms of adultery. If her church had taken the time to look into her relationship with Richard, the evil in his heart and his reprehensible actions, they would have been resolute that she remove herself from the relationship via divorce.

I could empathize with Leah. Even though I was not trapped by my church's doctrine, I was trapped due to my love for my children and had remained in a loveless relationship with some of the same problems she had faced. The differences between us is that the infidelity I was forced to live with was openly admitted to me, while for Leah the infidelity was hidden in back rooms, disguised as the religious right of man, and only later openly expressed via propositions to other family members. Leah's sister was victim to Richard's sexual solicitations, but even she remained silent, telling only her mother, who told her to keep her mouth shut as it was probably her fault anyhow. A travesty? Without question. A defilement of marital vows? Absolutely. An adulteration of love in the sight of God? Unquestionably.

Leah had lived the illusion of a competent business woman and a contented, loving wife, but as night fell, the fragile and frightened child of so long ago emerged. Unwillingly and through fear of condemnation, she had surrendered herself to the demoralizing and contemptible acts of a man, her husband, who was indifferent to anything other than perpetuating his contrived and morbid fantasy world. She became nothing more than an unwilling object, a toy of the night, believing she was commanded by her faith to submit. Defying all logic, she survived, holding tightly to her belief in God's love and praying that someday she would find the love missing from her life.

It's as though we had lived as one our whole life, with temporary understudies trying to steal a love they could not even comprehend. Our drives, our passions, our love for our children and our quest to find fulfillment had, by design, set us on divergent courses which have now crossed, reuniting us in love. Incredible, too impossible for words, perhaps, but I fervently believe this would never have happened if not for our faithful devotion to each other and with guidance from above.

The night was still young, and any blind man could see our hearts were racing with limitless expectations as to where this evening might take us. Leah, maybe as a way to lighten the air or possibly ignite it, asked me to sing to her. From our e-mails, she knew music was an important part of my life, and she had a great passion for it as well through her son Eddie. Although I agreed, I prayed she knew the pipes were not what they used to be, and I wished I had brought along my guitar. As I began to sing, she settled back in her chair and closed her eyes.

Something happened between us, for as I sang to her, she reached out to me with a soft touch and said, "Honey, sing another one." I realized this was something she had craved and that what she was really saying to me was court me, woo me, let me know you want me, and as you serenade me, seduce me. Leah is a passionate woman who would offer complete devotion to any man who shared with her the tenderness of love. As I sang to her, I was thankful beyond words I had been offered a second chance to be that man to her. I wasn't sure if we were moving too fast or too slow, but I felt as though I had been with her all my life and could think of nothing more natural than giving my very being to her.

She told me more about her married life that night than I feel comfortable with exposing at this time, and thankfully she told me how she kept me alive in her daily life and in her prayers all those years. She asked me to tell her the truth about what happened in Vietnam, and as painful as it was to me, we talked about those times for hours. I told her many times how she had been a beacon holding me through endless terrible nights, caressing me with her words.

Tired at last from the flow of words and emotions that had occupied our day, Leah rose to return home. I had a deep longing to keep her through the night, and I knew if I initiated intimacy, she would follow my every move with great zeal and passion. But again, this was not the time; although I knew our joining as one would happen soon. I kissed her goodbye with a passionate kiss that rocked me to my toes and lit a fire that will burn in me the rest of my life.

Not long after she left, as I lay there alone in the still cabin, I experienced a sudden burst of energy and a craving like I had never experienced for anyone else, and I knew I would ask her to marry me. I would not do so on this trip, and I wasn't sure when it would happen; but I could no longer picture us apart. There was only one hurdle left before us, and although I knew it would tear me apart, I also knew it must be done to bring closure to her past.

18

Boundless Love

$\mathcal{O}$n a matter of days, I would fly back to the West coast, and Leah would return home and try to make her marriage with Richard work. It was important for her to move into a relationship with me with her eyes wide open, with no reservations and no lingering "what if" questions. She had to feel she had given her marriage every chance before she ended it. She needed to be clear-headed and aware of the consequences our actions would bring, not blinded by the pure excitement of chasing her dream and rekindling our love. Painfully, I needed her to return home, look at the pictures on the walls, peek into her son's rooms, remember their childhoods and then realize it might all come to an end once she chose me.

Am I afraid? Of course, but my love for her is too strong to let her make life-altering decisions unless the love she has for me matches my love for her, unless she is willing to challenge all and give all to make us one with each other and with God. I do not believe she will stay with Richard, but we both need to be completely sure we are meant to be together and confident God will bless our union. I fear her boys will not understand what drove her to this decision. She told me she believes God will open their hearts and they will remember how much she loves them and will accept her happiness. I am not so sure as they have led such sheltered lives they may be too naïve to understand the power of our love and God's will to protect his children through love. All I can do is pray she is right.

The next day she welcomed me in the morning with what I guess is another Southern treat, a breaded pork chop on a biscuit. I looked at it, and all I could think about was a simple bacon and eggs breakfast. But to be honest, it wasn't half bad and tasted a lot better than grits. After I wolfed down the biscuit and some coffee, I asked Leah what she wanted to do. What she said was, "I just want to be alone with you."

"Perfect! That sounds great to me; let's go to the mall."

"The mall? Are you sure it's a good place to be alone?"

"Trust me, honey," I said. "I promise you a day of love and being alone."

She frowned but agreed, so with some mixed feelings, we were off to the Decatur Mall. At first she seemed disillusioned and hesitant. I'm sure she thought I was more than a little off, but I asked her, "Where can you go to meet people better than a mall?"

"Meet people? I thought we were going to be alone?"

"We will be, just alone with all those people who so far don't know us but will love us."

"Are you sure about this?"

"Just hold your breath; I'm going to show you a miracle."

"A miracle?"

"That's right. One you should have known all your life."

I love a mall. You can walk, talk, hold hands, window shop, take in a movie, try new things and grab a bite to eat. As we strolled the mall, I felt like a young buck of old taking "my girl" on a date. This was obviously something we had never done before; yet it was something so simple and compelling, it drew us closer together. We were alone in a place over-flowing with people. We were on our own planet where the pressures that surrounded us felt distant and removed as we walked, talked and shared the warmth between our hands. Leah had never just strolled through a mall without a purpose in mind; she had never taken the time to watch the lonely people that drifted by like zombies, never seeing the simple pleasures in life hidden in the mall; their only concern was searching out one final if not fatal discount.

We came across a Belk's department store, which I had never heard of, and went in. After browsing through several areas, we met the most amazing saleslady in the perfume department. She said she had been watching us for a while and we seemed to her to be different from the other shoppers.

"You two look like you are on cloud nine," she said, and then asked, "How long have you been together?"

Leah and I looked at each other and with a chuckle in our voices and almost in unison said, "Since yesterday!" I think I heard her jaw hit the floor.

Leah said she needed to visit the ladies' room, which gave me an excellent opportunity to tell the lady our story and how we were on a mission to build new memories. She was so taken back she almost cried, and when Leah returned she rushed over to her and hugged the both of us like a mom welcoming her kids home from summer camp. With her assistance, Leah tried out a few scents; none really excited her, so I asked if they carried Opium.

"Yes, we have Opium," the lady said, "but you know I don't think I have ever sold any. Let's try it."

When Leah spritzed the perfume on, she surprised herself as well as our new friend behind the counter, who said, "Wow! This perfume must have been made for you; you're like a whole different person and very alluring."

Leah blushed and said, "Stop it."

Leah had never thought of herself as alluring, but I knew. Opium is an expensive but ageless fragrance designed for lovers, and Leah was thrilled. I bought it for her, knowing it was going to make it very difficult on me once we got back to the cabin. Leah also knew it, for after she said "Thank you," she gave me a little wink.

After thanking the saleslady and receiving another hug from her, we continued our mission, I mean our stroll, through the mall, acting like young lovers, peeking into shops, making comments about the people around us and even looking at furniture. I wondered what was going through her mind. I could have spent the whole day shopping with her just to see that look in her eyes as we met people or her reaction when she saw something she liked. From what she told me, Richard was never outgoing, and she could not remember even one time when he struck up a conversation with anyone, even people he knew. He felt more comfortable avoiding people and talking under his breath about them. My perception is that he either needed to tear everyone else down to make himself look bigger or he used his comments to keep Leah from developing relationships.

I must have been quite a shock to her as I love people and cannot resist talking with anyone as though we have been friends for years. She had a bit of a problem with this at first, but after a while she seemed to enjoy leaving her shy and sheltered ways behind. As we were leaving the mall, we passed by the Belk's perfume department on our way out, and the saleslady who helped us called out, "Bye, Ryan and Leah. I love you."

Leah's face lit up. She treated me to the biggest smile I had ever seen, and in a faint voice whispered in my ear, "I love you, too."

Following our mall date, we drove through the hills around Huntsville. At first she had no idea where I was going or what I was looking for, but it soon became apparent I was looking for homes, and more importantly, a home for us. We found several, but one really stood out. It had an "Open House" sign out front, and we went inside. It was a new construction with over 3,800 square feet above ground, fashioned like a small castle. We had fun strolling through the different rooms, Leah imagining how she would place furniture or what art would adorn the walls.

We drove for hours through places like New Market, Gurley, Ardmore, Madison, Athens, Huntsville and even Skinem (this really is a town). We turned down side streets like Poorhouse Road, You Take It Road, Meeting House Road and even Butter & Eggs Road. As we traveled through these areas we listened to music, and Leah implored me to sing along with most of the songs. She found out something about me during our travels. I have this passion for exploration and will turn onto roads that seem to go nowhere just to find out what is at the end. I love to stop and talk to folks, maybe just to say "Hi," but all my life I have tried to live up to the sentiment expressed by Will Rogers: "I never met a man I didn't like."

The time slipped away from us and darkness began to fall. As there was so little time left on my trip, we headed back to the cabin. We settled in before the fireplace, and Leah spoke of the loneliness she lived with day by day and her longing to fly away from it all to a place where she could express her desires fully, desire not as in a passion such as lust but in a passion for love and the yearning to be loved, an eternal commitment to give herself like she had never done before and then to delight in knowing she was adored.

She was emerging right before me, coming to life and experiencing the desires she had never felt before. This is how I had pictured her so long ago, a teenager flirting with becoming a woman, waiting only for me to come home to her and fulfill those personal and intimate experiences in life she longed for. Her ideal life would be one where she could cast off the problems and the frustrations of the past and soar with new purpose, without intimidation, without denial, but with the freedom of expression that all of us hunger for.

I could see it in her eyes and feel it in her touch and I could not help but ask myself, how could I be so lucky? I was in a secluded cabin nestled in one of the most beautiful parts of the country with the woman of my dreams, who was now reaching to me in ways I could have never even imagined. Her words were not tempered by the past nor by biblical restrictions; genuine emotion flowed freely as she related the depths of her passion, her irresistible need to be loved and provide love and her desire to have me complete her dream. I believe she was reading my mind as she all but mirrored the words I had been hesitant to say to her.

I had felt these emotions since my first day with her, and now it took her to explain why we should not wait, not even for a day, to join our love. For the first time in my life I felt helpless; I could not resist her. I knew it was wrong since we were still legally bound to others, but in our hearts, we have been united since 1971. I told her she held a wondrous power over me, but this time she responded quickly that I held the same power over her, a power born in love which will be there no matter how guarded we might try to be. There was such clarity in her words and such honesty in her desire to love me, all I could say was. "I know how your heart speaks to me and mine to yours, and I promise, after tonight, I will never let your go."

She seemed to grow in strength with my declaration. Although I had not said much before, the small stutter in her voice and the shyness I noticed at the airport had faded into the distant sky, along with every inhibition I had ever seen in her eyes. There were no words to describe how I felt for her and what she meant to me, so in the silence of Cabin #10, I walked over to her, took her in my arms, and looked into her eyes as I softly said, "Leah, I love you."

I was as frightened as I could be; time had stopped and she remained motionless. It seemed as though an eternity passed before she spoke back to me in a gentle and compelling voice, "Ryan, I love you, too."

My heart soared, and I felt all was right. We did not grow to love each other in these few short days; we had loved each other all of our lives, and we were about to take another step in our journey to become man and wife. Although thirty-five years had come and gone, it seemed like 1971 was just a single day ago as I kissed her. It was a passionate kiss that had remained dormant far too long, and she responded to it with great eagerness. I felt her body quiver and her legs weaken as she kissed me again and again. With this single embrace, the longings of a lifetime were within my reach, and I knew she was mine.

She held me closer and closer, allowing me to sense her unbridled thirst for love. Our coming together was not to be an evil act hidden in the night; it was the consummation of our boundless love. Her eyes glistened as she tilted her head slightly, her lips barely touching mine, inviting me without words to even greater pleasures with nothing held back. As the scent of Opium danced around me, I could resist her no longer. Her lips were rich and full, playfully tempting me to go farther and farther. As I did she echoed my every move. I have been kissed by many women before but never with greater urgency or purpose. As we drew together, I could feel her body bonding with mine, revealing the fullness of her womanhood and the ever warming glow within her.

Her body moved with pleasure as I caressed her neck, and I heard her sigh with anticipation of what was to come. Her hands pushed against the arch of my back, and I found my self-control lost in her desire. All I had dreamed of and longed for, for so long was inviting me into the very being of her soul. My passions were all but uncontrollable, but I held her like a feather, a tender and gentle woman awaiting my love.

Longing for the comforts within her, I led her back into the bedroom, knowing this would be a night we would never forget. Then before anything happened, I was pulled back into the reality of our actions. I felt a ripping in my soul, an unfathomable need to stop and control my passion. I had waited a lifetime to make love to her, but my desire for her was overcome by the compassion and love I held for her. I could not put her in harm's way or allow her to become the object of what many would consider an act of lust. I vowed to never take her until she is wholly mine and we have a life commitment between us that places our love above all, not for a single night but forever.

I pushed away from her and said, "Leah, stop."

"Honey, what's wrong?"

"I can't do this; this is not right."

"Ryan, don't you want me?"

"Honey, I want you with all my heart, but until we decide we are going to be together forever, I will not take you, knowing how you will be treated or labeled by those who cannot see our love and who would twist this beautiful evening into something evil."

Leah, stunned, put her hand to her face and said, "Richard took me without love, and now you will not make love to me because of love. Don't you understand; I love you with all my heart and soul."

"Please, Leah, I love you more than you will ever know, but I will not sneak around behind closed doors in the dark, take you in lust, or dishonor our faith."

As I looked into her eyes I knew I was right, that the sharing of our love must wait. I wanted her desperately, yet I knew in my heart this night of pleasure carried with it the possibility of destroying us. I could not make love to her without her commitment to share with me every tomorrow. She was that precious to me, and I could not take her like a thief in the night.

I felt her dismay and disappointment like a knife in my side. She took my hands in hers and reassured me our making love was to her a natural expression of the love she wanted to share with only me. I knew she was emotionally invested in our time together. She had welcomed me back to her, provided a place that was special to her and one in which she knew we would come together in love. Because of this, she could not grasp that it was not that I didn't want to enjoy the pleasures of her love. It was because I was in love with her that I was not willing to place our future at risk for one night of love making that could cause her feelings of guilt or regret. In a few so fleeting days, which now seemed like hours, I would leave for California, placing two thousand miles between us, and she would return to a reality where I fear she will be persecuted if not harmed if I allow this to happen between us.

I know I am right, so why do I feel so awful?

Later that night she pleaded with me to let her stay; she even offered to sleep in the other twin bed, but I knew I would weaken with her that close. I wanted to give into her wishes and my passions as well, but this was not the time. Not long thereafter I gently told her it was time for her to return home. Imagine that? I don't think anyone who knows me would believe this, but I sent her away.

Just before leaving she told me of a fear she had, from a line in a movie she once saw. "Ryan, I am afraid if I walk through that door, this night may never happen."

"It will," I said, "and more. My heart is with you and has always been with you, and I promise that soon you will never have to walk out that or any other door alone as long as we both shall live."

Despite my words, as she walked toward her car, I felt like the best part of my life was leaving me. That night was maybe one of the longest and loneliest nights of my life. I had turned down my chance to fulfill the dreams I had held precious for so long. My mind wandered back and forth, recalling the dark times in Vietnam when she was the only reason I felt like staying alive. My mission then was to find my way back to her, praying she would wait for me, to have her touch my face, hold my hand and give to me the beauty of her passion as she lovingly and enthusiastically welcomed me home. We had found our way to each other, finally, and my prayer tonight went much the same.

Not able to sleep, I walked out the cabin door and looked around at the sights and the sounds of this wooded area. I searched the road, hoping she would drive back to me, but she did not; and in my mind I pictured her tears as she drove back to her home. She was no longer a dream; she was the essence of my life. Her love had transformed my reality into one bright and alive with exploration and excitement. Even in the chill and darkness of this night, I felt her presence like the warm glow of a soft fire.

I no longer felt alone and was certain I would not settle for a casual relationship with Leah in the future. Two strangers emerged from the past, neither knowing what to say or do, and now two lovers knocked at the door of eternity, searching for ways to fulfill each other's dreams and with prayers for endless tomorrows. I stood under the night sky in this timeless place and saw our lives joyously bonding as the vines of nature that held and encompassed the hills and trees of this land. Leah is a new person, ready to embrace opportunities and challenges denied her in the past. All she needs is love and the chance to give love, which I will give her every opportunity to accept and provide.

19

Parting and Sorrow

The night faded and like clockwork, Leah was knocking at the door. She was getting to the cabin earlier each day, and I liked it! She looked like she had just walked out of the beauty salon, and after my sleepless night, I looked like a rag; unshaven, hair sticking up like I slept with the dogs and a breath that would melt paint. Neanderthal, cave man seemed to fit, but it didn't faze her; she followed me around the cabin snickering. She even stood at the bathroom door watching me shave and brush my teeth.

"Hold on," I said. "This is not something we are going to share."

I pushed her out, closed and locked the door and hopped in the shower.

Have I mentioned Leah loves to talk? I could hear her outside the door saying, "Are you sure you locked the door?"

"Yes," I yelled back. "I'll be out in a minute."

"Are you always this self-conscious?"

"Right now, yes, I am."

"I can hand you a towel when you get out," she continued playfully.

What I really wanted to do was throw open the door and see what would happen, but. . . .

I stopped answering but she continued talking, I guess to me. What I heard most was laughter. I bet she inherited this flap jaw syndrome from her Grandmother Lenna. Whatever, she took great sport in intimidating the heck out of me. She was so caring and so affectionate; she made even simple events fun and natural. I wondered if she knew what I was thinking; it was all I could do to keep my hands off of her, and like a teenager, I had visions of shared showers in our future. After I dressed, I made coffee and we planned our day. Nothing was said by either of us about the events of last night, but the air between us was still charged with so much raw emotion, I thought it might be nice to spend some time away from the cabin and just play.

Our first order of the day was a meeting with Leah's sister Rachel, which made me a bit anxious. We stopped at a local café for breakfast, adding another experience to our shared lives. Have you ever been with anyone or had a feeling of newness with everything you saw and touched? I felt the world was in tune with us, and the joy in our hearts and the promise of forever tomorrows colored everything we did.

We arrived at the hospital where Rachel worked, and once I met her, I was happily surprised. She was a kick, open and outgoing, strong in her resolve, not a bit judgmental of me being there, and from what I gathered, elated that her sister had found love. Physically, Rachel is Leah's opposite. She has flowing jet black hair, olive skin and deep brown eyes, in contrast to Leah's fair complexion, green eyes and blond hair. But those deep brown eyes, the deepest I have ever seen, coupled with her olive complexion and her obvious alluring side; she must have broken quite a few hearts in her past and I'll bet, probably a few still in waiting; must be a family trait? Though Rachel only had a fifteen-minute break, I could see in her eyes and through her words and actions she was a warm, giving person and a loving and kind sister to Leah. I was thankful for this brief encounter. I knew our relationship would face resistance, and it was a blessing to meet another member of Leah's family who was accepting of us and genuinely happy for her.

We spent the rest of the morning browsing through antique stores and even a general store patterned after those prevalent in the forties and fifties. We ate lunch at Logan's Roadhouse, known for its steaks, ice-cold beer, yeast rolls, and bottomless buckets of in-shell peanuts. I looked around and saw everybody cracking the peanuts and throwing the shells on the floor and concluded the South is a lot different from the West Coast. As usual, I was cutting up with the waitress, talking with the folks around us and enjoying Leah.

After gorging ourselves at lunch, we drove quite a ways up the mountain to a special place Leah wanted to share with me, Green Mountain Nature Walk. After we parked the car, we started up a path carved out of the mountainside that wound its way past natural gardens with flowers growing wild, though they seemed to be color coordinated and in perfect harmony with each other. As we topped a small hill, the path led down into a shallow valley where there was a good-sized lake with a few docks and chairs scattered about. Wild ducks swam across the lake, and two good ole boys were fishing for catfish. We talked with them for a few minutes, and I got a good lesson on how to fish the lake and what bait to use. If I'd had a pole, I might have given it a whirl. *I wonder if Leah has ever cooked catfish.*

We strolled around the lake and found a dilapidated park bench set under the shade of a mountain laurel. The water was like glass, reflecting the surrounding trees and the overgrown foliage. This was a perfect place for Leah and me to rest, hold hands and talk. We had covered just about everything under the sun; past lives, children, marriages, food, sports, religion, music and how we were raised. But we had not explored where we go from here.

I turned to face her and said, "Leah, I leave in the morning, and you will return to your home and Richard, but what if you didn't have to?"

"What do you mean, what if I didn't have to?"

"I mean, could you just pack a few things, get on a plane with me tomorrow and start a new life?"

"Ryan, are you asking me to marry you?"

"No, well, at least not yet, but could you leave everything behind, even your kids, just to be with me?"

"That's not fair, and honestly, I'm not sure you really want me to."

"I do, but we both have to be completely devoted to each other. I'm not sure I could handle the fear of wondering if a part of you would remain in Tennessee"

"A part of me will always remain here, not because of my home or Richard, but because of the boys."

"Leah, I know that, but my fear is this will become too painful for you to handle."

She took a deep breath and looked into my eyes. "Ryan," she said, "I want to assure you I love you with all my heart. I know what you mean; but I need you more than life, and I will never believe my boys would not want their mother to be happy and complete. My youngest is twenty-two; it's not like I'm leaving small children. Don't ever doubt my commitment to you, even without their blessing. Ryan, how could I stay with Richard, knowing now what it truly feels like to share love?"

"Alright, honey, I hear you. Maybe it's time to change the subject."

I honestly thought she might have fought me on this sudden change of subject, but all of this was still very new to us, so we spent several hours talking about the past, where we were now and where we should go from here. This was tough for me as this was my last night with her, and the hours passed quickly. I wanted to take full advantage of every single second I had left with her, but the sad reality of having to leave each other was rapidly wearing us down.

We drove back across the mountain to our cabin in the sky, but when we arrived however, everything seemed different, nothing was the same; even the cabin looked different. The once romantic and rustic getaway, the place where our past greeted the present, now loomed before us like a tomb. I suppose it was the anxiety we were both feeling, knowing our last embrace was now just a few fleeting hours away. I even had a problem opening the screen door. I feared that if I entered that door a part of me would never come out. The joy, the ecstasy, the love we shared may once again be sealed away and only remain within these walls. I knew this wasn't possible, but if we could only stay outside, the universe would still be attuned to us and our love would never end. I shook it off and entered, but the cabin was especially quiet; no fire, no music, just an ominous stillness.

We sat at the table inside the cabin, both of us afraid to utter a word. How could we leave behind all that had transpired over the last few days? We felt like kids who were playing in an amusement park, enjoying all life had to offer, only to be told it was time to go home. I did not want to leave her, and I did not know what to say to her or where to start. The air in the room felt heavy, like being ten feet under water. One of us had to break the silence; one of us had to begin. I hoped it would be her, but I wasn't that lucky. I cleared my throat, the sound loud in the stillness, and searched for the right words. They were not to be found and I said, "Honey, what do we do now?"

With no hesitation or nervousness, Leah replied, "Ryan all I want is to be with you. I need you in my future, my life, my world and in my arms. What I need to know is do you really want me?"

The answer was clear to me, but what if she was just caught up in the moment? What if she had fallen in love with playing out a role she had dreamed of for herself? *She was looking for a utopia of love, and hell,* I thought, *I'm just a man.* I flashed back to her asking Richard to marry her for no other reason than to escape her home life. Was she unknowingly repeating the past?

I had to respond to her and not knowing how this might come out of my mouth, I said, "Honey, you gave me a reason to live again; and I honestly believe I am in love with you, and I cannot envision life without you. But I will tell you this; I am afraid. I lost you thirty-five years ago and then again when you had second thoughts, and I remember the pain and despair I felt. It's not your being able to leave Richard that worries me, but I know how much your boys mean to you, and I know how much you mean to them. What scares me is that something will happen when you return home to make you feel you don't deserve the right to be free and to give your love without restraint. You may very well go home to-morrow after I leave, re-read what Scott wrote to you from I Corinthians 7 "The Principles of Marriage" and feel you must sacrifice our dreams."

Leah tried for the better part of two hours to assure me this would not happen, telling me she had never experienced a love like ours and that she had loved me all the time we had been apart. I was still cautious. I told her she should go home to Richard and try to make their marriage work. I felt pretty confident it would not, but Richard had been shaken to his roots; finding out Leah was desired by another man and that she was on the verge of leaving him could make him change his ways. I doubted he was capable of stopping the abuse and become the loving mate she desperately wanted, but I loved her to the extent that, if she could find real happiness with him and not have to worry about losing her boys, I would walk away, knowing she was loved and safe. At our age, a decision to move forward together would have to outweigh all other considerations, her kids, my kids, our extended families. I prayed it would not come to that, but I could not allow her to make a rash decision she might come to regret later.

I wanted Leah to leave a bit early that night, not knowing if Richard would return home sooner than he had said, but it was still quite late before she left. I kissed her goodbye with tears streaming down my face. She tried to comfort me, saying her love for me would never end, no matter what happened, and that she would try, although unwillingly, to do as I requested and make it work with Richard.

I gave her a final hug, and wanting to end the night with positive thoughts and motivations, I said, "Leah, you have a passion for life and an abundance of strength, so whatever happens with us, never allow yourself to be used again. Go home, put your business back together, take a trip, go to dinner and learn to dance. You deserve happiness, and if it is God's will, our path will be made clear."

As she drove off, my plea to her to go back and try to reconcile with Richard rang hollow in my ears. I was not testing her resolve in some morbid fashion; I'll leave this childish crap to Richard. However, I needed her to be completely committed to me and have no leftover feelings that would take her away from me again. I hoped my words had not destroyed her, and I prayed she could bring closure to her past life. If she did, I would ask her to marry me so fast the planet might tip on its axis.

The next morning I tried to put the last few days into perspective. Did she truly love me as much as she vowed she did, or was I simply an unfulfilled dream from her past? Would she decide it was not possible for her to complete our journey, or was this to be the beginning of a new life for us?

At the airport we held each other and she almost cried; I felt helpless and ashamed of myself for leaving her there. Few words were spoken, but I hoped she could see the anguish I was going through. I said goodbye and tried to reassure her everything was going to be fine and that our moment might be just a breath away. Later I found out Richard was watching us from a ways back; I never saw him and later Leah told me she had walked away with him. I am thankful I did not see this, as I probably would have made a fool of myself, knowing how this pathetic excuse of a man had abused her love their entire marriage.

I sat in the concourse waiting to board my plane and turned on my cell phone to check my messages. Leah had already left me several before she came to the airport, which I was able to listen to just before the plane departed. She was crying and telling me the last few days were the best days of her life, which made me cry as well. She said she was not sure how she would be able to try again with Richard because all she could think about was how I had brought new life back into her reality how she loved me even more today. She did say if there was to be any chance for Richard, it would have to be on her terms and she made it very clear, he will never again use her.

The stewardess announced that the doors were closing and to please turn off all electronic devices, so I had no time to respond. The plane took off, and much like the first flight out of LAX, I felt I was leaving behind the most important part of my life and vowed I would return to her very soon. As soon as the thought formed in my mind, the old feeling of despair crept back into my psyche, making me wonder if I had lost my mind. Leah was a woman and not a child. How dare I profess to understand what was in her heart? On the other hand, all she had done for the last four days was tell me how much she loved me. I had listened to her vows of love, but what had I done? Shoved her back into the arms of another man! It was going to be another long flight.

Part VI

Not Wanting to be in L.A.

20

Yes, Yes, Yes!

I have always enjoyed the sensation of takeoff, feeling the powerful thrust of the airplane as it races down the runway and lifts into the air. But on this trip there was no enjoyment, just thoughts of Leah and how during our short period of time together she had unveiled herself, opening her heart and exposing secrets and emotions to me as she had never done before with anyone.

I wonder if I will have second thoughts as Leah had done a few months ago. I hope not, for this gift of love that is Leah grows brighter and more alive every day. Who am I kidding? I will pursue her with enthusiasm for the rest of my life. She is a fire that detonated my passions, and after our few days together, I know she is everything a lover and a wife could ever be. Not to say she is perfect, although maybe for me she is; it's as if she holds the breadth of my being and has become my motivation to live again.

It is still a mystery to me how someone with so much passion and so much love to give could allow herself to be used and betrayed for all those years. I believe my mere presence is Richard's worst fear, as for the first time in his life, the woman he held all but captive has felt the warmth of true love and now understands the motivations behind his actions and morbid obsessions. It is obvious Leah wants me, but there are battles of will ahead she must fight. With or without me by her side, Leah is poised to retake possession of her moral being and her humanity.

During our time at the cabin, as we reflected back over the last three months, Leah and I realized our love might not be as private as we had imagined. As our love grew and became known, the faint ripples of malicious comments became tidal waves of sordid and twisted stories filled with harmful words, like lust, greed, infidelity, adulteress, home wrecker, damnation, Satan and so many others.

Through our e-mails and following our first ever meeting where we exposed all to each other, it has become painfully obvious that her family and friends remain in denial as to the cause of her need to leave, if not run from, her past life and to be in love with me. How could her family not have seen the disorder and instability in her marriage? Maybe Leah did not openly admit how she was treated, but surely someone must have wondered why she gained so much weight or why Richard cried every time he was asked to say a prayer in church. Instead of telling her, "It makes no difference how you were treated; you are married," why would not even one of them ask, "How could you have let this go on all these years?" I guess it serves some morbid sense of cruelty to believe Leah was simply out for a good time and a four-day romantic sexual experience with me. Or perhaps they believe, should they side with Leah, they would become outcasts because of their church's unwillingness to hear and believe the truth. What is more disturbing is that I have found out more in four days than any of them have in over thirty years. Either way, I find it hard to believe anyone could be blind to the truth, especially when the scars are so evident.

Richard and Leah seem to be two great actors in a well-played out farce Leah kept alive for the benefit of her children, church members, family and friends. This phony Camelot, however, was in actuality a loveless union conceived in deception and perpetuated through biblical passages that were used to control Leah through threats of damnation. There was no love and Leah was all but held hostage, having to subject herself to her husband's aberrant fantasies and acts of servitude so repugnant they made me cry. As mind-boggling as it seems, she was told in no uncertain terms by her church that the husband is the head of his wife as Christ is the head of the Church and whatever he wanted she must surrender to.

Over the years Leah was subjected to such degradation that she cowered as night fell and eventually lost sight of herself, falling into states of depression and suffering a great loss of self-worth. Time and time again Richard would enter their bedroom late at night, generally between one and two a.m., waking her saying, "I'm not a man, I'm not a man." Leah, believing that it was her duty, would try and console him, telling him he was a man, all the while knowing what would come next. She would cover her face with her hands so as to not see what was happening to her. She begged him to stop, but without compassion and without care for her, he would not. His actions were not the shared pleasures of love making; these acts were evil and dark. Far too often the nights controlled by his obsessions took from her even the will to live, but as she continued to plead with him to stop, all he would say was, "Please don't take this away from me. I'm not a man; I'm not a man!"

Given her beliefs, she had nowhere to turn, nowhere to hide and no way to escape as she had been taught that the only reason for divorce was adultery or death. Given her naïveté and the fear of eternal damnation that had been drilled into her from an early age, she painfully allowed him, like a thief in the night, to steal her soul.

At this point and still unknown to her, Richard was actually violating biblical teachings, repeatedly committing adultery via the Internet and other forms of pornographic material. What would possess a man to marry a woman knowing she did not love him and that she was and would always be in love with another? I can only conclude that if your only intent in life is to use and abuse another with disgusting tools obtained in filth laden stores, then why let a little thing like love get in your way as long as you have her convinced the Bible says the man can have his way with you, no matter how repugnant, artificial and unnatural, or you are condemned to hell.

Richard used his religion as a crutch to dominate Leah, and I do not believe he ever saw the beauty in religion and how it glorifies you and your mate, how it lifts you up and sets your soul on fire to achieve wondrous deeds. Richard professes to everyone he is a true Christian; yet time after time he told Leah he saw no reason to go to church as he knew he was going to hell. I was taught men should honor and nurture their wives, share and provide love, and that the bedroom is a sacred place of sharing and mutual respect. Any man genuinely in love would never expose his wife to degradation or servitude, hiding behind a religion he obviously did not believe in.

During the entire time of her marriage, Leah struggled with feelings of loss of self-worth and helplessness. She planned many times to leave Richard, and once her boys were grown, she had decided to move forward and live out the remainder of her life alone. As fate would have it, this was when my letters were sent out about my father's passing.

Looking back, Leah and I humbly believe it was at the moment of my mourning and laying my father to rest that divine intervention opened a door to the future, beckoning us to walk through and fulfill the destiny that was stolen from us. I also believe Richard had known for years the day would come when Leah would grow beyond his manipulative domination. *Is this why Richard used her,* I thought. *Did he know in his heart someday she would find me and his fantasy world would collapse?*

I don't know or care at this point. Now that we had met in Huntsville, the lies and deceit no longer clouded the past, and a window to the future where truth lives and where Leah and I can dwell together has been opened. Although we will always question everyone's motivations those many years, we have brought closure to the past and acknowledged to each other that our love will never die. I only pray that those who choose to not understand will come to see the joy in our hearts and recognize our love as we become one in the sight of God.

"Ladies and gentlemen, the Captain has turned on the 'Fasten Seat Belt' sign. Please put your tray tables in the upright position and remain seated as we are starting our final approach into Los Angeles."

Wow! Where did the time go? It feels like I just left Leah at the airport, and yes, I still feel like a dope for sending her back to Richard. As I looked out the window, I thought, *Do I really live down there?* As far as I could see there was nothing but houses and freeways; no pastures, no streams, no lakes and miles upon miles of cars barely moving. So many people rushing to get somewhere, probably the same place as yesterday and the day before, never stopping to see the trees, wet a hook or take the time to hold hands and walk together. *What a difference.*

It was early afternoon, and smog clouded the sky's blue radiance. The land below looked dry and barren, like a jungle of twisted metal and framed boxes connected together via miles of endless streets. As we touched down, I had an eerie feeling I did not belong here anymore. I sat there, thinking of Leah and her playful ways, as everyone else walked off the plane.

After about fifteen minutes, the flight attendant came over and told me I had to get off the plane. I walked through the airport, not noticing anyone and feeling like a zombie aimlessly being driven from one area to another. I reached the baggage claim area, picked up my suitcase and took the tram to the parking lot. Much like an omen calling out to me, "You are no longer needed here," I discovered my car had been towed. Talk about your "not welcome home" events! I considered returning to the airport and booking the next flight back to Alabama. [For future reference, when you park in the long term lots at LAX, make sure your tags are current (mine was in the glove box), or you will be towed.]

To add insult to injury, the impound lot was closed. I took the shuttle from LAX to Simi Valley, finally getting home some five hours later. I was exhausted, mentally and physically, and all I could think about was Leah. I had a mental picture of her being with Richard and then worse visions of his cross-examination of her. As soon as I checked my computer, however, I found e-mails waiting for me. I read the first one:

> *I couldn't help but cry on the drive home. I MISS YOU SO ALREADY, but you have lit a fire and a zeal for LIFE again in ME! I have already told Richard I will rebuild the business with or without him, and if he couldn't*

or wouldn't help me, then there would be no ME. . . . I also told him I would try but will not make any promises as to our future together and that I was going to call or e-mail you any time I wanted because if not for you I wouldn't even try with him again. . . .I WILL NOT GO BACK OR SETTLE FOR LIFE AS IT WAS AND I WILL NEVER AGAIN BE USED!!

He saw us at the airport, so I went ahead and told him that I kissed you. I am no longer going to slip around or try to hide things from him as I am 50, and he and I were having problems long before you came back into my life. If you wish to call me, then just call, at any time, day or night!

I told Richard that you have more LIFE IN YOUR LITTLE FINGER than he has in his entire body. I will not let him continue to pull me down. ONCE AGAIN I BELIEVE YOU HAVE SAVED MY LIFE!! I also told him if not for your strength and caring about not hurting me, we would have made LOVE, and I am sure it would have been the ULTIMATE experience of my LIFE, so he should really thank you. I also told him that if we were going to build our business, I would speak to you to help keep me motivated and on the right track. He is not happy about this, but my stubborn side has kicked in and he understands he has no other choice if there is any possibility for me to stay with him. I told him what I really wanted to do was pack my bags and hop on the next plane to you, but again you sent me back to reality. I owe you so much! You have brought meaning back into my life and brought me back from the dead! I have only been going through the motions without feeling for so long. You don't know how much I needed you in my life! Where this all goes, only the future can tell as I still want YOU, but I also don't wish to make snap decisions or least the wrong decision.

Curious that she wrote "only the future can tell." Was she in complete denial? Our lives have been irrevocably changed already, and we are but a step or two away from committing ourselves to each other. My guess is there is no way she will be able to endure the world of her past, knowing she is truly loved by a real man and not just a dream. Maybe I'm reading too much into this again, but she must know this passion she now feels and her new zest for life will not be supported by Richard.

The next morning, about ten a.m. my time, I wrote to Leah, telling her how much I loved her. Yes, I had told her to go back and try and work it out with Richard, but I knew it would never work and wanted to stay close to her so she had no reason to doubt my resolve to make her mine. She offered so much while I was with her; the gift of her compassion, the eagerness to be a part of my life and the dreams of countless days of her loving touch caressing me in the dark of night or in the light of day. I knew where she was right now and who she was with. I knew how she loathed him, and I asked myself how long it would take before one of us broke down and admitted we had to be together.

Hey there Little One,

What can I say that will make any sense? I had maybe the best time of my life just being with you. During our time together, I experienced so many emotions, all of which you are well aware, and I hope you felt them too. The place you picked out was perfect except for the squirrels. I still can't believe they wouldn't eat our peanuts. Sorry to tell you, though, I still hate grits and wonder who discovered them and then why?

When I first saw you at the airport, I knew I was in for a week (okay a few days) of changes in my life, and at first sight I knew I was going to fall for you. You were so shy and nervous, I thought you were thinking maybe this was wrong and I should not have come back to see you. Actually when we stopped for breakfast, I was really tired as I had been up for over 31 hours at that time, and I was fighting the need to sleep. But as you started to talk to me, boy can you talk, I found new energy and I guess you had an effect on me right away as I still could not sleep later that night until maybe midnight. Very odd, I have no idea where Lenna gets the idea that you are quiet and that you never talk much. Maybe I bring out something in you; I sure hope so.

You know I thought I'd had a pretty eventful life, but you blew me away with the story of your life. Throughout our e-mails, you painted this picture of you as this little farm girl and that's what I expected to see when we met. I was taken back and very impressed as you unfolded all the things you have accomplished and all the dreams you have held. I kept asking my-self how you pulled off all the things you have done while raising a family. There must be a raging fire in your gut and a passion to succeed in your heart.

You gave me great pain (wonder why), and you gave me great joy just holding your hand as we walked and talked about the past and about your life. It seemed everyone we met fit like in a movie; I especially liked the woman in the mall who cried and gave me a hug and helped us pick out your perfume and the girls in the restaurant catering to us like we were something special. Guess we are.

What did your sister think of me? You will never be taken as her twin; there is no comparison between the two of you or maybe I'm just one-sided. Well, that's a given. She did have a good idea, or should I say ideal, with the nature walk place up in the hills. I got a kick out of the two good ole boys at the dock; I still can't imagine trying to catch catfish with crickets. To me, that's like trying to catch ants with salt; we use liver and dough gobs.

Oh, by the way, I have a surprise for you. Want to know what? Too bad; can't tell you now. But I will give you a few hints. It's smaller than an elephant and bigger than an ant; it cannot be hidden though it's sometimes hard to find; you can find it in Japan and in France and in Alaska but you can't find it in the ocean. It can't talk; it can't walk; you can't unwrap it and you can't eat it. It's not something to wear, but you can experience it at any time during the day or night and it's very revealing and obvious. OH!!!! I'm such a tease. I guess I'm getting to be more like you each day.

God I miss you. I see you everywhere and I remember everything about you. The small mole on the right side of your neck, your little toe, the dimple on the right side of your chin, the cute sound of your (on again off again) lisp, the beauty of your smile, and the honesty you could not hold back. Wow! I think I'd better change the subject as you well know how you affect me. Anyhow, I've been trying to pick up where I left off on our book, but it's different now. Before you were just a voice on the phone or an e-mail that brightened my day, but now that I have felt your touch, seen the warmth in your eyes and shared a few silent moments with you, my thoughts explode with anticipation. Words are like water flowing into me from all directions.

Every time I start a new sentence, ten more thoughts come to mind. Last night I wrote over 50 pages simply trying to describe our first meeting and the effect you have on me. You're going to have to help me edit it down as I have only gotten to the morning of day two. Do you remember the reaction I had every time I held your hand and how you told me, 'Doesn't that tell you something?' I hope you recall what I am talking about because even writing about you makes this happen!

Oh Leah, I have fallen in love with you, and I realize we are 2,000 miles apart, but trust me, I know what to do about it. Just give me a few days to sort out my thoughts. By the way, my son came over last night and all he wanted to talk about was you! He went on and on about doing the right thing and the right thing for him was for me to do what was right for me. His future bride was with him, and she was pretty adamant about it as well. She said she knew I was in love with you over a month ago after reading only 15 to 20 pages of the book. I guess I carry my heart on my sleeve.

Well, honey, you just called, and I guess the cat's out of the bag now. I wanted to tell you how I felt when I was back there, but I was so worried how you might take it. I have started plans to sell my home and bring closure to everything that keeps us apart. I promise I will try and quit smoking, but that's going to be a tough one. Well, maybe not if it makes you happy. Some day you are going to have to tell me how a little farm girl obtained so much passion and how she, 35 years later and 2,000 miles away, stole my heart. I know I said 'no' before, but if you were here right now, I would race you to the bedroom.

Loving You Our Way!
Ryan

I tried to get some work done, but God, this was difficult. All I could think about was Leah and what she must be going through. Around one p.m. I left to pick up Mom from Skip's, who had taken care of her while I was gone. After thanking him for his help and fifty questions later, we finally got out of there and headed home. Mom heard what I had said to Skip, but she was eager to know, the nitty-gritty, the actual truth, what went on between Leah and I on that mountain above Huntsville and what was coming next? I took her outside and in the shade under the roof of my patio, and I walked her through the last five days. I told her all about Leah, her kids, her married life, her work and her love for me. I told her what Lenna had said, and Mom laughed and then, as though they were two peas in a pod, said, "So, when's the wedding?"

I told her as soon as possible, that is after and if Leah says yes. But I told her this might take a while as I had asked Leah to go back to Richard and try and work it out because I needed to be sure she was not making a snap decision and one she might one day regret.

Mom sat up very straight in her chair and pointed a finger at me. "Have you lost your mind?" she said. "Finally someone comes along that I know you have always been in love with and instead of being a man you sent her back to a life you know she hates. Why do you think she wanted to meet you in person? Did you think it was just to look at old pictures? I should hit you with a two by four. She even sent her husband away, putting her life in harm's way just to spend a few precious days alone with you. Did you think all she wanted to do was play cards?"

I was speechless. I sat and stared at her and knew she was absolutely right. I felt like such a cad. Mom was relentless, keeping up a non-stop barrage for the better part of three hours. No matter what reasoning I came up with, she had the perfect counter to make me feel like an uncaring, arrogant jerk. Mom may be in the twilight of her life and there may be a few things she doesn't recall correctly, but on this she was spot on! I guess no matter how old you get, you remember being a young woman—the feelings, the desires, the dreams and the passions you had. My mother is a great lady, and I was proud to have her teach me another life lesson.

I could see she was tiring, so I made her a cocktail and a cold cut plate with fresh fruit and sat her down in her old rocker. Twenty minutes later I was alone, pondering what she had said and knowing I had to call Leah as soon as possible. I struggled, torturing myself for not being man enough to stand up to my fears and love her the way I wanted to. I paced, talking to myself, and remembered Leah had said to call her any time.

Okay, I thought, *but what if Richard answers? What do I say? 'Hey Richard, I'm in love with your wife and she's in love with me, so how's it working out with you guys?'*

The day was fading and so was my time to call as she was two hours ahead of me. As my internal debate raged on, Mom peeked out from behind the screen door and gently said, "Ryan, she loves you. Don't be afraid. I believe in you and so does she; just tell her what's in your heart."

I dialed the phone number with anxiousness and anticipation, and as it rang memories of Huntsville raced through my mind. *She was willing to make love to me, opened her soul to me, placed everything she had or believed in, in jeopardy and committed her all to me. I will never again ever offer her less.*

Leah answered with a simple hello; at first this frightened me as I knew she had Caller ID and I expected a warmer reception. This made me a bit apprehensive, so I started slowly with how are things, where you are and how's it going with you trying to work things out with Richard? *Why did I say that?*

She responded very quickly, "Ryan, I will never be able to work it out with Richard. When you left, I thought maybe I should. I even told him I would, but honestly, in my heart I knew it wouldn't work. There is no way I can rebuild a life of lies. You may not want me, but the feelings I shared with you reawakened someone I let go of back in 1971, and I feel alive again. Maybe this makes me selfish and maybe I'm a bit vain, but to know and feel love is something I will never let go of again. I would have never believed anyone could, in four short days, bring back to me those feelings of love and adoration. I told you I had thoughts of leaving Richard for years, but I never felt I was worthy of them. Then in a small isolated cabin, you breathed life back into me. I will always love you."

Wow! What was I going to say now?

"Leah, I'm sorry for telling you to go back to Richard as this was the last thing I wanted you to do. I wanted so badly to hold you and make love to you, but it was my fear, not yours, that prevented this. Honey, I was a coward. I should have been a man and stood up and risked what I believe in and what I know is genuine and true. I was scared, and much like you, I had never felt true feelings of love before."

With a sob, Leah replied, "I believe you love me, and I love you so much; let's give us another chance."

"Okay, but this time, it will only be about us? What happened next I'm really not sure of, she said something about our time together or something about the cabin, but her words and my thoughts ran together? I could hear her talking and I guess I said something back, but my mind was racing between what Mom had said and memories of Cabin #10. I hadn't planned what I was about to say, but suddenly it all made sense, and I blurted out, "Leah, what did you say? Never mind. Just listen to me! I know we really don't know each other very well, and I'm sure I let you down; but there is one thing I can't change, overcome or let go. I love you with all my heart, and I never want to let you go again. It's only you now and into tomorrow."

At that very moment, A calm came over me, and with an amazing sense of purpose. I asked, "Where are you right now?"

"I'm standing in front of my office."

"Can you see the moon?"

A pause. "Yes, I can. It's right over my left shoulder."

"I can see the same moon, honey. Now extend your left hand just a few inches from your side, and I will extend my right hand. Can you feel me?"

"Yes, Ryan, I can feel your hand in mine."

"Good. Close your eyes and pretend I am there with you and answer this question for me. Leah, I love you. Will you marry me?"

It took less than a second for her to say, "Yes, yes, yes."

"Thank you, Lord!"

Special moments come in many different forms, and her long distance "yes, yes, yes" was as romantic as any moment could ever be. We talked for a short while more when she interrupted the conversation to say she had something she had waited thirty plus years to do. She said she loved me and that I had made her the happiest woman alive and then she hung up. What was so pressing? What did she need to do? I had asked her to marry me; she had said yes and then ran off?

Oh my God, I can't believe it. I just asked a woman I hadn't had any contact with in over thirty-five years and had spent just four days with, never even touched her, and now I ask her to marry me. Call me nuts, but for the first time in my life I knew I had done the right thing. My actions might appear insane, but for me, sanity had been restored. I believe our union will save both of us and restore our faith. I understood what had been missing in my life—a love so over-powering I would willingly give up everything and anything for—and I reveled in the fact she was willing to do the same. This love was not the passion shared on a moonlit night, for we had never made love, nor was it the memories shared on sun-drenched beaches, as we had precious few shared times together so far. Our love was as simple as it was powerful. We were two souls who came together and soon would be fulfilling a lifelong dream.

The phone rang, interrupting my musings. It was Leah. So soon? I answered and immediately asked her what the urgency was ten minutes ago.

"Ryan," Leah began, "I'm not sure how you might take this, but I needed to tell Richard the truth right away. I've dreamed of this day for so many years and to have you back is something I could not hide, even for a second. I told him I accepted your proposal and soon I would be leaving him to become your wife and we needed to file for divorce right away."

"Did he threaten you or say 'no way, no divorce'?"

"He just stood there; then he told me he always knew, even from the beginning, this day would come, that he knew I never loved him and someday I would leave him."

"Wait a minute, he just stood there? No reaction, no yelling or fighting, no trying to change your mind?"

"No, he did none of that. I also told him if he kept this from our boys, family, friends and the church I would give him the house, one hundred percent, without a fight. All I want is out of this mess and as far away as I can get from him. I do not want to go through the questioning or arguments or someone trying to quote the Bible to me. Can you understand?"

"Of course I understand, but it may take three or four months until I can bring you home with me. Do you really think he will live up to his part of the agreement?"

"If he says he knew this day would come, yeah, I'm pretty sure he will settle for getting the house."

"I hope you're right. I'm not sure I buy this, but we'll give it a try. If things change, you have to promise me you will tell me the truth. Deal?"

"Honey, I gotta go. My head is spinning like a top. I have to tell my grandmother; she's going to be so happy! I promise I will call you later tonight. I love you so much!"

"Bye, Lover!"

Well, brother, this was hardly the reaction I imagined, though it was all I wanted. Maybe Leah now saw through Richard and his true motivation. I still found it hard to believe he would let her go without a fuss. Obviously he wasn't in love with her, and it sounded like he had resigned himself to the fact their marriage was over years ago. Maybe in his mind this absolved him from any guilt about the past. The past! He knew I was alive all these years and remained silent, knowing I would return, this is why he kept the copied e-mails. I have to talk with Leah. This makes so much sense to me, for how could any man as much in love with his wife as he professed to be with Leah, simply let her go without a fight? I believe that I or any real man would fight tooth and nail to hold onto his wife. I like you, might not win, but at least I would try; and I would make the other guy meet me to face, man to man, before I let him take my wife away. Richard let his wife go without even lifting his little finger to keep her. I didn't understand him at all, but I hoped he would keep his part of the bargain.

I opened the door to my office and standing right outside was, guess who? Yep, Mom had listened to the whole conversation! Although she is all but blind, there is nothing wrong with her hearing. She stood there with the biggest grin I had ever seen on her face, and then she blurted out, "You stupid ass. You put that little girl through hell over the last week because of your lack of confidence in her and your inability to believe that someone could love you the way you love them, but Ryan, I'm so proud of you."

She had never talked to me like that before, and now twice and in the same day? But I took her words to heart because she was absolutely right. Why would Leah have invited me back to her, risked her whole life, possibly destroyed her marriage and made herself an outcast from her church unless she was convinced she loved me? "Stupid ass" sure fit! I could not put the milk back into the carton, or change what brainless fears I had, but when we meet again, I will make amends and love her with an enthusiastic passion she has always dreamed of and without question; never known!

21

Free to Truly Love

eah and I needed to plan our new home, which I assume will be in Alabama since I have no intention of taking her away from her boys or for that matter her grandkids, her daughter-in-law, her dad or her Grandmother Lenna. I decided to let Leah take care of planning our next meeting, since the last one she put together worked out so well.

The next day, Sunday, I was so consumed by the joy and exhilaration that Leah would soon be mine, I had forgotten what the following day had in store for me. Monday was the day I had to pick up my soon to be ex-wife from the airport, and with the realization it was tomorrow, I felt like I had been hit with the two by four Mom had threatened me with. I had known this day would come, but my frame of mind was far different than I had anticipated. I was happier than I had ever been and I may sound callus, but I felt joy for some odd reason and an urgency to close this final chapter.

I love Leah with all my heart and I know she feels the same way, but it is still going to be hard to blind side the mother of my children that not only am I going to file for divorce but I have also been in love with

someone else my entire adult life. Richard, back in Tennessee was privy
to Leah and e-mails and conversations and he knew how our love was
stolen from us, but Elaine had never even heard her name or that we
had been communicating over the last four months. I struggled with
how to handle this—over a quiet dinner, alone in the back yard, over
cocktails—but nothing was going to make this easy or painless. Finally I
decided I would be blunt and to the point, not open for discussion and
no turning back. I did not wish to hurt Elaine, but there were no other
options, and I believed handling it this way might cause her to hate me
and give her the strength to move on.

I rationalized that surely she knew this day was coming as she had
crossed the line too many times. This parting was not totally one-sided,
and I knew in my heart I could never go back and live the unsatisfied life
I had become accustomed to. Our marriage had its problems, and even
though I had just cause, it promised to be a painful fight and I suspect
a long and drawn court battle. However, I did not harbor any guilt, nor
was I ashamed in any way. I was not running to another woman; I was
freeing myself to truly love and allow myself to be loved. Was there fear?
Oh my God, yes. No matter what I say or how it is accepted, it will be
twisted and related in ways that will make me look like a complete bastard. I had faced the possibility I could lose my children over this if they
couldn't understand what really happened. I didn't see them accepting
Leah either, but this was the time for me to retake possession of my soul
and love anew. Concerning my children, I did have one solace which I
prayed would come true; I was the one they had always been able to rely
on; their friend, their coach, their father and one I hoped they would
always believe in.

I didn't sleep well that night, and as the sun rose in the east, I heard
the ticking of my watch pounding like a jack hammer as the hour neared
for me to pick her up. It was just after noon when I arrived at the Burbank
Airport. I carried her suitcases to the car and drove to the freeway. I was
very quiet and afraid to start the conversation, but then the warmth and
compassion of Leah's love engulfed me. I took a deep breath and knew it
was time. I had to be a man and tell her the truth.

RYAN MILLER

"Elaine, I've told you for years this day would come and I hope you understand, but our marriage faded away a long time ago, and to be honest with you. . . ."

"What? Are you saying you want a divorce?"

"Yeah, I guess I am. It's over, and you know it, too. It's time to stop the fighting, move on with our lives, find real love, and you know as well as I do I have every biblical right to end this madness."

"I just got back from Colorado and in a good mood and you tell me it's over?"

"Come on Elaine, you know we have not been happy in years. It's time."

"You've found another woman haven't you?"

"I guess I have, but she's a woman I've always been in love with. I just lost her over thirty-five years ago."

"You expect me to believe that?"

"I don't know, but it's the truth."

"You bastard!"

"Maybe so, but soon I will be leaving."

I tried to tell her I could not go on living the life we were living and how our relationship had diminished to the point where we all but hated each other. I tried to tell her the story of Leah and how we lost each other, and I also told her I had asked Leah to marry me. It was about this time she went ballistic; I was called every name you could imagine. Then there was a long period of calm, followed by, "How much money are you going to give me?"

I knew right then this was not going to end pretty, but like Leah, I simply did not care. I would give her just about anything to end this madness as soon as possible. After we got home, she stormed up the street to talk with one of our neighbors. She was gone for the balance of the evening, and from then on we had very few conversations, most of which were not pleasant and even involved her lashing out with vulgar slurs at my eighty-eight year old mother. I guess I should have expected this, and although it hurt my mom, it toughened me. Any compassion I had was now gone.

Through all of this and with the turmoil of Elaine moving out, Leah was always there for me and my mother. She comforted me, and as we talked, she filled the void in my heart and lifted me above the issues at hand. I knew she was having emotional problems as well, but she never let on. She just kept looking forward to when we would finally be together. I felt so blessed.

As the days moved along, I became stronger and my fears of losing my children diminished as I put more faith in their judgment and compassion. I knew they were having problems with the situation, and I understood the anguish they were living through. I was their father, and they were asked to cope with the fact the home they grew up in would soon be sold, and more importantly, with the vision of a new woman who would soon share my home and bed. They were in a difficult place, but I knew they were old enough to comprehend that I could no longer live my life through them and ignore my desire for happiness and love. I believed in them and their faith and trust in God for they were taught that "Faith is not in knowing what the future holds; faith is in knowing who holds the future." They had been raised to believe God has a path for all of us, and in my heart I believe they will eventually see this was the way my life had to go.

The days crept by, and the intensity of Leah's and my conversations were overwhelming. We openly expressed our love and our passionate desire to be one. Leah made me feel like a teenager again in so many ways; we spent countless hours on the phone and wrote love letters and poems to each other. Mixed in with this exuberance were painful feelings of separation.

According to Leah, Richard was busy as a beaver, almost manic. It is true that Leah downloaded the paperwork required to file for their divorce, but Richard was an anxious as a Cheshire cat to get this completed. He listed their separation date as April 22, 2006, the day I asked Leah to marry me. Their divorce agreement was simple but a bit one-sided as Leah agreed to give Richard the house. They split fifty/fifty all the non-permanent fixtures—furniture, personal belongings, family pictures, cars, business related materials such as desks, supplies, demo kits, display cabinets, as well as all the personal items that had been given to Leah as gifts from her parents, grandmother and her boys. She would get maybe upwards of $10,000 worth of personal items, and Richard would get the same as well as $75,000 in equity in the house. It didn't sound fair to me, but Leah wanted it this way. I hoped she hadn't made a bad call as Richard seemed far too eager to get the divorce done. When the papers were ready to file, I sent them the money as they could not afford to do pay the fees.

Here is what I don't get. Richard, who was dead set against Leah and me at first, now seemed almost thrilled with his divorce and with Leah giving him the house free and clear. He had insisted they file immediately and asked Leah to sign the house over to him rather than making it a part of the settlement agreement. I had a premonition something was seriously wrong and that he was hiding something. Here we were back to the same tired conclusion; Leah's business supported the family, most all of their belongings came from her parents, and Richard was eager to cast her aside with nothing to show for years of hard work other than some old furniture and her personal items if she gave him the house. His attitude seemed to be, "If you pay me off, you can go."

In retrospect this worked well for us as all we wanted was to bring closure to our pasts and embrace what the future had to offer. Leah was pleased with her decision as Richard would retain the house and then, per their agreement, pass it on to her boys. She was content to have keepsakes of her childhood and those things her boys had given to her. Leah was right when she told me of a saying she had always believed in, "When God shuts a door, He opens a window." The quotation is not biblical, but I recall Isaiah 22:22, which says, "What He opens no one can shut, and what He shuts no one can open."

There was one additional reason to file for the divorce at this time and it relates back to Leah's religion. Although not confirmed by the laws of man, in the sight of God Richard had tendered to Leah a writ of divorcement, thus freeing her to remarry under a biblical right given to her based on his actions and deeds as described in Matthew 5:27-28.

27 "You have heard that it was said, 'you shall not commit adultery; 28" but I say to you that everyone who looks at a woman with lust for her has already committed adultery with her in his heart...."

I knew some people would not accept this, especially her boys, but how could they or any Christian deny their own Bible? I have read the Bible stem to stern, and I found nothing that gives you a pass wherein you can reject the truth just because it may be too painful for you to accept and turn a deaf ear to your friend, relative or mother, shunning her without cause. I seem to recall a passage from Psalms that sums this up well, "Let them be ashamed which transgress without cause."

From what I have been taught, it is our obligation to seek the truth and not deny it, for if we do we deny God. To me the truth was crystal clear. If Richard truly believed in the Word and was without blame, then what could have possibly given him the biblical right to divorce Leah? It was he who was the petitioner on the divorce papers, so where was his justification? Could that secret and concealed truth and violation of God's commandment "Thou shall not commit adultery" rest in his lap? As a Christian, for him to divorce Leah without the presence of adultery forces her to live in solitude or become an adulteress should she remarry, thus condemning her soul! I spoke with a biblical scholar on this at length, and in the end he told me that even the most naïve Christian would come to a simple and yet wicked conclusion; one, Richard possibly cared nothing for Leah's soul and acted only out of greed, or two, he knew that his adulterous actions would free Leah via divorce if he confessed and freed them both.

On a lighter note, Leah's days are filled with moving some of her belongings into a storage unit she rented with her daughter-in law Sandra, searching for a place to live, and most importantly, writing to me. Richard was being supportive, telling Leah she could leave anything that would not fit in the storage unit in the house until we found a place to live. Sometimes I feel like I'm caught in a cartoon, bouncing insanely from one unbelievable action or comment to another. I try to communicate to Leah my serious doubts about Richard's motivations and urge her not to leave anything with him. Her response? "He's a Christian, and I know I can trust him." I can't imagine how she came to this conclusion, so I tried one last time, "Leah you say he's a Christian, right?"

"Yes."

"Then go to him and ask him to sign a first right of refusal for us to pick up the house should he, for any reason, get into financial trouble where he cannot afford to keep it. This way, we can keep it in the family and assure it goes to your boys, per your wishes."

"Okay. I'll ask him about it today."

Guess what? She got a flat 'no' for an answer. At this point there was nothing she could do as the house was already in Richard's name. This upset me quite a bit. I felt he had no intention of passing the home to the boys; it was all about Richard, as usual. Because of his refusal, I tried, one last time, to make her move her stuff out of the house, but again she said no. Trying to understand, I asked her again, "Why?"

She said, "Then everyone would know I am leaving."

I didn't say anything at the time, but I was thinking, oh my sweet little naïve princess, Sandra knows, which means her kids and two of your sons know, your father and grandmother know, as well as Richard. A better question might be; who doesn't know?

I can't quite put my finger on it, but there is something wrong with Richard; he has no obvious signs of income, has the house but maybe can't afford it, has filed for divorce, but now is begging Leah to stay. His excuse is he wants her to stay as long as possible so he can slowly come to grips with the fact she is leaving. I don't buy this, because if he still loves her, then her continued presence in the house will serve as nothing more than a painful countdown until she leaves. I have this gut feeling Richard is much more calculating than Leah gives him credit for. I want to give him the benefit of the doubt, but all roads lead me to the same end. Every well-calculated step in his plan brings him closer to disgracing her, and I fear Leah's boys are too trusting to see through his sham.

I feel like I'm back in high school with "the rumor hate mill" churning to tear someone down. What could ever compel a man to be so malicious toward the woman who is the mother of his children? How does one hate so much? In the future when asked what happened, he can say,

"I tried and tried; I even allowed your mother to remain in the house to give her a place to live until Ryan came back to take her away from us. I held my tongue to protect you and to make sure she was safe, constantly pleading with her to come to her senses and not throw her life away. I held her until the last moment to show her my devotion and love, but the devil that consumed her was too strong and she ran to another man's arms with promises of passion and wealth."

If this is his scheme, he is consciously setting himself up to look like the victim, and he will then use this against her at a later date so she is disgraced in the eyes of her church and her children. God, I hope and pray I am wrong, but even if I am, the fact she remains there, given all their past problems, drives me insane. Am I paranoid? You bet, but Leah reassures me that Richard's intentions are true, just and honorable and he is a Christian! Leah, honey, wake up!

Even with this undercurrent of fear, the next few days fly by, happily filled with e-mails and cell phone talks preparing for our time together in Nashville. I am light-headed, romantic, and even somewhat clever. The passions that were placed on a back shelf for so long will be explored and tested, I hope, over and over again. I just pray I am half the man I used to be, for I know she is twice the woman I have ever known.

Search late at night, look when the lights are dim, seek out and hear the gentle whispers of lovers in the night, and there you will find Leah and me. Her beauty is beyond words, her playfulness encourages me and her passion leaves me breathless as I relish in her enchantment. I will never again deny her or myself the love we are about to share. We are touched by the hand of God, and as one, in awe, we will share his love forever.

Part VII

Nashville to California

22

Two Lost Souls Become One

I am blessed to have been allowed to live out a dream; the beautiful fantasy world I imagined thirty-five years ago has become a reality. I asked Leah to marry me, and her response, ringing like bells from heaven, set my heart on fire as she said, "Yes, yes, yes." For the first time in my life, I am complete, happy and at peace. The long battle is won and has come, not to a conclusion but a beginning, and one I had longed for. Soon, but not soon enough for me, we will become one, not only in body and in mind, but in soul; and I will do whatever is necessary to make her life magical and will never give her cause to doubt her decision to marry me.

The next few months will be hard on both of us, but the reward will be a life together in harmony with the saints above and will give us the strength to put the past behind us as we discover new places for our love to flourish and grow. That which man had so foolishly attempted to alter has now found light and will not be dimmed or denied as it was so many years ago; it lives again and burns brighter than ever, like a brilliant phoenix rising heavenward.

The turmoil of our existing lives is all but meaningless now, and even with the frustrations of being apart, I draw from Leah a power and a force to push on, knowing soon we will journey hand in hand through time. To some, trying to make up for our lost years might seem an impossible dream, but I feel as though every step I take is another new exciting moment to share with her. I swell with pride just talking about her, and I beam with joy when she tells me how much she loves me. Leah has developed a playful side so uninhibited and free that I catch myself wondering just what she will come up with next. Yesterday I woke up to a very special e-mail in which she wrote, "When we get together, watch out world!! I will allow you to live up to my love, and in doing so, you will make me the happiest woman alive!!!"

Just what am I supposed to do with "I will allow you to live up to my love?" I wonder if she has any idea how much pressure this puts on a man. I hope she means she is opening her heart to me and in doing so she will completely give herself to me and allow me to fulfill her wildest dreams. But if she thinks I am twenty-five again with the strength and stamina of a young man, I may be in for a bit of a problem.

Her transformation is amazing. She now speaks freely of love and the oneness she feels between us. I picture her in everything I do, the same as I did in Vietnam. She is with me every minute of my days and nights. This may sound a bit wacky, but I take her shopping with me, asking her what I should buy as I go from aisle to aisle, and to Red's for lunch, discussing the menu with her, trying to choose between the Tri-Tip plate or the Tri-Tip sandwich. We share these moments in real time when we talk on the phone, but she is always in my mind. She seems to understand this is who I am, so proud to be with her, so happy to share our love and our story with everyone and to show them how my heart swells that she is in my life. As Leah so playfully said, "Look out world," and now I know what she meant. Look out world, for ours is a love like you have never seen.

The day has finally come. I caught the redeye again, and all I can think about as I settle into my seat for another long night is how much I need this time to convey my love for her and be the man she has always waited for, just as I have longed for her and dreamed of her all my life. I will give and bring to her all that I am and then promise that whatever I shall become, it will be for her and no one else. Wherever I go, so shall she go, and wherever I stay, so shall she stay, now and forever more.

During my last call to Leah I jokingly told her she'd better bring a blanket with her to the airport in case we couldn't find our way out of the parking lot fast enough. All she said was, "Does the color matter?" She caught me off guard with this one; what have I created? When we talk, she challenges me and inflames my desires; those passions that lay dormant within her are now kindled, and I know she hungers to share her love with me.

The plane ride feels like an eternity, and we haven't left the ground yet. *God, please make this plane fly. You must know how anxious I am; are you testing me?* Finally we are airborne. Maybe I can get some sleep—in a pig's eye! There will no sleeping for this boy, not this night. I recall every word she has ever said and the effect they had on me and how she reacted to my slightest touch. I know she has a wonderful time planned for us in Nashville, and I want to pick out the perfect place to ask her to marry me. I will go down on one knee, take her hand in mine and ask her in front of what, I hope, will be at least a hundred people. Then I will . . . .wait a minute. Oh my sweet God! The ring—I left her ring on my upstairs desk. How could I be so dumb? What can I do to get out of this one? I sure can't sleep now.

I arrived in Nashville, looking for her on my way through the terminal. I felt a liveliness within me and a playfulness that has not motivated my actions for a long time. Boy, I feel good, and now I know why. There she is, as beautiful and as tempting as I imagined. She is wearing a white sundress, with her blonde hair glowing.

I said as I walked up to her, "Is that a halo I see?" (Sorry; I couldn't help myself.)

Her eyes filled with joy and her kiss hinted at the night to come and delighted me beyond words. I have never seen her this way; she is so beautiful. Mischievous thoughts creep through my mind; I have luggage—luggage, clothes. . . .for what? Jokingly I said, "So, good looking, what brings you to the airport this morning?"

She smiled teasingly and said, "Well, handsome, I usually come here to pick up guys. Feel lucky?"

"Lucky? Baby, luck has nothing to do with it, so just shut up and kiss me."

She did and then whispered gently in my ear, with a breath of a young girl's desire, "Honey, there's a blanket in the back seat!"

With those words, all the pain of the yesterdays that never were was replaced by the promise of endless tomorrows. I love her, deeply and above all others, so why are we standing in this damn airport?

Nashville is a wonderfully romantic city teeming with rich country traditions, lazy flowing rivers, green pastures and the warmest people you would ever want to meet. I cannot imagine a better place for two lovers to step into intimacy. I do not really believe we are any different than other couples, but how often has anyone had to wait thirty-five years to fulfill the dream of a lost love? We feel the joy in our maturity, and we fully understand the consequence our actions will bring back home, but the desires of our youth build within us.

We arrived at the Radisson and were given room 622 (remember this number). I could not believe the view from the room. In the distance was the splendor of rolling hills, and blustery cloud formations suggested a thunderstorm was brewing in addition to the one mounting in our room. I reached for her, but she said she needed to freshen up and maybe if I was lucky, she would slip into something a bit more comfortable. *Great*, I thought, *but make it quick.*

I was patiently waiting. . . and waiting . . . wondering what she was doing and checking my watch. Please try and understand what happened next. I'd had maybe four hours of sleep in the last two and a half days, and that bed sure looked comfortable. The blankets were really warm, and the pillows were fluffy and soft. . . and that's the last thing I remember! But, believe me, Leah remembers. Here's her side of the story:

> *I wanted to look amazing for Ryan, so I went into the bathroom to spruce up; hot shower, fresh make-up, brush out my hair, delicately yet strategically drown myself in Opium and then slip into a new little piece I had bought for our first night together, a little naughty and a lot nice! My brain was running at warp speed; just outside that door was the man I had dreamed of ever since I was sixteen years old. I pictured him propped up in bed, waiting for his first peek at me. I'm so bad!*
>
> *I gently opened the door, hoping to surprise Ryan. I tiptoed inch by inch toward the bed, as quiet as I could be; but what the heck was that noise? When I turned the corner, there was Ryan, balled up on the bed, fully dressed, and that noise? Take a wild guess! I sat there for almost an hour watching him sleep, and I have to say I got a bit scared. Did he really want me? Have I thrown away my life? Leah, what have you done?*

A noise woke me up. Leah was sitting in a chair by the bed, a glass of water in her hand and a confused look on her face. I was embarrassed beyond words and ran into the bathroom for a quick shower and shave and to brush my teeth. While I returned to the bedroom, Leah was not there. My first thought was to rush headlong into the outer room of our suite, but then I thought she might be so insulted she needed to be alone for a while, so I did not pursue her. I unpacked and sat on the edge of the bed, flipping through the "What to do While in Nashville" magazine that was in the nightstand drawer. Suddenly, there she was, and oh how she enhanced the ambiance of our room. I had pulled the curtains all but closed, allowing just a few rays of sunlight to permeate the room, and through these small gaps the sunbeams caught the waves of her blonde hair, surrounding her with an angelic aura. I was in heaven. What made this moment even more dreamlike was the reflection in the mirror on the wall in front of the bed; from my angle I could see her reflection in the mirror and at the same time see her standing there as well. *Wow, I thought, I have two of her!*

I was fully awake this time, but there was one more thing I was compelled to do, allowing the two of us to commit our lives to each other and in the sight of God. Prior to leaving California, I had written out a marriage ceremony from bits and pieces of vows from weddings I had either attended or been a part of. I ran this idea by my minister who, although he had some reservations, told me he believed God would approve. So I asked Leah to come close to me, and I said, "Leah, will you marry me right now in the sight of God?"

"Ryan, you know I want to marry you as soon as possible, but can we do this?"

"Honey, this has been done for thousands of years. I understand it will not be recognized by the laws of our land, and we will have to do it again to satisfy that requirement; but in the sight of God, Richard gave you a writ of divorcement and I gave Elaine a writ of divorcement, ending, in His eyes, our marriages and freeing us to remarry based on His laws. As an ordained Elder, I have the power to marry anyone, and I choose you. I told you once before I would not make love to you without a lifetime commitment and I now ask you to make that pledge to me. The consummation of our marriage, to me, is meant to be the final seal on our marriage covenant."

"Okay. How do we do it?"

"Just follow along, and I will lead you."

"Ryan," she said as she took both my hands in hers, "this makes me so happy."

"Me, too," I said. "Let's begin."

Dear Heavenly Father,

Leah and I invite you to be with us today to share and to witness the celebration of our marriage as we take each other through our solemn vows. We welcome you not to mark the start of our relationship but to recognize a bond that has existed for over thirty-five years. Our marriage may be only one expression of the many varieties of love, but to us love is being one where the expressions are infinite. We discovered all those years ago the truest guidelines to our quest when we realized love in all its magnitude. Your love to us is the eternal force of life. Love is the power that allows us to face fear and uncertainty with courage.

The foundation of our union is the love we have for each other, and our love for you, not just at this moment, but for all the days ahead.

Our love will never be blotted out by the commonplace nor obscured by the ordinary. We stand fast in our faith with hope and confidence, believing your loving hand will continue to guide our way. In this spirit of love, we will create a partnership that will strengthen and sustain us all the days of our lives.

Leah, will you have this man to be your husband and belong only to him in the covenant of marriage? Will you love him, console him, respect and keep him, in sickness and in health, and forsaking all others, be faithful to him as long as you both shall live?

I will.

Ryan, will you have this woman to be your wife and belong only to her in the covenant of marriage? Will you love her, cherish her, honor and keep her, in sickness and in health, and forsaking all others, be faithful to her as long as you both shall live?

I will.

God our Father, you have witnessed these promises, so do all in your power to uphold the two of us in our marriage.

I, Ryan, take you Leah to be my wife, to have and to hold from this day forward, for better, for worse, for richer, for poorer, in sickness and in health, to love and to cherish till death do us part.

Now, Leah, repeat after me.

I, Leah, take you Ryan to be my husband, to have and to hold from this day forward, for better, for worse, for richer, for poorer, in sickness and in health, to love and to cherish till death do us part.

May the love we have found grow in meaning and strength until its beauty is shown in a common devotion to all that is compassionate and life-giving. May the flow of our love help brighten the fate of the earth.

May the source of all love, our Father in Heaven, touch and bless us and grace our lives with never ending faith, courage and the ability to forgive.

Therefore now, and in the sight of God, I, Ryan Miller, by the power vested to me as an ordained Elder, declare that Ryan and Leah are husband and wife.

You, Leah, may now kiss your new husband.

We shared a gentle kiss, and Leah said, "Ryan, thank you. I feel free and blessed, no longer fearful, as I truly believe God is with us and believes in our union."

For the first time, I gazed upon Leah as my bride, and I was in seventh heaven. She gave me her true and natural beauty, adorned with her devotion and total commitment to the man she had wanted to share her love with her entire life. I was in awe, and I could see that her self-consciousness had vanished. Before me stood the most genuine and beautiful woman I had ever known. She moved closer to me, and as she did I sensed an uninhibited passion in the air. It was clear to see tonight there was only desire and deliverance in her eyes.

She reached out for me, gently touching my face with a slight tremble in her hands. She kissed me with such desire and compassion, I knew this night, our wedding night, would trigger the beginning of never ending and wondrous romantic adventures. She awakened in me the desires of a raging bull, but I held her with the tenderness of a dove as we began to express our love, our union, and our commitment to each other. I could feel the essence of her increasing with each touch as the sweet scent of her womanhood filled the air, and as we melded together, our desires became transfixed solely on fulfilling each other's passions, needs and dreams.

What happened throughout the night were the most wondrous, hallowed and fulfilling moments of my life! I was amazed with the miracles and the gifts of love she gave me as she took me to her soul, not only stealing my breath away but breathing renewed life into me time and time again. It was as though she had saved herself all her life to commit every ounce of her being to me. We responded to each other with great harmony and as vibrantly as I could have ever imagined. We enhanced each other's desires and needs as we echoed each other's every move; it was as though we had been one, in this way, for years and years. For the first time in my life I felt one with her, as I had never before felt with anyone, and I thanked God for this wondrous and timeless miracle; her love.

Later as we lay there holding hands, gently stroking one another and exchanging soft kisses, Leah told me she had never known that love could be so warm or fulfilling, and she promised me she would never fear the fall of night again. There was a special glow about her, and I knew there would be many more magical nights ahead.

The night passed slowly and yet it seemed to vanish in an instant, but it left within me a memory I will recall in humble reverence forever. The storm outside our window crackled in thunderous waves as lightning streaked the sky and sheets of rain blew against our windows, echoing our passionate embraces.

Leah laughed as she awoke to the off key musical arrangement I had unknowingly conceived and which had awakened me as well. "Do you know you snore like a full grown male moose?" she said, as she snuggled up to me. "Don't worry. It's another first for us, but maybe we can try and make this one a last one as well."

I didn't know about that, but I was awake and the sight of her enticed and stimulated me I reached for her and found her quite willing for a replay. I woke up again sometime around two a.m. and with a dim light shining in from the outer room, I lay there watching her sleep, remembering our last visit in a small cabin where each night I had to send her home crying, which now seems foolish and cruel. I remembered her first call to me, her first e-mail and then her accepting my proposal of marriage just shy of four months after I heard her voice for the first time. *Funny,* I thought, *it took her over three months to get the courage to call me the first time, and then less than four months later, she committed to be my wife!* Out of the ordinary? Maybe for most, but not for us, as the joy and love we felt and needed to share had been with us for decades. Some movement must have awakened her as she whispered, "Honey, are you awake?"

"Yes, love, just lying here thinking."

"About us?"

"Yes, lover, only about us."

"I love you, Ryan."

"I know, baby, now go back to sleep. I'll hold you until dawn."

— ⁓

The next day Leah and I drove around Nashville, taking in the rhythmic sounds of country music that emanated from local taverns, walking through the Gaylord Opryland Hotel and enjoying each other and the wonders of the city. It was during this drive we had our first picture taken as a couple. We stopped at a place called the Rainforest Café, which is quite unique with animated animals; large elephants, monkeys and many more. About every twenty minutes, the place comes to life with a tropical storm filled with lighting and simulated rain. As the animals came to life, they delighted every child. I decided I have a lot of child left in me as I was thrilled as well. It is also here that Leah had her first tropical drink, and as we joked with the waitress during lunch, Leah became quite happy.

Following lunch we went back to the hotel for. . .well you might take a wild guess at this one. . . and then a short nap, as we had a full night planned. Later that evening we got decked out for our dinner date and cruise on a remake of an 1817 riverboat paddle wheeler called the *General Jackson*. The cruise began with cocktails, coupled with live music and dancing, and the itinerary called for the old paddle wheeler to make its way up the Cumberland River, past the Grand Ole Opry and the Titans' football stadium, and then glide through downtown Nashville prior to returning to the docks.

Once on board Leah and I made our way to the upper deck, and as we reached the center of the dance floor, I knelt on one knee and took her hand.

"Leah," I began, "I did not get the chance do this before as I was two thousand miles away when I first asked you to marry me, and I know we have already exchanged our vows, but I believe you deserve this proposal. So, Leah, will you pledge yourself to me and become my bride?"

I loved her response, as she did not change a single word but shouted, "Yes, yes, yes!"

The small crowd around us applauded, which made Leah glow with pleasure. It was obvious she was waiting for me to give her something. Sheepishly I confessed that in my excitement to see her and my haste to pack I forgot. . . .She interrupted me and said, "I know, honey. You left my ring in California, but I forgive you and I love you so much, I won't send you home."

Then she laughed, pulled me up and kissed me. When I drew back, I saw a tear run down her face, so I asked, "What's wrong?"

"Oh, Ryan," she said, pulling me close, "don't you get it? You're the only man who has ever asked me to marry him, and now you've done it twice."

I'm the luckiest man alive. We toasted our new life together with a bourbon seven (me) and a Gilligan's Island for her. Seconds later, bells started ringing, not from heaven (though that would have been nice) but as the signal that dinner was being served and the live stage show was about to begin.

We were escorted to the Captain's Table for dinner, which included wine tastings and a perfectly cooked filet minion as the entree. I found out one thing about Leah at this dinner; she has an amazingly clumsy side. Right before the main entree was to be served, she dropped her napkin on the floor, bent over to retrieve it, and while trying to rise up as quickly as possible, caught the rim of her plate, flipping it almost to the center of the table. Here's the good part; this amazing feat was not done with her head, shoulders or hands, but with the part of her anatomy just below her neckline. This cracked up the other guests at our table, sparked immediate laughter, a round of applause and several shouts of "Encore, encore." A crimson glow spread on Leah's face, but we were an instant hit and now had a table filled with new friends as we exchanged stories about ourselves and our lives throughout dinner.

During dessert the lights dimmed, and "Let the show begin" rang from amplifiers around the room. We were treated to a live performance of the musical *Sing!*, which highlighted the best from country, swing, rock 'n roll and spiritual music. The musical was marvelous and moving; what a night for two newlyweds.

The next day we spent most of the time alone, walking and talking our way closer to each other. We drove to the Opry Mills Mall just outside The Grand Ole Opry to have lunch at a restaurant with the biggest aquarium I have ever seen. The tables were arranged in an oval surrounding the aquarium, and as we ate, we were entertained by hundreds of species of salt water fish, from great white sharks to manta rays, schools of tuna and an abundance of other smaller fish.

Leah and I may not have recognized it at the time, but we were re-living a past that should have been—the simple pleasures of youthful dating, the holding of each other, the playful pecks along the way and the endless stories about each other. I caught myself thinking that soon I must wake up. How could this be? I was holding hands with my girl, soon to be (legally) my wife! I suppose what I was trying to do was give Leah those things she had missed as a teenager in the dating stage of romance and those things that were denied her in her first marriage, which involved no courtship by her spouse.

We walked and window-shopped, talked with everyone around us and even took in a movie, Tom Hanks in *The Da Vinci Code*. With popcorn, a box of candy and a Coke in hand, my girl in my arms, I was back in high school and loving it. We should have sat in the balcony or at least in the back of the theater as the desire to make out was over whelming. We did "act our age" and decided we should try not to get thrown out of the movie, but that would have been one unforgettable memory. There was so much life in Leah and such happiness that I prayed for the world to stand still, just for a few more days, but the hours marched on and our time left together on this trip was fleeing far too fast.

Returning to the hotel, I no longer had the desire to venture out and had planned a romantic dinner for us in our suite. The meal consisted of a Cobb salad, shrimp cocktail, fresh breads and raspberry cheesecake, along with a bottle of very good champagne. The dinner started well but soon took a few unexpected twists. Maybe I forgot to mention the dress code I established for this dinner; Leah wore a negligee with a soft and all but transparent robe, and I wore pajama bottoms and a light tank top.

We toasted each other, and I watched her as she drank the champagne, I guess I should have told her to sip it! The effervescence, coupled with the alcohol, made Leah a bit tipsy. Here I was in a romantic setting with this woman I had dreamed of for decades, and everything we said to each other cracked her up to the extent we could not even kiss without her busting out in laughter. Still, I can't remember having so much fun on a date or being more at ease with anyone than I was with her. Then that twist I told you about happened. Leah loves shrimp and couldn't wait to dig into them. She dipped one end of a shrimp into the cocktail sauce and then attempted to take a bite, but as she bit into the meaty part while tugging on the tail, it suddenly snapped off and the body of the shrimp went flying straight up her nose. God, are we romantic or what? We doubled over with laughter and found ourselves playing like children, rolling around on the floor. All the fears of being together and trying to be perfect vanished. We were, due to this clumsy act, so in tune with each other it was incredible. The night evolved into an unmatched night of tenderness, adoration and love like neither of us had ever experienced. It was as though two people entered the room trying to please each other and now only one remained as our love, our commitment and our vows to each other molded us into one.

Her love is not easy to explain; but if you have ever felt love to the extent that you cannot breathe, cannot sleep, cannot control your passions, then you may have come close. Words were not spoken; yet volumes of emotions and expressions were accepted and shared. She countered my every move with almost poetic grace, compelling me to delve further into her delight. Loving her was the easiest thing I had ever done, and as we discovered each other, we found there were no limits between us; no fears, no anxiety, no apprehensions and no doubt. This night bestowed upon us the chance to explore our love in ways we had dreamed of for years, and yet in the blink of an eye it vanished into an unbelievable memory. Our union had magically come to life.

The night gave way to a simmering dawn, bringing visuals of sweeping clouds and dew-drenched meadows like textures in a Picasso painting. The sun found its way around the folds of material in the curtains, casting a soft light into our room. Although there was peacefulness and contentment between us, holding her was emotionally painful as I knew I must leave her soon. This feeling was unlike our first meeting when I was still in doubt about our future and her commitment to me. Leaving her at the cabin was heart wrenching; this time it was agonizing.

The drive to the airport, seeing the town and its people meandering about as though nothing was wrong, called out to me. I knew, once again, that here, with Leah, was where I needed to be. Nothing could stop us from being together, yet I knew there would be much work ahead to overcome the misgivings of our children and self-righteous naysayers. We sat in the airport holding hands, waiting for the final call and when it happened, loneliness seized my heart. Looking at her, I saw tears forming and all but heard her screaming in her mind for me to stay. I could not and she knew it as well, but I had this gut-wrenching fear that should I get on that plane, something tragic was going to happen, like an omen warning me.

As the plane lifted off and Leah headed back to a life she knew was over but which held painful times ahead for her, I felt helpless and alone. I was once again leaving behind the woman I loved as no other. I could not stay with her nor could I take her with me at this time, but I swore it would not be long until we were together forever. I tried to take my mind off her but instead found myself writing love poems and songs about her. *God*, I thought, *this is such kid stuff, but it helps me and allows me to share my thoughts about her.*

As the flight moved on, I composed a song for her called "Midnight Till Dawn." The song relived some of the past and some of the joy and playfulness of our new love. The words flowed from me as though I was a mere conduit for what needed to be spoken in a melody to her. The lyrics were simple but true and followed a love that began in her letters to me in Vietnam:

Midnight Till Dawn

    C   Am   Em
I found you in a far off land
        a million miles away
I found you in your letters
        they stole my heart away
I found you in a foxhole
        you probably saved my life
And someday you're gonna be my wife.

        Because it's
Midnight till dawn,
        I feel your hands a creepin'
Midnight till dawn,
        I feel your body a sneakin'
Midnight till dawn,
        I feel your love a peakin'
And there ain't gonna be much sleep tonight.

You were hidden in the back roads
        In a land called Tennessee
Sheltered from a love
        You knew was meant to be
But I knew someday I'd find you
        If it took eternity
And someday you're gonna be my wife.

Because it's
Midnight till dawn,
*   I feel your hands a creepin'*
Midnight till dawn,
*   I feel your body a sneakin'*
Midnight till dawn,
*   I feel your love a peakin'*
And there ain't gonna be much sleep tonight.

We met one night in Nashville
*   Thirty years had come and gone*
But the feeling that I held for you
*   Was growing oh so strong*
I held you in my arms and kissed you
*   And took you for my own*
And now you're going to be my wife!

Because it's
Midnight till dawn,
*   I feel your hands a creepin'*
Midnight till dawn,
*   I feel your body a sneakin'*
Midnight till dawn,
*   I feel your love a peakin'*
And there ain't gonna be much sleep tonight.

I am helplessly in love with her, and all that stands in our way is two thousand miles, no home to go to, no jobs, her ex-husband, my ex-wife, all of our kids and most everyone who has ever known her. Simple, right? Who knows? But the journey cannot be any more difficult than the wasted thirty-five years of not being with her.

23

Unbelievable Actions

$\mathcal{I}$t's been nearly three weeks since Nashville, and although these weeks began with some very anxious moments, Leah's new life has apparently become visible and irreversible to all. There is no more fighting, no more denial, and from talking with Leah, Richard appears to be relieved she is moving on. This is a tough time. For me, it's almost like being back in Vietnam, trying to fight an enemy I cannot see. But at least time keeps pressing on, and in a week, we will be together.

My divorce has been laden with greed and wrought with tribulations. I had hoped we could amicably resolve our issues; but this was not to be, and I have been forced to hire an attorney. Strange that my divorce is the one with complications and Richard's and Leah's was matter of fact. I still find it hard to believe how quickly Richard filed the paper work. Although I am elated matters are going so smoothly, I have this gut feeling something else is at play here. Though Richard has said to Leah over and over, "I love you, I love you," his actions said, "If this isn't going to cost me anything and I get everything, you can go away at any time." To me, his actions lend even more credibility to the fact he never loved her in the first place.

Their lives have evolved into a mundane routine, as if nothing had or was about to change. According to Leah, a dead calm has come over their home; no more fights, no more cross words and very little interaction. I tried to rationalize it away as Richard's greed to secure the home or the fact he had known all along this day would come since he had stolen Leah from me so long ago. Either way, it was nice to see Leah happily preparing to be with me and finally out of harm's way.

Leah ignored my pleas to the contrary and left most of her personal possessions with Richard to be claimed when we found a place to live. These included items that were most precious to her; her mother's wedding rings, spoon collection, maple hope chest, and a Bambi fashioned table she had as a child, her china cabinet, her grandparents' engagement rings, an antique bed from her childhood and dozens of other personal items given to her over the years by her parents and grandparents.

We focused on our next meeting, which was just a week away. We planned to meet in Huntsville and then drive to North Carolina for a Rainbow Rally for her business, after which I would take my bride home with me. I counted the days with every breath I took. Leah and I rarely e-mail anymore as it is so much nicer to hear each other's voice. This morning, like every morning now, I am treated to my wake up "I love you" call. As I am two hours behind her, she is generally in the middle of her daily routine, trying to make the clock move faster, cataloging her personal things, seeing her grandmother, and at night, setting appointments for Richard. In the evening, I get my goodnight "I love you" call, generally around seven p.m. my time. When the phone rang tonight, I checked Caller ID so I wouldn't say something inappropriate to an unsuspecting caller. It was Leah, right on schedule.

I answered with, "Hey there, honey. How's Ryan's girl tonight?"

There was a long pause, and I could hear a car running in the background. A moment later I heard Leah crying, then another long pause, followed by Leah's hysterical scream. "Ryan, Richard tried to kill me. He pulled a gun on me!"

As calmly as I could manage, I said, "Leah, stay right where you are. Lock the doors, and if you see his car coming, drive straight to town to a busy location, but stay in the car. I am going to call the police on the other line."

Leah screamed again.

"Ryan, please don't call the police. My boys, my boys, they will not understand, and I will not be the cause of them seeing their daddy in jail."

Although bewildered by her words, I was fearful. Was she in shock and could not visualize the magnitude of what had just happened?

"Alright, honey, calm down. I'm here; tell me exactly what happened."

What she told me frightened me as I never thought Richard would come close to something like this. From what I could gather, Leah was in their basement office setting appointments for Richard and was not aware he had gone out. Shortly thereafter she heard him return and come into the house. A moment later, she was startled as their preacher came walking down the stairs to her office and in a very demanding voice, said, "Hang up the phone, Leah, and come upstairs right now."

Leah followed the two of them up the stairs and sat on the couch As Richard sat down next to her, the preacher asked her two questions: Have you slept with Ryan, and are you staying with Richard? Leah simply answered yes and no, I will not be staying with Richard. Stunned and in disbelief, she moved to walk away when the preacher spoke up, telling Richard these things never work out and that Leah would run back home to him sooner than he thinks. Then he looked at Leah and said, "I guess this conversation is over."

Leah, shocked at his callousness and one-sided comments, left the room, running down to hide in her office, but the minister was close behind and all he said to her was, "I will never be seeing you again and I just wanted to say goodbye."

This so-called man of God never asked what prompted Leah's decision, why she would want to leave after so long a period of time, or had she talked with others in the church. He hadn't even asked an Elder contact her. Based on their religion, he acted inconsistently as he should have had at last two others (Elders) speak with her. Apparently he could have cared less about her as he condemned her without even asking a single question of why?

Richard had once again done a great job conning this preacher. He apparently had told him nothing about his and Leah's pasts or the fact he was the one who had filed for divorce almost two months prior and had told no one. This man of God had falsely accused without cause one of the most supportive members of his congregation and one of the most loving mothers on the planet. He did not seem to care if there was any biblical reason for her leaving. He heard what he wanted to hear, and his actions fell in line with his church's underlying agenda of treating women less than men.

Good job, Richard. You just set up a minister to unknowingly defile that which he should uphold—the truth—and then, based on your denial or silence gave him cause to turn your sons against the only one who never lied to you. I hope you rot in. . . . I think I'll leave this one up to God.

Leah wanted to expose Richard, but she knew it would become a "he said, she said" fight, so she held her silence. Then as abruptly as he entered, he left, repeating to Leah, "I will never see you again."

I suppose this was said to intimidate, no, I think to terrorize Leah. She remained in her basement office thinking about what had just happened and why now, less than a week before she was leaving? Hundreds of thoughts raced through her head. If Richard really loved her, would he not have called their preacher in prior to her leaving for Nashville or the day she returned home from my first visit or even after she told him she was going to marry me? The more she contemplated the timing of this, the angrier she became as it was clear that Richard, in addition to getting the house and having no problems with her leaving, wanted to make sure that the preacher would support his position; Leah was an adulteress! What a bastard!

Leah, no longer able to hold in her emotions, grabbed her purse and keys and took off for her car with Richard close behind. In a fit of rage she rolled down her car window and told Richard she hated him for what he had done and that she was leaving right now and would forever hate him.

Richard bolted for the house, screaming, "I'm going to kill myself." Leah, in fear he might follow through with his threat, raced after him. As she ran down the hallway, Richard came out of their bedroom with a gun in one hand and a box of shells in the other, pushing her aside as he ran down the stairs and out into the night. Leah and her son Brent ran after him, but he vanished into the trees. Terror tore through Leah's mind as Richard's father had committed suicide at about the same age after finding out his wife was leaving him. She knew she could not live with that on her conscience.

The two of them searched and called out for Richard, but they could not find him, nor would he respond. After a short while, he reappeared into the light that shown from the window of their living room. He held the gun shoulder high and pointed it directly at Leah, standing maybe ten to fifteen feet from her. As he moved forward, Brent frantically ran at him screaming, "No, Daddy, no Daddy, no."

Leah shouted at him, "What are you going to do now, shoot me? Do you really want to kill me?" Leah's daughter-in-law, frozen in fear at her side, looked on when, in an almost childlike manner, Richard, pointing the gun, said, "Bang. She's not worth it."

He turned slowly and walked back into the house as Leah, horrified and trembling, ran to her car and sped off in search of a good spot to call me.

— ~ —

Later that evening, Richard told everyone the gun was never loaded and that it was just a joke. Just a joke? I guess no one ever realized Richard set this whole melodrama up to insure that everyone present would see he was willing to commit suicide or kill her should she leave him; then dismiss it as a joke. What kind of man would create such an act in plain view of his grandchildren? Could he not see what they must think? Obviously he cared nothing about them or the woman he openly professed his love for. A joke? Hardly. This was another calculated risk planned by an evil and cunning man willing to expose little children, his grandkid's, to emotional harm and trauma.

Maybe this was his last ditch effort to make sure they would be on his side and to dispel any doubts he was the wounded party. But what he failed to realize, I hope, is that those who witnessed this farce would be smart enough to put two and two together. Richard accepted the house, had filed for divorce months earlier, had never looked for marriage counseling, and told no one knowing (from our knowledge) Leah was leaving in a week. To me, this was a pathetic attempt to gain the support of his family and his church. To my amazement, they bought into this sham. "Poor, poor Papa; he's willing to die for her." They told Leah that if she called the police, they would deny it ever happened.

By this time Leah had calmed down; well, at least the hysterical screaming had stopped. I hoped she could feel my words and gain comfort and strength from my compassion. Following a long pause, she said, "Ryan, something else happened two weeks ago that I did not want to tell you or anyone."

"What, honey? What else did he do to you?"

"He tried to strangle me after a fight we had in our bathroom."

From what she told me, Richard made one last ditch effort to try to frighten and control her, screaming at her that she had made a promise to him before God to love him until "death do us part" and by leaving him, she was condemning herself to hell. As he again and again reminded her of her vows and her duty to him, Leah lashed out at him, screaming, "I lied; Richard, I lied."

At this point Richard grabbed her by the throat and began strangling her until she was limp in his hands. Leah was struggling to stay conscious, and as she lay all but lifeless in his clutch, his madness faded into the reality of what he was doing and he released her. She caught herself on the edge of the vanity and gasped for air, trying to regain her strength. Richard then fell to the floor in a fetal position, sobbing and saying, "I'm sorry, I'm sorry."

This was a side of him she had never seen, and although she had never feared him before, this was not something to be overlooked. Leah regained her composure and started to leave with Richard saying, "Please don't leave. Please stay. I have no idea what came over me, but I promise I will never touch you again."

Leah, for reasons I will never understand, agreed to stay and later, as so many times before, tried to convince him that she understood. She told him over and over that he had done nothing wrong; it was just that she had always been in love with me and had tried to love him but could not. He told her again that a life without love was good enough for him. I guess he never stopped to realize Leah needed to be loved and to give love and total commitment, something she could never give to him. His offer to continue in a loveless relationship was what she had lived within all those years. She could not continue to live with the lies and abuse.

"Ryan, I did not tell you because I thought this was just his frustration boiling over. I believed him when he said he would never touch me again. I had no idea just how far he would go or what he is capable of, but now I do."

My mind was racing with places for her to go, but Leah had one more thing to tell me. "Ryan, Richard said one other thing that showed me he never loved me and just how he used me."

"Okay, honey, take your time. I'm listening."

"He told me that if I would stay with him, it would be alright if I pretended he was you if we ever had sex again."

What a pig, I thought. Here again he showed he is something less than a man, with no compassion, no love and obviously no regard for anyone other than himself. With this attempt to keep her only as a sexual object to feed his sadistic addictions, he openly revealed his disdain for her.

The calculating and logical side of my brain kicked in; this was normal for him. He had for years pretended Leah was someone else or someone he viewed in his porn magazines. To have her pretend it was me having sex with her and not him, in his twisted mind, made perfect sense.

"Leah, do understand what you just said?"

"What do you mean?"

"You spent years in fear, terrified by his threats of damnation as he used the Bible as his weapon of choice against you. Now, he turns his back on God and the Bible, asking you to continue to be his sexual slave by pretending you are with me. Honey, get out of there, get out of there now. This man is sick!"

It was about this time Richard beeped in on her cell. She placed me on hold, and after about two minutes, she came back on the line.

"Ryan, Richard has asked me to come back until I leave with you. He said the gun was all a bad joke and swore he would never touch me again."

"Are you nuts? He said that before, remember?"

"What is he going to do now that Brent and Sandra witnessed it?"

"Honey, he's off his rocker."

"I know him, and this is over. Please trust me on this one; I'll be alright."

"Leah," I begged, "you do not know him. Get out of there!"

"Ryan, I'm going back. I have to, not for me, but for my boys. Ryan, my boys, my boys, PLEASE help me keep them safe!"

What was I to do?

I guess I should have seen it coming. She did not fear losing her life; it was her sons and their love for her she was afraid of losing. She would not leave Richard until the last minute, solely so that she could see and communicate with her boys. I wonder if she has told me the truth. Does she really want to be with me, or will her beloved sons take away her life with me? Time will tell, but today I am very afraid as I have committed myself to a woman who protects a man who threatened to kill her and who used her like a prostitute. She is willing to endure this for her sons? I know in my heart Richard will lie about anything, and her precious sons may never know or accept the truth of what she endured for them.

We said goodbye for now, with the promise she would call me as soon as she could later that night. About an hour later, the phone rang. I answered and Leah said, "Ryan, everything is okay. Richard is in the other room, and nothing was really said; but I promise, no matter what, I will tell you everything in the future."

"Okay, honey. Please lock the doors and try and get some sleep."

But sleep was not for me that night, no way. One thought kept crossing my mind. *If he ever touches you again, I promise you he will live, but only to pray that his final breath comes soon!*

Over the next few days, things smoothed out considerably. Leah and Richard had few conversations and for the most part avoided each other. As Leah was packing her great grandmother's Aladdin's Lamp that dated back some one hundred twenty years, Richard asked her to leave it with him so it would not get broken. He also told Leah he wanted her to leave her family's jewelry as he wanted to repair her grandmother's wedding rings, saying this was the least he could do for her.

In my last phone call to Leah, I had asked her to reconsider her position on telling her boys goodbye and explain to them why she was leaving, but she was stubborn as always. I even offered to do this with her. But Leah said, "Ryan, absolutely not. I will not bring them into this."

"But honey," I countered, "if you don't do this, then Richard can make up anything he wants, and I don't mean tell the truth."

"I don't care. Don't you see; I cannot turn them away from their father, no matter what he has done to me. If my boys want to hate me, I can live with it."

"Leah, please think of the pain and humiliation he has caused you over the years and remember how your preacher acted. I think not telling them will only make it worse."

"I don't care. I believe in them, and I believe God will give them the truth they need to know."

"They may turn their backs unknowingly on God and fall prey to Richard's lies," I said.

"Ryan, I love you, and I believe in my boys. They know I would never lie to them nor would I ever leave them. In time they will come around."

"Alright, honey, you win. I'll shut up."

We ended the conversation with a rather tough goodbye, not that we were mad at each other. It was just that in less than twenty-four hours we will be together with no more goodbyes but with problems and heart-aches we knew would come.

— —

It is now June 22nd (remember this date), and I am flying into Huntsville airport to take my lover with me on life's new journey. Leah gave her home and her past life away without any goodbyes, apologies, guilt or an ounce of regret. I sincerely pray she reconsiders talking to her boys, but I suppose this is out of the question. She honestly believes that someday they will challenge their father and uncover the evil within him and understand why she could not tell them how he drove her from him. I sense she takes too great a risk here, as their denial will be to overpowering and Richard's lies will be too easy to accept. I can only pray their love for their mother will guide them beyond whatever advice or counseling they may receive from the self-serving hypocrites who rely on hearsay and not the truth. I have spent hours pondering if it is the truth that frightens them, or are they just fragile naïve sheep simply willing to abandon their mother to avoid the truth that their father was capable of such acts? I believe this is a simple question to answer for Christians.

— —

Leah met me at the airport in Huntsville. This was the first time I actu-ally believed it to be real; the true beginning of our life together. Our first stop before flying to California was to attend a Rainbow business meeting and rally in North Carolina. We had decided it would be fun to drive, so we loaded my bags into her car, turned on an oldies station and took off for parts unknown. We needed time away from everyone, and this gave us a chance to escape, though we did not feel like we were running away from anything, more like we were running toward a new life without limits and without lies.

After several carefree miles, Leah turned down the radio and told me of an out of character almost atypical conversation she had had with Richard right before she left for the airport.

"Richard stopped me as I was walking out the door," she said, "to tell me he was going to hell unless I forgave him He said if I forgave him then God would forgive him as well, and he would forgive me for leaving. I was a bit stunned at such a request and asked, 'Forgive you for what'?"

Richard then said to her, "Leah, do you remember all those nights after you went to bed when I would go downstairs to use the computer?"

"Yeah."

"I wasn't playing games or looking up information; I was searching for and viewing internet porn. I first got the idea from our preacher who told us not to look at this stuff as it violated God's laws and promoted lust in men. At first I was just curious; but then I could not stop, and I viewed it almost daily. Can you ever forgive me?"

At this point I had to weigh in. "Honey, I don't get it, why would he ever admit this and why now, just as you were leaving?"

"I guess he thought if I forgave him he would go to heaven because he asked for forgiveness and repented."

"I'm not sure I buy into that. I think he was trying to clear his conscience and using internet porn as his excuse for how he treated you. He's still in complete denial."

This conversation again gave me cause to challenge his religious ethics as I do not believe, no matter how hard you try to rationalize it, something as precious and everlasting as forgiveness is not something you can barter for, it's something you pray and endeavor for, through deeds, actions, accepting and telling the truth, and repentance!

As bizarre as it sounds, Richard continued and confessed to Leah that he had been viewing this garbage for quite a while, and that their son actually caught him one day watching this graphic porn. He told her that if she stayed with him, he would never do this again. All I could think of was, you're just in avoidance, lying to yourself pal; you're hooked and you know it.

"What did you tell him?"

"I told him I forgave him and then asked, 'Now are you willing to forgive me'?"

Typical of Richard, his reply was, "Well, I'll have to think about that one."

Leah said fine and left, but this was the first time Richard had openly admitted he had used the Internet for such purposes. Leah flashed back to the time when she found a hidden stack of explicit pornographic magazines in their old workshop. When she confronted Richard, he told her they belonged to an ex-employee of theirs. Without any further probing and without any follow-up questions, Leah threw them into the large dumpster outside their shop. One week later, guess what? They were back. When she asked him a second time why they were there, Richard said he was afraid his employee would get upset, so he retrieved them. Strangely enough, Leah accepted his answer; she honestly believed he would never lie to her or anyone.

Following Richard's confession of viewing internet porn, it all made sense to me. All the abuse she had endured over the years flowed from things he found in the filthy magazines, on the pornographic websites and from sex shops where he purchased items to satisfy his sadistic cravings.

Leah turned toward me. "Honey, why would an employee who lived alone and just down the street from us, keep those magazines at the workshop? It doesn't make any sense, does it? Wouldn't he want to keep them at his home, to use them in privacy?"

"I think you can figure this one out, honey, and finally accept the truth."

She replied with a tremble in her voice, "They were Richard's all along!"

She started to cry, so I pulled over to the side of the road and held her as her tears flowed. I could see the truth of her past was becoming clearer, and it was tearing her apart.

Leah started talking, even though her words were all over the map. She rambled on about Richard's despicable treatment of her. Her comments centered along the lines of, "I feel so used, I am so ashamed, how could I have ever been so stupid? He betrayed God's love, he never really loved me, and he just used me."

She took a deep breath to compose herself and continued. "I trembled every night knowing what might soon happen, but I was told this was my place and my duty as his wife to submit to my husband's wants and needs no matter what. I never knew I was only an object to him; I didn't know, honey, I didn't know. I honestly believed this was my marital duty. Ryan, my mother even told me this is what I had to do! I begged him over and over again to stop, but he never would; all he kept saying was, 'Please don't take this away from me; I'm not a man, I'm not a man.' I wasted thirty-three years of my life, and I gave him everything I have ever worked for, only now to find out he never really loved me; he just used me!"

This was not a time for me to talk but a time for her to vent and come to grips with the sadistic, dark side of this soulless man. She cried and cried and told me, for the first time, the graphic details behind the many painful acts of servitude she was forced to endure. At this point, I tried to console her, telling her that this was now in the past. "It's over, honey, and he will never touch you again."

"But why, why did he use me so cruelly when I gave everything to him?"

"I don't know, maybe the way he was raised, maybe because he never had a father to guide him or maybe he's just a sick little man who felt bigger through hurting others. But let it go; it's over and believe me, I will never need foreign objects or any other form of outside influence to stimulate my desire for you; I will just love you."

Richard's denial and lack of care for Leah's feelings obviously took on many forms, and his addictions became too powerful for him to control. In the aftermath of his actions, he had almost destroyed Leah as she came to know she was nothing more than a convenient victim in his lurid obsessions and exploitation of the dark side of sexual domination. Years ago I read an article about pornography in a religious journal. Although I do not recall it verbatim, the gist of it went something like this: *Pornography conditions men to view women as things to be used only for pleasure and not as they really are, which are creations of God, each unique and having a ministry the Lord gave them to fulfill.*

I believe this relates to I Corinthians 7:2-5, which describes the marital duties of both husband and wife and their relation to each other as each has power over the other's body. But this, as I see it, is the benevolence of sharing love and does not step over the moral boundaries of each other. Pornography distorts and defiles this ministry that God gave us and turns us away from God, begging the question, Did Richard even for a minute ever really love God or his wife?

Leah, following the scriptures pounded into her, knew she had a biblical right to divorce Richard and love me; but what would this do to her precious sons who hold Richard up as some sort of hero and a champion among men? If she speaks out, she would be worthy of her church's love and support, but she would also tear a father from his sons. No matter the anguish of the past or the bitterness and anger she now feels she, she chose not to do this, believing faithfully in God's love and believing in her sons' love for her. One outcome was that her boys might abandon her, her friends might turn their backs on her and her church might revile her; but God knows the truth and in the end, when the life within her fades, she will rejoice forever within God's love and reside by his side. Leah is truly a remarkable woman; she was willing to sacrifice herself to protect a man so guilty of sin and crimes against God that he will ultimately be condemned, not only for his actions but his inactions as well, to shield her boys from things they may not comprehend or be emotionally strong enough to deal with.

It was time now to move on again, but she made me promise I would not speak of this facet of her life. She pledged to place it on a back shelf and never allow it to come between us. I hope she is right and these words are never spoken out loud, but I have a feeling someday they will come to light.

For the most part we drove straight through to North Carolina and to her business meeting, which I admit I was not looking forward to. We checked into the hotel, freshened up and went downstairs to grab a bite to eat. We were both a bit apprehensive about being there as Leah has been involved in this business for twenty-two years with Richard.

Surprise! We were greeted with open arms, like family members not seen in years. I was dumbfounded, as was Leah; it was so amazing I thought there must be a fatted calf turning on a spit outside the hotel. Leah was completely blown away. For the most part those who had heard of our thirty-five year plight were in awe of our love, and many suggested we either write a book or try and sell our story as they felt it should be made into a movie as one of the greatest love stories ever told. I had folks I had never heard of come up to me in droves and introduce themselves as though I had known them for years, which was weird, but gave me an enormous sense of pride, knowing I was with someone who was loved and cherished by all of them. Most of the people I met kept saying how happy they were that Leah had finally found the love she needed and desired.

This made me feel wonderful, but it also seemed rather odd, as everything I was led to believe through Leah's e-mails was that in everyone's mind, she and Richard were the perfect couple. I found this was not even close to the truth, as everyone I talked to held an opposite view of them. Most of them made a comment or two, but some of them went into detail. They perceived Leah as a woman who embodied a desire for life and one who, if she ever tried, would find the sky is really not that high. They felt she was tenacious and vivacious and could always beat the odds, but for some reason she could never quite take that final step to reach her dreams; they thought there was something missing in Leah, and they all said it was love.

They told me Leah and Richard seemed like the odd couple, with Leah outgoing and enjoying life and Richard showing reserve and a lack of social graces, seemingly avoiding the enjoyments of life. None of them saw any love between the two. To a few they acted more like a brother and sister, with Richard being the possessive big brother. In their minds, Richard held Leah back, denying her and in some ways crippling her from enjoying the zest life can bring. I guess in Richard's defense this may have scared him or maybe he was jealous of her and could not envision that this woman who lay beside him was destined for greatness. Either way, they were never seen as the perfect couple Leah thought she was portraying.

Wow! Did I ever get an earful? All the comments made me feel better, for now I had opinions from people outside of Leah's hometown who genuinely cared for her and viewed Leah's past in a totally different light. They fortified my strength and alleviated my fear that I had destroyed Camelot. Quite the opposite. In her hometown, she was perceived as only a housewife who sold Rainbow vacuum cleaners. Here people thought of her as an intelligent, strong businesswoman and leader with enormous talent and an endless desire to succeed.

However, to make a very long night and this segment of the story a bit shorter, let me start with "These folks are seriously nuts!" I kept telling myself these folks sell vacuums, not cars, not houses, not boats, but vacuums and yet they were all having a ball, singing songs, poking fun at each other and giving away numerous, and expensive, prizes. The stage was half filled with these prizes, and in addition to handing out money like water, they provided encouragement with some of the most outstanding motivational speakers I had heard in years.

I remember one, I think his name was Billy, who was full of energy and charisma and one the best motivational speakers I had ever heard. He started out by asking how many in the audience were attending for the first time. Maybe seventy–five to eighty stood up. Then he asked if there was anybody in the room who had made over a million dollars selling Rainbows. Over two hundred stood up. When he asked how many had made over ten million dollars selling Rainbows, to my astonishment very few sat down. I was blown away. Here's a business you can start with zero cash outlay, dictate your own hours, start part time and become a millionaire simply by following what they call their Total Program. *Only in America*, I thought.

Later that night, back in the hotel room, Leah was bouncing off the walls. She had believed everyone would shun her like the upright and pious Christians had back in her neighborhood in Tennessee and was elated with the reception she had received. What she did not realize is that most people find joy in happiness, understand change, do not tolerate abuse, and believe that God is love and forgiveness and not hate, despair and servitude as she was taught to believe. On this night, Leah's eyes were opened to who she was and who she will become, without limits and without persecution. She can look forward to nights with a loving mate and to waking up to each new day, without guilt, looking forward to new adventures.

The next morning we took off for a romantic adventure to Gatlinburg, which rests within the majesty and radiance of the Great Smoky Mountains, slow-paced, peaceful and warm. Gatlinburg epitomizes where a romantic rendezvous should take place. It combines the splendor of old-fashioned small town life coupled with amazing waterfalls, gourmet restaurants and five-star hotels. The rooms are picturesque with running streams just outside the windows and balconies which catch the cascading spray from rambling waters that rush down the mountain side.

Gatlinburg is about twelve miles out of Pigeon Forge, which is a great family fun town with attractions like Dollywood, Dollywood's Splash Country and wonderful stage and comedy shows for all ages. This was a perfect spot for Leah as her life thus far had been so sheltered; other than a few trips she won via her Rainbow business, she had traveled very little and had few outings other than with her boys. Painfully she had not done much of anything, as many activities were either out of reach financially or against her religion.

After a glass of wine in our hotel room, we ventured out to explore the night life of Gatlinburg, take in the sights and enjoy a late dinner. We chose to walk this quaint town as it was filled with novelty shops, candy making shops, local craft stores and breweries. This was a good idea, and at the same time, a bad idea. As we walked and walked, the night slipped away and many of the better dinner houses began closing. Then, down a side street, we found a great little bistro specializing in lobster tails and fine wine. After we were seated, Leah started to read the menu, but to her amazement the prices were not listed, replaced with a new term for her; "market price." To her way of thinking there was something wrong with this. How do you choose a meal not knowing what the final price would be? She looked a bit dumfounded, so I asked her if something was wrong.

"Ryan, they don't list any prices. What should I order?"

"They specialize in lobster, so why not try that?"

"But there are no prices!"

"Trust me and order the lobster."

To order dinner this way was strange to her, and after she ordered the lobster, she called the waiter over to find out how much her dinner would be. I thought she was going to faint when she heard the price. I smiled, squeezed her hand, and said, "Honey, we're not in Kansas anymore."

I ordered a dozen oysters on the half shell as an hors d'oeuvre. Leah had never tasted them before but she was game. When the waiter arrived with a tray of raw oysters, lemons, cocktail sauce and crackers, I thought she was going to lose it.

"Remember you said you'd try anything once," I reminded her.

I still thought she would turn her nose up and say "no way," but she loved them and ate so many, I ordered a second dozen. Our ramblings earlier in the evening and this dinner made me realize something about Leah I had not expected; she had an inexplicable desire to explore and discover the unknown. I felt like I was unleashing a whole new world to Leah, one she was never allowed to experience. She loved the idea of making new friends and setting off on adventures. It was very obvious she was becoming more and more outgoing with everyone we met.

Later that night as we were enjoying each other and listening to the sounds of the stream outside our room, I asked Leah what had come over her. She told me she had lived her whole life surrounded by people living day to day, never challenging life, content to take the same vacations year after year and never turning down a road just to see what was at the end. She had lived through books and movies, dreaming of new adventures and challenges but never being a participant.

As I kissed her goodnight, all I could think was, if you are looking for adventures, you're about to meet a few head on. Los Angeles has a population of over three million, opposed to her hometown, which has a population of just over two thousand. Then there's the challenge of putting up with my soon to be ex-wife's wrath.

"Good luck, honey," I whispered as we drifted off to sleep.

The next morning I awoke feeling a bit apprehensive, knowing this would be Leah's last day in the South for quite a while. *This must be really tough for her,* I thought, *as she is leaving everything she has known behind with nothing more than a dream and a prayer.* I lay still, waiting for her to get up, trying to give her another thirty or so minutes to sleep in, when out of nowhere Leah popped out of the bathroom.

"What are you lying around for? There's a plane to catch and I'm starved, so get out of that bed and let's go."

Oh my God, I've created a monster!

Needless to say I was knocked off my feet, again! What a woman; what a mate. I'm still the luckiest guy around, but I better get ready or she might leave me behind. We grabbed a quick bite and headed back to the Huntsville International Airport for our flight to California. We left her car in the overnight lot, where her daughter-in-law would pick it up the next day. As we were walking to the terminal just minutes away from our journey to California, Leah stopped me and said, "This is 1971, isn't it?"

I know it sounds dense, but all I could think was, *All my bags are packed, I'm ready to go, I'm standing here outside your door. . . .*I hummed the tune and said, "The way I feel, it couldn't be any other time."

She said it all at that very moment as I was thinking the exact same thing. As the plane took off, Leah looked out the window, not with sad eyes but as a farewell, not to her boys as they are with her at all times, but to a life filled with bad memories that was rapidly fading into the vacant past. She rested back into her seat, held my hand and closed her eyes, saying, "I love you." I thought she would be scared or depressed to be leaving all she had known behind with nothing more than two suitcases, no money and flying into a possible hornet's nest in California. Instead she seemed relieved and relaxed.

24

A New Beginning in California

After we arrived at LAX, we still had to drive several hours to pick up my mother, who was staying with my cousin in the San Diego area, and then begin the long trip back to my house. Once we arrived it was like a bad joke. My wife had gutted the house. We had no pots or pans, no plates, no silverware and even the mattress cover on my mother's bed was gone. I guess this was justice for me. Since Leah only had two suitcases of clothes, why should I have anything more?

Obviously, it was time to regroup and quickly, and although I knew why everything was missing, Elaine actually did us a favor as we could start our new life with our own stuff and with no possessions laden with prior memories. I found out the next day that my son wasn't talking to me, my daughter wasn't talking to me and, of course, my soon be ex-wasn't talking to me. Here we were, in California, with a car, an empty house, Mom and her damn dog, and no job, and yet I am the happiest I believe I have ever been.

When it comes to my kids, I understand and respect their reservations as I raised them to be who they are, but throughout their lives I did my best to instill in them a desire to handle life's problems on their own, to not judge without compassion and to hold onto those things which are the most important, family and honesty. I could demand their attention; I could even insist they hear the truth about what happened between their mother and me, as I had every right before God and man to make this change possible, but I will not provide them with any cause to judge their mother nor will I suggest that anyone other than I motivated our divorce. I will never dishonor the love they have for her, and I will not force them to see the truth. This is something they must seek on their own, and when and if the time comes, I will be there for them with open arms.

Leah and I are on the same page here, as she has every right to discredit and bring shame on her sons' father and open wide the door biblically to divorce him. My only fear is that through waiting for them to see the truth on their own, she may be called a liar for waiting so long. In other words, her boys may think that if this really was the truth, why did she not come to them right away so they could confront their father after they became adults? Seriously, though, how could she have mustered the strength to tell her children the sordid facts of her marriage? As for her church, the preacher had made it very clear he was unwilling to hear the truth; he had already condemned her, so why bother him with truth?

A few days later, my son Patrick started coming around, using his grandmother as the excuse to come over, but I knew he really wanted to see what this woman in my life was like. What was amazing to me, and I'm sure to Patrick as well, is that Leah and Patrick hit it off from the very start, and soon thereafter we saw him on an almost daily basis. My daughter April was a different story. I expected this as she was the stubborn one and she loved her mother deeply. I hope I taught her that. I made a conscious choice to give her space and did not attempt to call her. But with Leah pushing me, asking me to contact her on a daily basis, I finally (thank God) called her. I'm not exactly sure how it happened, but within a week, I was at a ball field where April was playing. This was a perfect setting for us as she and I shared a twelve-year career playing softball (her playing and me coaching) from the time she was six until she was eighteen. I make no bones about it, and I mean no disrespect to my boys, but April was always "Daddy's little girl."

It took four innings, but she finally came over, ostensibly to grab some sunflower seeds, and she actually said "Hi" to Leah. It was one word, but it was a start, and at this point I would have taken a slap in the face just to feel the warmth in her hand again. I wanted to cry, I wanted to hold her like this was my last day on earth, but stupidly I did not, I just sat there, proud fool that I am. A million thoughts raced through my mind, all the good times with her that are burned into my mind and soul, like the time my coaches and I were hitting fly balls as deep as we could hit them and April was flagging them down like it was nothing and throwing strikes from deep center field to home plate. I remember a coach coming up to me to ask who the number 6 kid was. "That's my life out there, my little girl," I replied. I knew that although I would not be with her much longer, she had the talent, the guts and passion to over-come anything. I hope I taught her well enough that she will eventually accept Leah, though it's obvious the situation makes her very uncom-fortable now.

As I said, April is stubborn, and it took her four months to get to the place where she accepted Leah as her father's future wife. I guess she could see the love I held for Leah and the love she brought to me. By the way, Leah and April are best friends now, and I am as proud of my daughter as I have ever been. I knew she would see the truth and in her heart know this was what had been missing in my life.

I was busy taking care of Mom and showing off Leah to my friends and family. Then something very peculiar happened; Leah received a call from Richard asking if she was going to come back to him. As she had many times before, she said no. Then out of the blue, Richard said, "Well, if you're not coming back, I am going to marry Shelly."

As a precaution I had convinced Leah to let me listen in on all her conversations with Richard to make sure he did not threaten or try to bully her in any way. But this call was stranger than fiction; Walter Mitty has nothing on this guy. After she disconnected the call, I asked her what the date was.

"I don't know," she said, "July 6th or is it the 7th of July?"

"Think back to the beginning of the month. Do you remember a letter Richard wrote to you saying how deeply he still loved you and always would and how he would love to have you back? 'In a heartbeat,' I think, were his exact words."

"Yes, I remember."

"Doesn't it strike you as a bit odd that only three weeks later he tells you he's going to marry someone else? Honey, I thought we moved fast, but this guy just broke the sound barrier."

"Ryan, do you mean. . . ."

"Yep, he's been either seeing her, e-mailing her, talking to her or whatever else for quite some time."

She paused for just a second and then blurted out, "This is great. I hope it's true as my boys will surely see through this."

"Don't get your hopes up. I think he will hide this as long as possible and then, knowing him, somehow turn it around to where it was caused by you."

— —

For the next two months every ounce of our time was devoted to making the house presentable for sale, buying some basic necessities, and looking for a home in Alabama. I had gone back several times looking for houses for Leah and me to share with Mom but had found nothing suitable. I fired four real estate agents who just didn't get it or could not understand what we were looking for. Then, while were surfing the Internet, bingo! We came across a home we both fell in love with, located where we wanted to live, maybe a bit over our price range, but the home Leah had dreamed of. We made an offer the next day, and they accepted. We had not seen the home in person but relied on our gut instincts and the dozen or so photos posted on the website. At this point all bets were off, and we were in a dead run to get things settled and move back to Alabama.

This took a bit more time than I had anticipated; two weeks and a lot of effort working twenty hours a day. Finally, we were ready and the next day, lock, stock, (damn dog) and a few more barrels, we were on our way to our new home.

Boy, I feel like a little kid again! Thank you, God.

Part VIII

Our Dreams Come True

25

Home Sweet Alabama

*L*eah and Mom left today for Huntsville; they flew, and I have the dubious privilege of traversing the better part of the country on a road trip with the damn dog and a car so packed I can't see out the back window. Leah and Mom are somewhere thirty-six thousand feet above me cruising at around four hundred fifty miles an hour, and I am stuck in LA traffic with a map, a dog between my legs, a few sandwiches, snacks and some soft drinks. Despite all that, I feel great. I'm not crazy about country music but stuck in the back of my brain is "Sweet Home Alabama," where I knew my lover would be waiting.

After two days of all but non-stop driving, forty or so pit stops, a few hours of sleep and a car that smells like the damn dog, I finally made it to Athens, Alabama. It's amazing how the adrenaline kicks in when you know someone special is waiting for you. Athens is about fifteen miles outside of Madison (Huntsville area) where our new home is located. We are set to close tomorrow, but for tonight we had booked the cheapest hotel room we could find. After totaling our funds, we had just under fifty dollars between the three of us, but Leah was there and shortly thereafter she made me feel like a king again.

RYAN MILLER

Buying a house off the Internet is very out of character for me. Normally, I wouldn't buy a pair of shoes that way. Leah and I joked that the wire for the money from the sale of my house in Simi Valley had better arrive tomorrow or we wouldn't be able to pay for the hotel room; what a perfect start.

Leah was up at the crack of dawn and filled with excitement; she even wanted to skip breakfast, which if you knew her, you would understand how keyed up she was. We called the escrow office and the agent told us the money came in late yesterday; big relief. We drove to the attorney's office to sign a few papers (dozens), picked up the keys, got directions to the house and then broke every speed limit in Alabama. When we arrived at our new home, I was shocked; you can't imagine what you can buy back here as opposed to what you would get for the same money in California. The house was gorgeous, and I could tell Leah was overwhelmed and delighted.

The home came with quite a bit of furniture, which is a good thing as we still had a few days before the truck would arrive with our furniture and my Mom's things. This also gave us time to pick up Leah's belongings left in the care of Richard, and she had quite a few things we could use. So far we had no cause to doubt Richard's honesty or integrity, but this was soon to change as well.

This long journey has come down to a final quiet question that has yet to be asked. The question could not have been heard by anyone other than us, yet it was so powerful, it resonated in my heart. As we stood in our home, Leah took my hand and said, "Was it worth the wait?"

I couldn't get the words out fast enough. "You've got to be kidding me. Leah, honey, we've waited a life time for this day, and now it feels like it was only a blink in time."

Looking at her standing there with that mystical squint in her eyes, I knew what she was thinking, but that would have to wait for a few hours as I was far too philosophical right then. I felt like everything I had done in my life now had meaning and purpose, for the events that transpired over the last six months, as rough and as callous as they had been, had brought me to this journey's end to be with her. This house, our home,

226

symbolized the fact we had righted the altered past and brought closure to it; the love that had eluded us for so many years would now grow
within these walls. Here, I pray, we will begin to rebuild those relations
that were turned upside down just a few short months ago and open our
doors and hearts to all who wish to enter. I said a short prayer of thanks
to our Lord for providing me with all I had ever dreamed of and asked
for forgiveness for my transgressions and vowed to fill our home with
love and compassion for all.

Enough being philosophical! I told my Mom it's time for her to go
into her room, as there were some things I should never put on hold.
Mom is great as she knew exactly what I meant, and without any discussion all she said was; "take your lover son, there's no better time than
the present". So I called out to my lover Leah, "Woman of the House,
where's our bedroom?"

The reply came a second later. "The room I'm in. . . .you better
hurry." What a woman!

Later that day Leah led me all over the house, showing me where
and how she would blend together her things with mine. We had decided
that the second story would be used as office space, and at the top of the
stairs there was an open space Leah had appropriated as her office. She
planned to put the cherry desk that her father had given her in this spot
and then build a few display shelves, one to house the Aladdin's Lamp
given to her by her grandmother and others to display some of the trophies she had won over the years. In the back area she would put some of
her office furniture for the dealers and telemarketers. In the adjacent
room, which was previously a TV room, she would put her antique sofa
and chair along with some high back chairs that were her mother's.

Ecstatic that I have agreed to rent the truck tomorrow, she is flying
around the house. Moving downstairs, she showed me the place where
she would put her mother's hope chest and hang a picture, "Amazing
Grace," that was given to her when her mother passed away. She had
dozens and dozens of other beads and bobbles I knew were precious and
sentimental to her. I suppose she felt it was her duty, as the woman of the
house, to show me exactly where each of them would fit, down to where

her mother's spoon collection would be displayed. We will also get her clothes out of storage, though I'm not sure why she wants them. She has lost so much weight I bet most of them will not come close to fitting her anymore. She is so happy, bouncing from room to room, I think I've married some wacked-out kid. When she stopped to take a breath, I said, "Whoa, honey, it's getting late; you don't have to plan out everything tonight."

She replied, "I remember the look in your eyes when we were in California after your wife gutted your house, and I know many of the things she took were precious to you. So try and understand that most of the things we are going to pick up tomorrow aren't worth much, but to me they are cherished memories of my mom and dad, my grandparents, and my boys, as well as my childhood."

A chill ran down my back at the intensity of her feelings. Lord, I pray I'm wrong, but Richard knows this, and I fear the worst. I shouldn't have these thoughts about anyone, but I believe he is capable of doing just about anything to hurt Leah.

The next morning, Leah was awake before the roosters, and although I told her it was too early, she couldn't wait any longer and called Richard to make the arrangements to pick up her personal belongings and her half of the Rainbow business materials he was keeping for her, per their divorce decree. To her utter and complete shock, if not anguish, Richard told her he had lied to her and that all of the belongings she had left with him were now his and she could have nothing. Leah was devastated as she had trusted him with things precious to her and fell to the floor sobbing in disbelief. It may have been minutes, but it seemed like hours, until she regained her composure. When she did, her sobs turned to rage, and she began shouting, "What kind of a man would steal my mother's jewelry and my grandmother's wedding rings, the glass etching from my grandfather, pictures of my boys and my treasures from them. They don't mean anything to him. Why is he doing this?"

Leah cried most of the day, hiding from me, if not from herself, in our bedroom. Later that night I did my best to console her, but this time the loathing and contempt ran too deep. Time and time again she lashed out. "I gave him the house and trusted him; now he wants everything? He lied, he cheated on me, he used me for years and now steals from me. He's no Christian, just an immoral vile man and a common thief."

Leah did not sleep much that night, falling in and out of conciseness as I held her in my arms fully dressed. All I could think of at the time was what could possibly motivate Richard to do this? Could he not see that his actions would only reflect what a pathetic coward and liar he was? I thought he had a new love and was engaged to marry her. *If I were her,* I thought, *and he had said he was in love with me, I would question why he wanted to steal his ex-wife's personal belongings.* Maybe I'm completely stupid, but my question to her would be, "Is this the type of a man you seriously want to marry?"

I did not sleep either but held my bride tightly in my arms until she awoke the next morning. Once she was fully awake, I told her we should not play Richard's childish games, that we should take him to court or get the Sheriff involved and go pick up her belongings. Leah's answer bewildered me and showed me that part of her was still trapped, just as she had been for so many years. She said she would not take Richard to court to force him to live up to his agreement nor would she cause a scene by getting the Sheriff involved.

"I will pray Richard comes to his senses," she said. "But even if he does not, I won't sue him. I'm afraid that would only drive my sons farther away."

I believe just the opposite would happen, exposing to his sons just what kind a man he really is. I viewed them as adults who are smart enough to add two and two together and get four. Personally, I was enraged by Richard's actions; here was this sanctimonious and supposedly God-fearing man who had used the church as his personal band of mercenaries to destroy and discredit Leah and who turned out to be a liar, a thief, and a bearer of false witnesses. His obsession to condemn and vindictively punish her damns him; anyone with any sense must be able to see this and clearly see how his past actions all but destroyed her soul and her faith in the beauty of God's love. *I guess he was right all along,* I thought. *He's not a man; in fact he brings shame on the meaning of the word.*

I felt guilty at this latest indignity suffered by Leah. How could I have been so blind? There were so many warning signs—snide remarks, secret files, weird phone calls—yet I allowed Leah to let him keep her belongings. He must be laughing his head off right now, and I'm getting madder by the minute. Leah wants to believe he is only doing this out of greed; but I don't think so, and I am coming to understand how maliciously he uses people. Richard did not take Leah's possessions for money but to cause emotional suffering and heartache for her.

It wasn't enough for him to threaten her with a gun, disgrace her in the eyes of their church and turn her boys against her, he craved something more—trophies. Like the taxidermied heads of fallen prey to the big game hunter, he wanted his trophies strewn about his house, hoping all would see how Leah could never defeat him and how he had put her in her place. To me this was a hollow victory. He may have pilfered man-made trinkets, but the real prize, Leah's desire and love, he would never enjoy, possess or hold. God forgive him as he's beyond pathetic.

I can only pray, given the fact Leah will not turn me loose on him, when time has passed and if he does marry Shelly, he will change his ways. But then again, I don't know her. She may be cut from the same cloth as Richard, and his ex-wife's personal possessions may excite her in some twisted way. However, if she is a Christian, I simply cannot imagine how she, the new bride, could sleep with her husband under a roof that houses so many of his prior wife's personal and treasured possessions and not ask why they are there and why on earth do you want them?

Through all of this, Leah has carried herself like the Christian lady she has always been, holding her silence and trying to do what is right for everyone. You can't imagine the strain this has placed on her, for all she had ever worked for has now been stolen from her, even her business. Here again he lied as he was to retain, via their agreement, only half her Rainbow business—stock, supplies, desks, etc. So for now, Richard walks away with the house, Leah's personal possessions, her business and her children's love. I'm not sure what evil created a narcissistic man like this or how with such disdain for the truth he professes his Christianity, but I do know the guilt of his immoral life will resonate within his soul every night for the rest of his life. His futile and cowardly attempts to betray the truth and his lies of ill repute will never tarnish or disrupt the miracle and splendor of Leah's love for me and mine for her. What is surprising and foreign to me is that I would have thought someone in the family would have the guts to stand up and say, "Wait a minute. Why do you still have Leah's or Mom's stuff, and for that matter, why did Leah or Mom leave you?"

If this was my mother and she left my father, I would want to know every detail and not just assume that the stories given to me by my father were true. For those of you that still don't get it, let me spell it out for you. Leah and Richard had been married for over thirty years, owned a very nice home, had three great kids and two grandkids, owned their own business and went to church three times a week. Why then would any mother just up and run off, committing to marry a man she had not heard from in over thirty-five years, had only met once and had e-mailed and talked to for barely four months? I had no money and a job that paid commission only. All I had to offer her was true love, something she'd never had or felt. For God's sake, folks, someone ask why.

Apparently, compassion and empathy are words missing from their Bibles, and although I really did not expect them to completely understand, I did assume her sons and close family members would, after all the years of love she provided, have the courage to seek the truth. However, it appears to be much more expedient to condemn your friend, church member or mother without asking why and to turn a deaf ear to the one whose love has always and unconditionally been there for you. I have never been subjected to such a band of hypocrites in my whole life. I guarantee you Leah and I would ask questions if the tables were turned. Our God would expect nothing less from us.

Obviously I am a bit upset about this as it was just a few months ago that Richard sent Leah a letter begging her to come back, underlining "I love you" several times. Then just a couple of weeks later, he called to let her know he was going to marry Shelly if she was not coming back to him. A few months later, he even gave Leah an e-mail from Shelly to him with the subject line "Loving You Always!!!!!" I suppose he sent it to Leah to show her he was adored and desired by another woman, but to my way of thinking this was not an, "oh by the way" e-mail. It was a love letter and shouldn't have been shared with anyone, let alone your ex-wife. Shelly was very graphic in her references to her desires for Richard. She told Richard she wished her daughter was already in college so that Richard could, be with her more often, and what a blessing he was to her in this cold and selfish world. I wondered how her opinion might change if she knew he was flaunting her love letter as some form of trophy, with his ex-wife? Other than a liar and now a thief, it became obvious to me now he is a card carrying narcissistic, and maybe this was the underlying cause of abusive ways.

Her e-mail made it perfectly clear to me that Richard's "Woe is me" is just an act. This was no recent relationship. It had to have been going on during the times he was putting on his act of not eating or sleeping and crying all the time. After reading Shelly's love letter to Richard, I thought someone should have a talk with her before they get married. Based on his treatment of Leah, I am not sure he even comprehends the meaning of love. One interesting thing we found out from Shelly's e-mail love letter, was that she was about to receive a sizeable inheritance. She told Richard that now she would be able to get new caps and Lasik eye surgery and still have enough to invest in their retirement. Funny I thought, Richard, during this time was in the middle of foreclosure proceedings on the house Leah left to him and now Shelly, his new fiancée, was about to come into a bunch of cash? Go figure! I bet Richard sure had.

I pushed Leah to go back to court and have the divorce amended and take back her house. Leah, however, would not budge on this. *Blessed are the peacemakers*, I thought. Although I completely disagree with her and would take great pleasure in visiting Richard once a day to stomp the self-pity out of him, I let it go. I didn't want their house, but it sure galled me he was getting away with what is essentially robbery.

Over the next few months, some of the animosity lightened, but for the most part there remained an undertow of resentment from most of Leah's side of the family. On a brighter note we finally met Shelly,

Richard's new fiancée, at one of the grandson's baseball games around May of 2007. Shelly was sporting a diamond engagement ring, although they hadn't set a date. A glimmer of hope crept into my mind as I prayed for her to be a Christian and help Richard find the courage to repent. When he told Leah in California he was going to marry Shelly, I thought it was a joke, some contrived attempt to make her jealous. Maybe I was wrong.

Richard did a pretty convincing job on Leah's kids; all but one will not even talk to her. She has been labeled as an adulteress, and their religion mandates they not speak with her or acknowledge she is alive, while their father is being touted as their hero. I guess his lust for other women, which he confessed to, his thieving ways and continual lies (if they have any knowledge of this) are overlooked by them because he's a man. I had been taught to believe the truth is what you are to seek, even if you know the outcome may hurt you or change your way of thinking. But Leah's church apparently teaches if you have what you believe is the truth, look no farther and do not question a man's word. I was raised to believe in "Judge not lest you be judged."

As the months rolled by, nothing changed, and Leah became madder and madder. Mother's Day came and went, her birthday, Thanksgiving, Christmas and Easter, and still no calls from her beloved boys. Having endured so many days of crying and longing for her sons, she decided it was time to seek the guidance of her old preacher. She poured her heart out to him, and as painful as this was, she needed him to know the facts of her marriage to Richard. Throughout a three-page letter she detailed the truth about what her parents had done to her and a how she had endured a life where she was forced to live in servitude and sin. She ended the letter with a pointed question to this man of God. If your daughter was strangled, kicked so as to have a miscarriage, had a gun pulled on her and was sexually abused, not made love to, for years, would you advise her to grin and bear it or to file for a divorce and move on?

This man of God did not reply to her letter but gave this personal confession of deceit and abuse to Leah's youngest son, who was engaged to his daughter, to share with all concerned. All Leah was looking for was a chance to bare her soul and ask for understanding and guidance, not for forgiveness as she had every right to divorce Richard. She simply sought compassion. However, not one call was made to bring her back to her church and not one mention of why. As I said, Leah's youngest son is engaged to this preacher's daughter, so how could he allow the truth to come out?

I'll give you another insight; he will not be performing the wedding ceremony of Richard and Shelly, nor will it be held in the church. Are you getting the picture here? He perceives them both at fault but advises that only Leah be condemned; he needed to hide this from his flock.

Despite this, things were not all bad. I got to know Leah's father and his new bride, and I know this may sound strange, but Leah and I went on their honeymoon with them. We spent some marvelous times with Lenna, whom my mother adored. Finally, the ice was beginning to melt with some of Leah's family. Her daughter-in-law had started coming around, and Leah and I welcomed her and the grandkids with open arms. In time, Sandra and the kids ended up living with us, on and off, for the better part of two years and brought us great joy. Sandra became another daughter to me. We laughed together, cried sometimes, and as I watched her grow (she worked with me in the telecom business), I found a compassionate caring person much like Leah, only wanting love and a true feeling of self-worth.

Sandra's son Trent is a bit of a wildcat and a loose cannon. I say this in a good way because Trent is all boy and one who takes great pleasure in beating me at a game of horse or out-fishing me at the lake. I had forgotten just how much energy boys of his age have, and I generally wound up with aching muscles and bruises. Love that little man. I only wish he would eat something other than chicken.

Her daughter Mercedes (although I never really told her) became my pet and wove her way into my heart. She unknowingly helped fill the void of not having my daughter April beside me. She is an amazing kid; she loves simple things like "food fights" and "marshmallow wars." She does have a stubborn side, but deep down she has a kind and loving sprit that I believe will propel her into becoming something great. I pray I am still around when she blossoms. Sandra's family spent holidays with us and even invited Leah and me to several parties to meet their friends. I can't say enough about them, for without them I would have had a much harder time being so far away from my kids.

I also got to know some other very special people who a hand in shaping Leah. Lenna had two other children who were much younger than Leah's mother, Aunt Sherry and Uncle Bobby. Aunt Sherry is a kind and loving woman who has a wonderful talent for ceramics and who had made many sculptures which Leah proudly displayed for years. (It's really sad that Richard kept them). There is a warmth about Aunt Sherry that makes you feel at home. She has strong Christian convictions and a way of making you feel you have known her for years the first time you meet her. Sherry's husband Jimmy is a giant of a man with a sense of humor a mile long, but you need to pay attention to him as his humor is witty and may get your goat. He was the first one I got to know after we moved to Alabama, and I believe him to be one of the few standup guys left who speaks his mind freely and believes in the American way of life; I took to him right away.

Uncle Bobby had always been one of Leah's favorites as he was the one who took her on trips to California, out to dinner, was always there for the holidays and never let her down. Bobby is a strong man with a very strong will and a great belief in God. He is the type of person you can always rely on to do the right thing. He is there daily for his mother Lenna and would never turn his back on anyone. His door is always wide open, and if you are in need, all you have do is ask and he will give you the shirt off his back if you need it. It might not fit, but you would be welcome to it.

Leah and I held open every Friday as "date night". We took trips to Gatlinburg, did some motel hopping and spent many nights on the patio writing songs and being alone together. For New Year's Eve, we booked tickets for the festivities at the Huntsville Holiday Inn, which included a private suite for the night. Leah got all dressed up in a beautiful evening gown, and I, well let's just say I didn't look as good as her. They had four ballrooms with bands in each playing different forms of music. We picked the band playing good old rock 'n roll and settled in for an evening of fun. Leah didn't drink much in her past life, and even with me, she generally only had a single glass of wine with dinner or maybe one or two drinks over a four to six hour period at a party. On this night, however, as everyone was having such a good time, she got caught up in the festivities and had a few more than usual.

It was getting close to midnight, and the band was playing "Hit Me With Your Best Shot". I was clowning around, like everyone else, faking throwing punches as we danced. The next time the lead singer sang "Hit me with your best shot", I stuck my chin out, playfully taunting Leah, and you probably can guess what happened next. She hit me with her best shot, which spun me around and almost dropped me, as she kept dancing like nothing had happened. Couples around us lost it, and between fits of laughter, came over to see if I was alright. I learned a valuable lesson that night. Leah is the love of my life and the greatest lover I have ever known, but I will be careful not to make her mad.

The months flew by and Leah's Rainbow business picked up steam. Our legal wedding was to take place in Hawaii, but we hit a bump when we were working out the arrangements with our travel agent. She pointed out that my California driver's license had expired, which might cause problems at airport check-in.

"No big deal," I said. "I'll get a new one here in Alabama."

The next day I took what I thought was my birth certificate to the DMV. After examination they informed me what I had was a certificate of live birth dated several years after I was born. I told them it was all I had ever had. They referred me to a company, Vital Check, for assistance in obtaining a State certified copy of my birth. About three weeks later, the company sent me a notice that there was no record of my birth in the State of California on November 11, 1950, and there was no record of me being born at any time from the periods of 1949 through 1951. The only record they found was a certificate of live birth filed in Sacramento in 1953 listing my birth parents as a Mr. and Mrs. Miller. I was completely baffled. I knew I was adopted and thought I had been born on the date on the certificate.

My father had told me I was adopted before I was even born, which explained why my adoptive parents' names were listed on the certificate of live birth and not my biological parents. As the story went, my biological father, a fighter pilot, died in the Korean War and my biological mother, not able to handle the loss of her husband, committed suicide shortly after my birth. Recently I found a letter from an attorney that said she was killed in auto accident a month after I was born. What actually happened? Am I who I think I am, and was I really born on November 11, 1950?

The problem facing me was who do I turn to and what questions should I ask? I searched through my mother's storage boxes, her safe and important file folders. I even checked her dresser drawers; but nothing showed up, not even my adoption papers. I had not asked my mother directly, hoping to find some evidence myself and spare her having to talk about something that was obviously difficult. As a last resort, however, I went to my mother to ask for her guidance and support in finding out where I came from and to locate the records of my adoption.

I could see the pain in her eyes when I asked her, and as she began to cry, the story she unfolded seemed so farfetched, it was hard to believe. She told me she had tried for years to conceive, but in the end there was no hope as she was barren. Desperately wanting a child, she attempted adoption, but their income level and some strange law that remarried couples could not adopt at that time made this avenue impossible. She turned to her doctor, a long-time family friend, for help. He told her he would find her a baby, but she would have to have the money in hand when one became available, so she mortgaged her furniture as collateral for a loan and drained her bank account to pay for me.

Very shortly thereafter, the doctor called her to say there was a young and talented girl who needed to give up her baby as soon as it was born and he believed he could make this happen for her. A few weeks later, arrangements were made for her to meet someone at the hospital. She was to look for a young lady holding a clip board, who would be waiting for her. After an exchange of money, she was told where to pick up the baby, who would be in a basinet on a bench with a tag reading "Baby Boy Miller." She was also instructed to file in Sacramento, three years later, a certificate of live birth that her doctor actually signed as proof I was her child. Mom told me that for the next three years she lived in constant fear of her crime being found out and someone taking me away from her. Given the circumstances, she told no one how she got me or that I was even adopted.

I asked my mother, "Is it really true I was bought on the black market?"

She said, tearfully, "Yes." Then she hit me with another bombshell. "Ryan, I only wished we could have taken both of you, but we did not have enough money. Please try and understand. I wanted a baby so badly, I would have done anything to get you."

Oh my God, do I have a brother or a sister somewhere in the world? Do they know about me?

I went back to the DMV with this new information. After a long wait they told me they would issue me a license if I could produce a passport. Saved! I did have a passport and finally got my license, but the process took us over two months.*

*I have added this to the book for one reason. If anyone knows of a family member, wife, daughter, aunt, etc., who knew of a baby born into their family on November 11, 1950, in Los Angeles, California, that was given up, please try and find me as I would like to know just who I am and if I have siblings.

26

"I Do" Forevermore

The driver's license obstacle was behind us, but my divorce was dragging on and on. Leah and I were becoming quite concerned as our wedding ceremony was planned for June 22 in Hawaii. The problem was June had arrived, and I still did not have final settlement papers from the court. We had paid for the airfare, reserved the hotel room and had our wedding planned through Rainbow Weddings out of Kauai. Rainbow Weddings fit as Leah loves rainbows and Leah is my pot of gold at the end of my rainbow. I know it's corny, but if you have not guessed by now, that's how I feel and how much I love her. Maybe someday I'll start a business and call it Rainbow Dreams.

I called my attorney every day, and every day I got the same answer—nothing today. I didn't understand the holdup. Elaine had gotten everything she asked for, the attorneys had signed off on the terms and they had been paid. Leah was more nervous every day and said she would pray it comes in time. The next day's mail came and no divorce papers. There was not a lot I could do as we are in Alabama and my attorney was in Simi Valley, California. I asked Leah to pray harder.

Later that day we got the call. For some reason I got the feeling God was testing us, making us wait until the last possible day to fulfill our dreams. My attorney said the papers were in and did I want him to mail them. Obviously my loud reply was "No!" Explaining the situation, I made arrangements to pick them up prior to getting on the plane in Los Angeles. Fate, prayers; am I getting through to you yet? So now with my divorce papers complete, Sandra, Mercedes and Trent watching Mom and the damn dog, Leah and I are finally going to get married, legally and blessed again by our God!

The next day we flew into LAX, rented a car, picked up the papers, drove back to LAX and took off for Kauai, acting like young lovers. The flight was pleasant enough, but there was heavy cloud cover and very little to see until we were on our final approach into Kauai. The island first appeared out of our window, lighting up like a paradise simply waiting for us to arrive and offering the most wondrous, fulfilling and exciting time of our lives.

As we deplaned, a blast of warm humid air mixed with the sweet aroma of the islands filled our senses and enhanced our dreams of endless nights of love and adventure. We picked up our suitcases and Leah's wedding dress and rented a car; not just any car, no, no. I had my girl, and I needed a fine ride, so I picked out a retrofit convertible Mustang with over 350 horsepower and a kickass sound system. The car looked like a throwback to the late sixties or early seventies, which made us feel like we were back to where we should have been from the beginning. Everything was right in our world.

We drove to the hotel, and I goosed the Mustang a few times just to make Leah squeal. The sound system blasted old Beatles, Credence, Eagles and Beach Boys tunes, and we belted them out along with the bands. Leah was so full of life she was like the perfect date, the girl you never thought would give you a second look. *In two days,* I thought, *I'll have a little piece of paper showing her name as Mrs. Leah Miller!* I wanted to cry at this point as the dream I had held silent for so many years was about to come true. I figured I must have done a few things right in my life to have a girl, okay, a woman, like her, who truly makes me feel like the luckiest man alive. Here I was cruising with my girl in one of the most beautiful places on the planet, basking in the sun as the wind blew her hair back, revealing a face that Michelangelo could never have topped. What did she want to do? Pull over and neck! Best idea she's had all day.

When we pulled into the hotel guest entrance, we were attended to like dignitaries, pampered at every turn. The hotel was magnificently landscaped with beautiful pools highlighted by waterfalls and lush tropical plants and flowers. This was a place for lovers to share their lives or maybe like us to take that first step as husband and wife.

For the balance of the day and into the evening, we relaxed and drifted into the ambience of this magical land, taking walks down to the water's edge, stopping at the pool for a Mai Tai and enjoying the Hawaiian music that playfully filled the air. Just as the sun was setting, thunderous drums began to beat. A native Hawaiian stood atop a man-made mountain in the center of the pool area, where he began blowing into a very large Pu, a Hawaiian conch shell that emitted a loud low pitch. This triggered the arrival of two dozen scantily clad Hawaiians, men and women, carrying torches, who moved around the resort singing what I guessed were traditional Hawaiian chants, as I could not make out a single word. This turned out to be the nightly lighting of the torches that illuminated the pathways and gardens of the hotel. Leah beamed with enthusiasm. Maybe it was my imagination, but I seem to recall her hips moving to the music. At the time I thought, you better stop this or we will miss the show.

Hawaiian nights are among some of the most beautiful in the world; they draw out your passions and allow you to let everything go, sort of like the feeling you have right after a gentle massage. Your mind is no longer in high gear, the stresses of the day vanish, the problems of life that have all but haunted you fade and your heart opens like the blooming of a fragrant flower, beckoning you to give and receive love. Later that night and in our room with the roar of the ocean in the background and the lit torches casting off an array of flickering lights that transformed the shadows of our room, all but bringing them to life, I found myself never wanting to sleep again, just hold her and offer my love to her throughout the night.

The light of day took the place of the moonlight much sooner than I wished, but it brought me one day closer to making Leah mine. First and foremost, we needed to get a marriage license. I assumed we would go to City Hall, see some State official and have some papers drawn up and blood testing. It's a little different in Kauai.

After asking a few questions, we were directed to an address off the beaten path. Following several winding and narrow roads, we came to a small hamlet and a smattering of shops. The signs showed we were on the right road, and I searched for the address while I looked for a parking spot. 124, 120, then the number we were looking for, 110. We thought there must have been some mistake because 110 was painted above the local delicatessen, but we were here, so we decided to go in and ask for directions to the right place. I strolled up to the counter and asked for the address of the marriage license office. The butcher behind the counter looked up and said, "Hey man, you are at the right place! Let me finish this order, and I'll be right with you. Go have a seat."

We sat down in the lunch room with other tourists and locals enjoying their food, and I told Leah this must be a joke someone was playing on us, but nope, here comes the butcher with some forms, and (I'm sorry) I busted up. He had us fill out and sign a few pieces of paper, asked to see Leah's divorce papers, and said, "That's fine, Wahine." Then he asked for mine, pondered for a bit, and said, "Hey man, you cut it awful close, didn't you?"

Still chuckling, I replied, "Not really. I have waited thirty-five years for this woman, and I will not let even one more day pass without her as my bride."

He then took out the Seal for the State of Hawaii, pressed it to the paper, handed us our marriage license and asked for his money. Before we left I asked him where I could get a wedding outfit for a beach ceremony as I did not want to wear a tux or suit.

"Over there just down the street. My cousin will take good care of you. He's a good boy and will not cheat you."

He was right, and I found exactly what I was looking for; white string pants (which made me a bit nervous as they were all but see through) and a white cotton shirt that had a sort of a wrinkled look to it. The cousin then said, "You need this too, man. You wear it at the wedding, very traditional. Your minister will explain."

This was a puka shell necklace with a shark's tooth formed into a hook hanging from it. We said aloha, and with license in hand and outfit complete, we were set for our big day. . . .tomorrow Leah will be my wife!

We are entering our journey's end, and as odd as it may seem, we always knew this day would come. The dream had lived within us and survived. Our paths may have led us away from each other for a time, but as we are on the verge of becoming man and wife, we see that what is truly meant to be will never be denied. Each of us has a purpose in life, which is to live in love and to light the path for others to follow and thereby glorify God's name.

Our truth is simple and has been the same since Leah's first letter to me in 1970; I am within her and she is within me, and in God's name no man will ever find cause to destroy or deny our love for one another. I promise, on this day, to love her with all my heart in faith and in adoration until the day I die. It will be my lifelong pleasure to share my life with her, breathing back into her the love she desired, nurturing and fulfilling those feelings that were stolen from her through fear of damnation and deceit. I will also restore her belief that God is kind and forgiving and loves us today as He did so long ago when He gave to us the greatest gift of love the world has ever known. Today God will finally allow me to say those words I have so long been denied; today I will make her my bride.

She has brought me a joy like I have never felt, and she is the very essence and meaning of who I am. She brought to light the purpose of my existence and reignited the flames of passion which had lain dormant. She holds in her heart every song I will ever sing and gives me a reason to arise each morning, just to hold her one more time.

One last thought, one last poem I offer to her:

Like castles in the sky that compel you to soar
Like the eyes of a child peering through the
Window of a candy laden store,
So now our love hungers to take flight
With dreams of love and never-ending delight.

Still hearing those echoes of a lifetime past,
Like silhouettes that fading memories cast,
Sail now with me my love without fear on the turbulent seas of life
As I commit myself to you, my forever loving wife.

In awe we shall stand together in silent reverence
Before the greatest gift to man and whose loving guidance
Gave us strength as he guided us on our way
So that our love through his grace may begin again this day.

Today is June 22 (that would be 6/22). Back in Chapter 22, I asked you to remember the room number in Nashville, which was 622, and exactly one year to the day when I first brought her home to me. Still don't believe in fate? Am I getting closer?

— —

I am standing on a secluded beach on the Island of Kauai, dressed in a white traditional Hawaiian wedding outfit adorned with the puka shell necklace. Standing next to me is the minister, who is about to commence a part Hawaiian, part Christian wedding between Leah and me. I am facing the turquoise waters of the Pacific Ocean, and the white sand beach is lined with tropical trees. Foam bubbles from the sand as the waves move in their eternal rhythm onto the shore and out again. A light breeze is blowing and behind us are tall peaks and sharply chiseled cliffs that give off a roaring sound as the waves rush to them. The sun is brilliant, and small puffy clouds have formed just offshore. Hawaiian music sets the mood for paradise, and I cannot believe my dreams are becoming reality in such a beautiful place.

The minister motioned with her Bible, and Leah emerged from the trees and slowly walked toward me. I had never seen Leah like this before, and I knew right then I would carry a mental picture of how she looked on this day forever. She was dressed in a stunning white wedding gown that lit up her green eyes. Her hair was pulled up with small tropical flowers so delicately placed they transformed her into an angel with a purple and white orchard lei around her neck falling onto her breasts. She wore just a hint of makeup that accentuated her tan and soft pale pink lipstick. She was more beautiful today than I had ever seen her, and she had a look of anticipation in her eyes that made me feel like a king, albeit a speechless one as I was in complete awe.

The minister positioned us in front of the ocean's rippling waters, asked us to face each other, and then told us a story of Hawaiian love and the meaning of marriage, speaking some of the story in traditional Hawaiian language and interpreting in English as she went. Following this she read from the Bible and called us to believe in God, to forever honor our union and to keep this day and our love alive in our hearts, bodies and souls.

She turned to me and asked if I had prepared wedding vows. I had been waiting a long time to tell Leah how I feel about her. I thought this would be hard for me, but looking into Leah's eyes, I felt strong and with great conviction said,

I, Ryan, ask you Leah to be my partner,
my lover, my friend, and my wife.
Time and space may have taken my youth
But could not deny my love for you.
I have held you in a special place for so many years,
Always knowing somehow this day would come,
And with it I give you the deepest friendship and love,
and in doing so commit my life to you

to share and to shelter, to give and to receive
to inspire and to respond, to speak and to listen.
A commitment which I make in love
I will keep in faith, live in hope
and hold eternally only for you renew.
I commit to be with you forever
in a holy partnership of the soul,
and I know that we will always share
all that is good within us with all those
whose lives we touch.

From my heart to your hand,
With this ring I thee wed and join my life
With yours forever and then forever again.

It was here on this isolated beach and in the presence of God I placed a symbol of my love on her finger, not like a moment in time, but a moment for all time. I felt my heart secure and my life fulfilled, but there was one final step to take as now it was her turn.

The minister turned to Leah and asked if she had prepared her wedding vows, and Leah said softly and filled with love,

I, Leah, ask you Ryan to be my wedded husband.
In doing so I give you all that I am and ever hope to be.
You hold my life and my dreams as you stand beside me.
Where you go so shall I go,
Where you stay so shall I stay,
And I will be there with you come what may.
As I have so long awaited this special day,
You took my heart many years ago
And now I take you to my soul.
Be my lover, be my friend, and hold me in the night
As for all that was wrong is now forever made right.
I promise to hold you as our love unfolds

And then again love you more as we grow old.
I will answer your whispers in the night,
Embrace you at every dawn
Complete you when you feel alone
And make our house a welcome home.
My life is now made whole with you
As I never dreamed before.
So with purpose and joy,
I commit myself to you today
and then through eternity.

From my heart to your hand, with this ring
I take you as my husband and join my life with yours forever
And then forever again.

Following Leah's vows to me and the presentation of the ring on my left hand, the minister turned to us and said, "In the Hawaiian language we say *Aloha au ia oi mauloa*, which means 'I will love you forever.' Ryan and Leah, this is the commitment you two make to each other this day. It is a lifelong commitment to love each other in your marriage. We have come here in this beautiful setting to celebrate with you and to offer support and encouragement to both of you, for today marks the beginning in your lives and your relationship with each other, for from this day forward you will always be looked upon as husband and wife.

Love is something beyond the warmth and glow, the excitement and romance of being deeply in love. Real love is not the absorption in each other, but it is looking outward in the same direction together. Love makes burdens lighter because you divide them. It makes joys more intense because you share them. It makes you stronger so you can reach out and become involved with life and with people in ways you dare not risk alone. Let your hearts always be ready to ask for forgiveness, as well as to forgive, for a marriage filled with tenderness and built on trust and giving is what brings the deepest meaning and greatest joy to living.

Ryan, you are truly blessed to have Leah as your wife. You are to love her in such a way that the acceptance, understanding and support she finds in your love will provide the security she will need to express her inner light and beauty to you.

With this understanding, Ryan, do you take Leah to be your wife, and pledge your faithfulness to her in all love and honor, in all faith and tenderness, to hold her above all others and be faithful to our Lord until death do you part?"

"I do."

"Leah, you are truly blessed to have Ryan as your husband. You are to love him in such a way that he may find within himself a greater sense of who he is meant to be. It will be your devotion and lifelong commitment to him and him alone that will make your love grow deeper as the years drift by.

With this understanding, Leah, do you take Ryan to be your husband and pledge your faithfulness to him in all love and honor, in all faith and tenderness, to hold him above all others and be faithful to our Lord until death do you part?"

"I do."

The minister then turned us back to face the island and said those magical words I had waited so long to hear, "By the power vested in me by the State of Hawaii and through the grace of God, Ryan and Leah, I now pronounce you man and wife. Let the world rejoice; let the heavens sing. Allow me to be the first to introduce to all mankind Mr. and Mrs. Ryan Miller."

I stood there in shock, unable to speak or move, remembering the lost thirty-five years of our lives, which now faded away as though they had never happened. I am so content with her hand in mine that I care not to look back anymore, for in this moment Leah and I have brought into the light a love that was hidden yet always there, our living testimonial to what love is all about.

The minister, seeing I was either in silent reverence or simply speechless from wonder and amazement that Leah was actually my wife, said, "Ryan, Ryan, it's okay. You can kiss your bride."

I kissed her with the most delicate and yet most fervent kiss of my life, and tears ran down my cheeks as I held in my arms the girl of my dreams and now my wife. Resonating in the back of my mind was a song from long ago, one that I asked her to find while I was in Vietnam, "Till Then". When she did, she told me in a letter that "Burning Love" by Elvis was playing in the background, and she felt it was an omen of what was meant to be.

Till then, my darling, please wait for me
Till then, no matter when it will be
Some day, I know I'll be back again
Please wait, till then

Our dreams will live though we are apart
Our love, I know it'll keep in our hearts
Till then, when of the world will be free
Please wait for me

Although there are oceans we must cross
And mountains that we must climb
I know every gain must have a loss
So pray that our loss is nothing but time

Till then, let's dream of what there will be
Till then, we'll call on each memory
Till then, when I will hold you again
Please wait till then

The minister asked us to stand apart and face each other. She told Leah to take off her lei and blow into it as a symbol of her giving her life to me and place it over my head and around my shoulders, and in turn, she had me do the same. She told us this was a symbolic gesture of our lives now being intertwined and a reminder to always freely and openly give ourselves to each other with a simple "Aloha".

She then turned back to Leah and said, "There is but one thing left for you to do. It's another Hawaiian tradition. The necklace that is around Ryan's neck has a shark's tooth shaped like a hook. You need to break off the barb from the base of that hook."

Leah took it in her hands and broke off the barb. The minister continued, "Leah, this signifies that Ryan is no longer a fisherman and will no longer have a reason to troll the waters of life in search of a mate, for it is you for all time."

Funny, I thought at the time, *troll? Are you kidding me? I knew in my heart I had just landed the catch of a lifetime.*

Right after the ceremony the minister's assistant brought out a small but nicely decorated table, along with two glasses and an ice cold bottle of champagne for us to toast our union. I had some trouble opening the bottle, but when the cork flew, it soared as if it was trying to reach the heavens, which seemed fitting. We toasted each other and then the festivities began. Maybe it was just the two of us, but we played like children up and down the beach. As we walked in the sands where only our footprints appeared, it felt like no other man or woman had ever been there before.

We were photographed in trees, hollowed out logs, holding each other on the beach and wading in the warm waters of the ocean like lovers lost in time. At one point the photographer called to me, "Ryan, take Leah in your arms and dip her; then give her a big kiss."

Little did I know he was setting me up. He knew as soon as I dipped her, the sand would start to give way. As it did, I thought, *Oh My Lord. I am about to take the most beautiful woman I have ever seen, wearing a stunning tea length gown, and drop her into the foamy tide of the Pacific Ocean.* But just then my strength doubled, and I lifted her up like a feather, not letting her fall. Leah roared with laughter, and the photographer said, "Too bad you didn't let her fall; it would have been a great photo."

Over the next few hours, he took several hundred pictures of us, holding hands and kissing (which we did a lot). As the sun was setting far out in the ocean, a rainbow appeared as if in testimony to our union and new life together. We said a prayer of thanks and hand in hand took our last walk back to the water's edge. Leah looked back over her left shoulder, and I looked back over my right; and with the photographer snapping maybe thirty pictures a minute, he captured us in a way that will live with us forever.

As I look at those pictures, we seem to be saying, "We are headed on our own path now and to everyone who has ever touched us or has been a part of our story, you are welcome to come along, for the life we share is open to all. Join us as we venture to new and wondrous lands. The past is just that, the past, and we will never look back, for the future is all we will ever need. Past memories of all of you will live in our hearts forever, but I pray that new memories await all of us. As for Leah and me, our destiny is back on track."

We bid our alohas to the minister and walked to the car, where we shared another kiss. As she leaned back in my arms, Leah said, "Mrs. Ryan, Alfred, William, Hodges, Jefferson, Kesterson, Miller I like that." (this is actually my full name)

"So do I!"

— ~

We drove to the top of a cliff to a dinner house called Bali Hi nestled within a tropical forest with gorgeous views of the gardens of the Hanalei Bay Resort. Leah and I felt like we had either taken a page out of or added a new one to *South Pacific* as there could not have been a more romantic spot for us to share our first dinner together as husband and wife.

After dinner we drove back to the resort, hand in hand, like two young lovers should have done thirty-five years ago. Leah and I basked in the reverent adoration that God had, on this day, blessed and confirmed our love. There was still one last thing I needed to do before

Leah and I consummated our union, which was to have my first dance with Mrs. Miller.

A single guitar entertainer who played Hawaiian love songs asked that everyone take a seat because the next song was only for two. There was complete silence as we danced, and oh how we danced to the "Hawaiian Wedding Song" performed in a way Elvis would have been honored by:

> *This is the moment*
> *Of sweet Aloha*
> *I will love you longer than forever*
> *Promise me that you will leave me never*
> *Here and now dear,*
> *All my love,*
> *I vow dear*
> *Promise me that you will leave me never*
> *I will love you longer than forever*

After the song I kissed Leah in front of everyone, and the crowd came to their feet applauding. We bid them farewell with a heartfelt aloha and now it was time, oh was it ever time, for me to take my new bride for my own.

[Sorry. . . .This part is not censured; it is simply held in reverence. On this night we consummated our lifelong dream, but I will tell you this; our first night in Nashville, as breathtaking as it was, paled in comparison, for on this night my love was accepted by my wife!

I awoke the next morning feeling completely fulfilled, warm and at peace as the woman of my lifelong search was in my arms and wearing a special ring, a symbol of the eternity we began to share faithfully with each other and with God. The tattered and stormy paths that joined the past to the present and brought us together are hollow memories of someone else's lives. The torment, the lies and the deceit are no more, and the evil that filled Leah's life has been defeated and will never again hold her back or deny the beauty that lives within her.

Over the next few days we toured the islands, basking in the sun, exploring the Pacific Ocean, shopping, dancing (you should see Leah doing the hula). We took in shows, attended luaus, and Leah even said okay to a helicopter tour. The only mistake was taking Leah out on the high seas. The photo of that day clearly said, "Get me off this boat!"

For the remainder of our stay on the islands, we loved each other as though the earth would end the next day. I will carry this feeling forever, and if you have not felt this passion, find it! As our adventure ends and we head to the mainland, I carry with me a treasure trove of picturesque memories and unforgettable passionate nights! It's hard to leave paradise, but I see life ahead as a series of new voyages merely waiting to take sail for us. As we fly back home, I do so without a care in the world, for her hand will rest in mine forever.

I have one final thought for you to ponder. Life deals some weird and wonderful hands which maybe you cannot understand, but if you believe in your dreams and you believe in yourself, nothing can alter your final destiny, destroy your dreams or leave you wanting throughout the night for what might have been.

You may be compelled to follow many paths, but if you truly believe in the wonder that is you and if you are willing to challenge many, if not all, things as you grow up or grow older, you will not be denied. If you feel your life has been altered through no fault of your own, believe in God and refuse to deny your dreams, and you will find them, for they are destined to be yours. Pursue all your dreams, no matter how small, no matter how daunting or impossible, with passion and conviction, casting off all fears of self-denial. Reflect upon yourself and your deeds, for this is your life and no one else's waiting to unfold. Trust in the power of the Lord and never deny His will, for He shall open doors and paths for you to walk on and through that will lead you to eternity.

Hopefully our story has inspired you to live not for today but forevermore! Let your heart begin to live, let your sprit sing, let the hand of God lead you along your way and then allow your life to begin anew.

Leah and I found our path. Hopefully yours will not take as long, but we believe the new light we bring into the world, our union, glorifies our Father and our God, and we give Him praise. I say a prayer just before I kiss my wife good night to let God know how blessed and thankful I am that through His love and compassion, we are now and forever complete in His name.

I leave you with a statement taken from the greatest book ever written, which in any language and any culture remains the same in my heart and around the world. In Hawaiian it would read:

> *E kolu mea nui, Ame kealoha kealoha kai oi ahe, po maikai, na mea apua.* Translated into English it reads: "The three greatest things in this life are faith, hope, and love, and the greatest of these is love."

Just for Fun
"Numbers and Patterns"

Humor Me??

The number 22 appeared throughout our journey—I asked Leah to marry me on the 22nd, our first meeting where we would give ourselves to each other was in room 622, I flew back to bring Leah home with me on 6/22, and we were married on 6/22, which leaves us with 3 sets of 2s or 6. Our wedding date is June 22, the number of kids we have is 6, the number of grandkids we have is 6, the number of years Leah was in business was 22, and I was born on 11/11, = 22.

— ~

22 is also known as the master builder. It is potentially the most successful of all numbers, and it can turn the most ambitious dreams into reality. 22 has the intuitive insights of the 2 combined with the practicality of the 4. 22s have to be practical; otherwise they waste their potential. 22s can deal well with a great variety of people, and they are inspirational and intuitive, practical, self-confident, visionary, idealistic and have good common sense.

Like 11s, 22s have to work towards the realization of larger goals that are beyond personal ambition.

— ~

ALOHA!

Reading Group Guide

A Q & A with Ryan Miller

Q. What was your inspiration for this book? It seems odd that you and Leah have been together for over nine Years, and only now you are publishing your story, what factors motivated you to tell your story?

A. Echoes in the Rain, in the beginning, was solely a vehicle to communicate with Leah. Put it this way; after hearing Leah's voice for the first time and realizing she was the missing part of my life I needed a way to let her know how I had loved her, seemingly forever. I knew I couldn't just blurt out "I love you", at this time we were both still married, so after a few calls and several e-mails I decided to tell her how I felt via a book I began writing about our story. I guess it was about chapter three when Leah called me with a single question; "Ryan, are you in love with me?" After that, I lost interest as our story was still incomplete and I now had Leah; so the book had accomplished its goal. However, several Years later after a few disturbing things happened that harmed Leah, the motivation to make our story known became overwhelming.

Q. Echoes in the Rain is very intense from an emotional stand point, and a very passionate romantic journey that obviously, in the beginning, frightened both you and Leah. Do you believe that the passion you and Leah feel for each other is obtainable for everyone or are the two you the exception?

A. Exception? Absolutely not! Too often so many become indoctrinated into a belief that this is their lot in life and discard their true feelings. I have met so many folks who deny God's calling, maybe out of fear or they have just become numb and accept the status quo. Passion and destiny are entwined and require the same trust and eagerness, as well as, the honesty in believing that a power greater than they have ever known guides their way and always provides.

Q. At one point in the book I got the distinct impression you were attempting to vilify the Churches in the south; was this by design?

A. Unquestionably no! However, as a parent I questioned the motivation of any parent and any church consenting to the marriage of a seventeen year old naïve child to a man whom she had never dated, held, or even kissed knowing she would forever be obliged too, based on their religious beliefs, submit to his domination or be condemned. Also, when the Minister came to Leah the night before she was to leave with me, he asked only two questions, he never asked; have you and Richard filed for devoice, have you sold the house, why are you leaving, how has your marriage been, why are you unhappy, do the kids know of this, are you sure? So no, I do not wish too nor would I ever attack or vilify the churches of the south, but I will forever harbor resentment for this one Church's Minister who placed himself above the true Judge of Mankind, turned children against their Mother without even questioning why?

Q. You told me of a woman named Pam from Hartselle Alabama who gave you a meaning behind what your book represents; can you share that with me?

A. Pam is a true friend and one who reads hundreds of books a Year, and she was aware of Leah and my story. She pleaded with me to allow her to read one of the first copies of the book, finally I gave in. Two days later she called and posed a question to me; "do you know what you have here?" Honestly, I wasn't sure how to react. Then she asked me "how many guys got Dear John Letters while I was in Viet Nam?" I told her "Lots!" She went on to say that my book is an inspiration to those in war who have lost their loves via, fear, youth, disbelief or other wise; "your book gives them hope and if they have faith, their dreams must come true; it's destiny!" She blew me away!

Q. In writing Echoes in the Rain, what would say was your biggest challenge?

A. The first part of the book was pretty easy, the View Nam days, but once I began to delve into Leah's life after I was supposedly was killed, things got really difficult. Imagine having to interview your wife knowing she was betrayed by her Mother, terrified of night fall and forced to marry a man she did not love? Every time I talked with her about her life, it brought back to life all the abhorrent memories and the repugnance she was forced to endure based on their religion.

Q. The book does not describe what motivation Leah's Mother had that led her to create this fantastic story of you being killed in Viet Nam, did you ever uncover her reasoning?

A. Frankly, no! We discovered many underlying factors but with her Mother being killed in the car wreck there was no way to confirm the truth. The most logical through, was her Mothers affection for Richard. By forcing Leah to marry Richard she could continue to dominate her daughter, and as Richard was so weak, she could control his life as well.

Q. You portray Leah as a shy and naïve woman who never dated, and then after the two of you got together she shed her insecure ways. Can you explain this?

A. I could publish a book solely based on our e-mail exchanges; many of these will be on our web page as they demonstrate just how sheltered and how fearful she was about being condemned. But yes, it is true that Leah never had any dates, had very limited social skills and was completely naïve, especially when it came to relations between men and women. Watching her bloom was astounding, she seemed to grow from one e-mail to the next. Put it this way, after thirty five Years, it took only two and a half months for us to meet and then two days later I ask her to marry me. Light speed? Maybe, but the woman that Leah had locked away all those Years over powered every doubt and every fear she ever had and what emerged was the most caring, loving and passionate woman I could have ever dreamed of.

Q. You write of destiny and fate and how all of us should never give up on our dreams and how, if we believe, all things that are destined to happen will happen and without question. Do you truly believe this?

A. Without question! Think of it this way, without faith what really do we have? Going to Church is not about us; it's about Him! Believing in yourself works for a while, but believing in him is the first step on the road to eternity. I'll give you an analogy; picture a white rope a thousand miles long with six inches painted red on one end. The red part represents your time on earth and the rest represents eternal life. Why would you ever allow God to control eternity and deny him, and his will, while you are alive? Destiny is in his hands and through him your fate is guaranteed. How many seemingly impossible things had to fall into place, and at the same time, for Leah and me to find each other?

Q. What's your next move????

A. Tough question, as a first time writer, other than training manuals and motivational pieces, I will be trying to bring awareness to the book via radio stations, social media and word of mouth advertising. Frankly, I have a very limited budget, but I have a passion that is uncontrollable and a drive to bring our story to life, epically for the veterans of this great Nation and those who believe in destiny and the one true love that was meant to be there's.

Ryan Miller On Ryan Miller

I was born in Los Angeles, California, on Veterans Day and as fate would have it, sold the next day to a couple who lived in Lawndale, California. Back in the fifty's there was a disgusting, yet profitable business going strong, that of selling babies on the "Black Market". I was a product or maybe I should say a consequence of the times. This revelation obviously shocked me as I had been told, and believed for over five decades; I was lawfully adopted.

It was also here in Lawndale where I first saw Leah. I guess she was about one year old, but she was the most perfect thing I had ever seen; I was five at the time. Her Grandmother ran an "in home" day care center that we both attended. Her Grandmother had known me from birth and when I held Leah, she glowed with pride. There are countless stories of the mischief I got into carrying Leah around, steeling bananas, hiding, and playing games.

I lost Leah when her family moved to Tennessee, and about the same time when things were about to change for me as well. My Father was a tough, two fisted man, working in the construction business as a Crain operator for the Department of Water and Power, and as his jobs changed, from site to site, so did we; move that is. Our next move was to Lone Pine California. This was a very small town at the base of Mt. Whitney and home to the Owens Valley Paiute Indian Reservation. Obviously this was a complete culture shock for me, but one I will remember and cherish for the rest of my life.

Here, in this small (less than one thousand population) town I would learn how to farm, hunt, fish, ride, rope and get into my fair share of fights. I loved this town! The locals, my buddies, the Paiute Indians at school, called me "Talulah" which meant "Leaping Water", I guess because of how I could ride and jump most creeks on horse back. Today, when people ask me where I came from, I proudly tell them, Lone Pine California, the gate way to the great Mt. Whitney and the home of the historic Paiute Indians!

I loved this town, but again, like so often before, it was time to move on. Dad was re-assigned to Scatter Good Steam Plant and we picked up and moved, this time to Manhattan Beach California and still another culture shock; Farm boy to suffer? It was here I left, for the most part, my calf roping skills behind, for a new set of skills, surf board riding at Manhattan Beach, Hermosa and Redondo Beaches.

Over the next five Years we moved seven times, living from homes mom and dad bought to make shift flats and even motels, but we always remained happy and as a close nit family. In 1964 Dad made a stand and decided he had traveled enough. We ended up in Inglewood California, where I began **junior high school**. This was my eleventh school in the last seven Years.

Two Years later my High School life began with about as much flare as the long awaited fire works show that started with a dud, I had friends, but being a freshman in a large California school was a bit overwhelming. However, things were about to make an amazing about face. I was love-struck "puppy love of course" with a girl named Paula, a dancer, who pleaded with me to audition for the Senior Musical "Music Man". I tried out for the lead, but as a freshman I stood little chance; I did not get the part. However, Paula started pushing me to try out as a dancer, a dancer? This was the farthest thing from my mind. She made it perfectly clear; "if you ever want a chance with me, you better dance". So I danced!

Ironically, I got picked to be a dancer. My Father was all but mortified! When the final show was over I was cornered by the choreographer asking if I would like to take part in some summer stock shows "musicals by Gilbert and Sullivan"? At first I said absolutely not. Then he said he would give me private dance lessons if I would take the part and I would make $50.00 per show. Let's see, $50.00 a show, seven shows a week, three months guaranteed, WOW!

Following that summer, Fred (the choreographer) lined me up with several auditions. It was like a fantasy, everything seemed to fall into place. I was picked up by Universal Studios, made appearances on the Hollywood Palace, the Carol Burnet Show, and even landed a part on Bonanza. Life was good! I was the lead singer in a rock n roll band, had passes to every show imaginable, making much more money than I could spend and even had a nineteen sixty four and a half Ford Mustang with a blue printed engine! Like I said "life was good!!!!"

At the end of my High School days, life for me drastically changed. I was almost nineteen when the welcome letter arrived, "ORDER TO REPORT FOR ARMED FOACES PHYSICAL EXAMINATION". At first I thought, this must be a joke, but no, it was real and like so many time before I had to move again. It was less than three weeks later I was ordered to report for a physical, and then loaded on a bus headed for Fort Ord in California; basic training.

After basic training I was sent to what they called AIT "Advanced Individual Training". I was assigned an MOS (Military Occupation Specialties) of radio operator. During AIT I received my orders; Viet Nam. At first I thought "what the hell, I'll be on the air, in a well secured bunker", but when I got in-country I found things were going to be a quite a bit different; Morris Code and PRC 25 (field radios) to sixty and fifty caliber machine guns, almost over night, I would say is a bit different?

That Year in Viet Nam brought to light the realities of life, memories I can never forget, and Leah back into my life. It was also in this hostile land that I first became fascinated with writing. Letters were our only form of communication and each word needed to be absolutely precise, depicting feelings, emotions and painting word pictures of the surroundings. Today, now that I have finally started writing, seems almost like a lost art. Letters now are replaced with texting, and statements like "Oh my God I love you, you are so great" have been replaced with "OMG I <3u U R so GR8".

Following Vietnam, and for the next seven Years, I attended several Colleges; El Camino, California State University, Dominguez Hills and UCLA obtaining several degrees that still remain as meaningless scraps of paper lost somewhere in the attic. Over the next three decades I worked in the telecommunications industry doing everything from selling systems to installing equipment. I enjoyed this industry as there was always a challenge as it transformed from one company "AT&T" to hundreds and from copper wire to fiber and then onto SIP trunking "VOIP".

In 2004 I was offered a forced retirement, completely unexpected, but this set up what was going to happen in 2006. 2006 is the Year my life began, and if you've just finished the book you'll know what I mean.

Today, my bride and I live on the Gulf Shores of Alabama and the Gulf of Mexico. I spend a great deal of my time writing about and searching for those allusive new characters that intrigue, compel and possess life altering qualities like my Father in Law! There's not much more to tell, but know this, when God calls, answer the phone!

"Jericho"

†

Jericho is a novel inspired by a real life tragedy that was originally written as a memoir. However when arriving at "Part III" I was inspired to create a novel. Life's paths are many; doors open to bright new beginnings while others lead to destruction and entrapment. Jericho tells the story of could have been if Patricia and her love child Jericho would have followed God's plan and not the sanctimonious path of her Mothers selfish and immoral desire to conceal the families secret even at the price of her own daughters soul.

†

Available in paper back

July 2016

CPSIA information can be obtained
at www.ICGtesting.com
Printed in the USA
LVOW10s0650091117
555624LV00036B/1245/P

9 781533 100559